DIVE GU
COZUMEL, CANCUN
& THE MAYAN RIVIERA

LAWSON WOOD

**Photography: Lawson Wood
Series Consultant: Nick Hanna**

**NEW
HOLLAND**

Lawson Wood has many years of experience as a diver and is one of the world's leading underwater photographers

This second edition published in 2002 by
New Holland Publishers (UK) Ltd
London • Cape Town • Sydney • Auckland

86–88 Edgware Road	80 McKenzie Street	14 Aquatic Drive	218 Lake Road
London W2 2EA	Cape Town 8001	Frenchs Forest, NSW 2086	Northcote, Auckland
UK	South Africa	Australia	New Zealand

www.newhollandpublishers.com

Copyright © 2002 in text: Lawson Wood FRPS FBIPP
Copyright © 2002 in Underwater Photography: New Holland (Publishers) Ltd
Copyright © 2002 in The Marine Environment: New Holland (Publishers) Ltd
Copyright © 2002 in Health and Safety: New Holland (Publishers) Ltd
Copyright © 2002 in photographs: Lawson Wood (all photographs except for those credited separately below are by Lawson Wood).
Copyright © 2002 in artwork and cartography: New Holland (Publishers) Ltd
Copyright © 2002: New Holland (Publishers) Ltd

All rights reserved. No part of this publication may be reproduced, stored in a retrieval system or transmitted, in any form or by any means, electronic, mechanical, photocopying, recording or otherwise, without the prior written permission of the publishers and copyright holders.

ISBN 1 84330 251 9

Publishing manager: Jo Hemmings
Series editor: Kate Michell
Design concept: Philip Mann, ACE Ltd
Design/cartography: ML Design

Typeset by ML Design, London
Reproduction by Hirt & Carter, South Africa
Printed and bound in Singapore by Tien Wah Press(Pte) Ltd

Photographic Acknowledgements:
All photographs are by Lawson Wood except: page 15 Ethel Davies/Mexican Tourist Office; pages 35, 142, 149b, 153b Ron Winiker; page 143 Mike Madden; page 80 Keith Cunningham; page 153t Lesley Orson.

Front cover: *The reefs off the Mayan Riviera offer some of the best diving in the world.*
Spine: *Erect rope sponges* (Amphimedon compressa).
Back cover top: *Cancún's hotels spread along a narrow sandbar overlooking the Caribbean Sea.*
Back cover bottom: *The author, Lawson Wood.*
Title page: *Huge sponges make vivid splashes of colour in the coastal waters off Cozumel.*
Contents page: *Yucatán divers discover a moray eel.*

The author and publisher have made every effort to ensure that the information in this book was correct when the book went to press; they accept no responsibility for any loss, injury or inconvenience sustained by any person using this book.

Author's Acknowledgements

Writing and compiling information for this book involved a great deal of of support and help from many local experts in their field. Of the many people who have provided time, effort and assistance in the region, I would like to extend my sincere thanks and appreciation to the following:

From the Mexican Ministry of Tourism – Dr Gerardo Hemken, former Director for the UK, Ireland, Scandinavia and the Netherlands, and Manuel Diaz Cebrian, Regional Director for the UK, Ireland, Scandinavia and the Netherlands, and Lupita Ayala, without whose help and support, this project would not have been able to get off the ground. Alejandro Zubieta, Marketing Manager for the Cancún Hotel Association who organized my accommodation and provided many of the contacts required to make this work. Javier Aranda Pedrero of the Cozumel Hotel Association. Clara Angulo of the Cozumel State Tourism Office. Carlos Maldonado of the Mexican Ministry of Tourism offices in Cancún who acted as unofficial driver and guide along with César Rodríguez and José Hernández Magaña. Guilelmo Velasquez, and his boat *Ecológica I*, who took me to Isla Contoy, and Juan José Cadena of the Mexican National Park Service who explained the complex ecology of Isla Contoy. Luís Gomez of Dive Mexico, author of the excellent booklet 'Dive Mexico', gave much of his valuable time. Rene Applegate 'Apple', Daniel Ayala Díaz and José M. Castello 'Pico' of Dive Paradise on Cozumel. They were excellent hosts and I have no hesitation in recommending their dive centre. The Cozumel Hyperbaric Centre. Dive House at the Fiesta Americana Cozumel Reef Hotel. Mike Madden of CEDAM Divers, who provided me with information and photographs from Nohoch Nah Chich, the largest underground cave system in the world. Steve Gerrard, Tony and Nany DeRosa from Aquatec who took me diving in the Cenotes and allowed usage of their years of experience. Jeff at Dive Aventuras who helped with the updated list for this edition. Don Brewer of the Akumal Dive Shop for his insights into the Yucatán reefs. Phil Kennington and Alex Schweizer of Quicksilver Dive Cancún. Daniel and Michelle Quezada of Manta Divers Scuba Centre, Cancún who provided me with the list of diving operators and gave me some great diving on the outer reefs of Cancún. Xcaret Ecological Park. Xel-Ha Natural Aquarium. The Manager and staff of the following hotels: Fiesta Americana Cozumel Reef Hotel, Ocean Club, Pok-Ta-Pok, Cancún, Marina Club Lagoon Hotel, Cancún, Maranatha Hotel, Playa Del Carmen. British Airways, Aero Mexico and Aero Banana.

Diving equipment by The Shark Group, Amble, Northumberland, England and Sea & Sea Ltd, Paignton, Devon.

And last but not least, my diving buddy, partner and wife Lesley who acts as a 'spot' underwater and without whose help, support and encouragement this would have been even more difficult.

Publishers' Acknowledgements

The publishers gratefully acknowledge the generous assistance of Nick Hanna for his involvement in developing the series and consulting throughout and Dr Elizabeth M. Wood for acting as Marine Biological Consultant and contributing to The Marine Environment.

Photography

The author's photographs were taken using Nikonos III, Nikonos IVA, Nikonos V, Nikon F-801 and Nikon F-90. Lenses used on the amphibious Nikonos system were 35mm, 15mm, 12mm and varied extension tubes. The lenses for the housed Nikons were 14mm, 50mm, 60mm, 105mm, 28-200mm zoom and 70-300mm zoom. Housing manufacture is by Subal in Austria and Hugyphot in Switzerland, and Sea & Sea Ltd in Japan. Electronic flashes (supplied by Sea & Sea Ltd), used in virtually all the underwater photographs, were the YS20, YS50, YS200 and YS300. For the land cameras, the Nikon SB24 and SB26 were used. The film stock was Fujichrome Velvia, Fujichrome Provia and Fujichrome RDP. Film by Fuji and Calumet Ltd. Film processing was by Expocolour and Eastern Photovisual Ltd in Edinburgh, Scotland.

CONTENTS

HOW TO USE THIS BOOK 6

INTRODUCTION TO COZUMEL, CANCUN AND THE MAYAN RIVIERA 9

TRAVELLING TO AND IN COZUMEL, CANCUN AND THE MAYAN RIVIERA 23

DIVING AND SNORKELLING IN COZUMEL, CANCUN AND THE MAYAN RIVIERA 33

CANCUN 45

ISLA MUJERES AND ISLA CONTOY 59

COZUMEL 73

THE MAYAN RIVIERA 105

DIVING THE CENOTES 143

THE MARINE ENVIRONMENT 155

UNDERWATER PHOTOGRAPHY 164

UNDERWATER VIDEO 166

HEALTH AND SAFETY FOR DIVERS 167

BIBLIOGRAPHY 174
INDEX 174

FEATURES
New Frontiers 14
Angelfish 56
Queen Conch 66
Fish-Feeding 80
Toadfish 100
Xcaret 112
Manatees 122
El Matancero Wreck 133
The World Ocean 140
Nohoch Nah Chich 152

How to Use this Book

THE REGIONS
The dive site areas included in the book are divided into four main regions: Cancún; Isla Mujeres and Isla Contoy; Cozumel; and the Mayan Riviera, where the main dive sites described in the Cenote Diving chapter are also located. Regional introductions describe the key characteristics and features of each area and give information on climate, the environment, points of interest, and advantages and disadvantages of diving in the locality.

THE MAPS
A map is included near the front of each regional or subregional section. The prime purpose of the maps is to identify the location of the dive sites described and to provide other useful information for divers and snorkellers. Although certain reefs are indicated, the maps do not set out to provide detailed nautical information, such as exact reef contours or water depths. In general the maps show: the locations of the dive sites, indicated by white numbers in red boxes corresponding to those placed at the start of each dive site description; the locations of key access points to the sites (ports, marinas, beach resorts, and so on); reefs and wrecks. Each site description gives details of how to access the dive site. (Note: the border round the maps is not a scale bar.)

MAP LEGEND

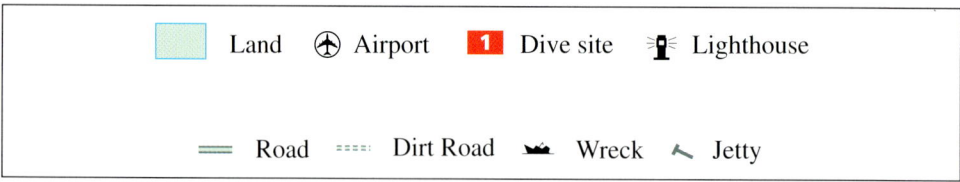

THE DIVE SITE DESCRIPTIONS
In the geographical sections are the descriptions of each region's premier dive sites. Each site description starts with a number (to enable the site to be located on the corresponding map), a star-rating (see opposite), and a selection of key symbols (see opposite). Crucial practical details (on location, access, conditions, typical visibility, and minimum and maximum depths) precede the description of the site, its marine life, and special points of interest. In these entries 'typical visibility' assumes good conditions.

How to use this Book

THE STAR-RATING SYSTEM
Each site has been awarded a star-rating, with a maximum of five red stars for diving and five blue stars for snorkelling.

Diving
★★★★★ first class
★★★★ highly recommended
★★★ good
★★ average
★ poor

Snorkelling
★★★★★ first class
★★★★ highly recommended
★★★ good
★★ average
★ poor

THE SYMBOLS
The symbols placed at the start of each site description provide a quick reference to crucial information pertinent to individual sites.

 Can be done by diving (applies to all sites except those that are good purely for snorkelling)

 Can be reached by swimming from the nearest shore (even if, in order to get to the shore, you need to take a boat)

 Can be reached by local boat

 Can be done by snorkelling

 Can be reached by live-aboard boat

 Suitable for all levels of diver

THE REGIONAL DIRECTORIES
A regional directory, which will help you plan and make the most of your trip, is included at the end of each regional section. Here you will find, where relevant, practical information on how to get to an area, where to stay and eat, and available dive facilities. Local non-diving highlights are also described, with suggestions for sightseeing and excursions.

OTHER FEATURES
The first chapters of the book introduce Cozumel, Cancún and the Mayan Riviera and give practical details and tips on travelling to and in the region. They also provide a wealth of information about the general principles and conditions of diving in the area. Throughout the book there are features and small fact panels on topics of interest to divers and snorkellers. The chapter on the marine environment at the end of the book describes and illustrates fish, corals and other marine creatures that are commonly seen in the region and explains the need for divers to help preserve the undersea environment. There are also sections on underwater photography and video, health, safety and first aid. The book ends with a useful guide to further reading on diving in the waters around Cozumel, Cancún and the Mayan Riviera.

INTRODUCTION TO COZUMEL, CANCUN AND THE MAYAN RIVIERA

Protruding like a giant thumb from the southeast coast of Mexico, the Yucatán Peninsula is a huge landmass which divides the Gulf of Mexico from the Caribbean Sea. Most of it is low-lying and covered in dense rainforest and swamps criss-crossed with rivers. It is scattered about with the intriguing ruins of the great Maya civilization, which arose around 400 BC and endured until the 14th century AD. Situated 115 km (65 miles) southwest of Cuba, and bordering Belize in the western Caribbean Sea, the Yucatán is blessed with sophisticated resorts, superb beaches of white sand lapped by warm, crystal-clear waters – and some of the best diving and snorkelling in the Caribbean region.

The name 'Yucatán' is something of a misnomer. When the Spanish conquistadors landed on the peninsula in 1530, they asked the locals what the area they lived in was called. The locals answered *yucatan* in the Mayan language, which means 'we do not understand you'. The name stuck.

The whole peninsula is called the Yucatán, but Yucatán is also the name of one of three Mexican states within it. Yucatán state straddles the north of the peninsula and has at its heart the city of Mérida, which was built on the site of an ancient Maya city. The state of Campeche is on the peninsula's western seaboard, with its capital, Campeche city, on the Gulf coast. The state of Quintana Roo runs down the peninsula's eastern side, with its capital, Chetumal, overlooking a bay on its southern border with Belize. All the diving areas covered in this book are off this coast, for parallel to the Yucatán peninsula's entire eastern seaboard from Cancún in the north down to Guatemala and Honduras in the south runs the world's second largest barrier reef.

THE OFFSHORE ISLANDS

The peninsula's most established coastal holiday area is Cancún, which was purpose-built in 1970 as a resort town along a sand bar on its northern tip. Offshore from Cancún are three coral islands, of which the largest is Cozumel, a popular holiday destination and the most famous diving destination off the Quintana Roo coast. The island of Cozumel is

---

Opposite: *A Cancún tourist gets a very special view of a Caribbean sunset.*
Above: *Mariachi folk singers in Mexican dress performing in Cancún.*

10 INTRODUCTION TO COZUMEL, CANCÚN AND THE MAYAN RIVIERA

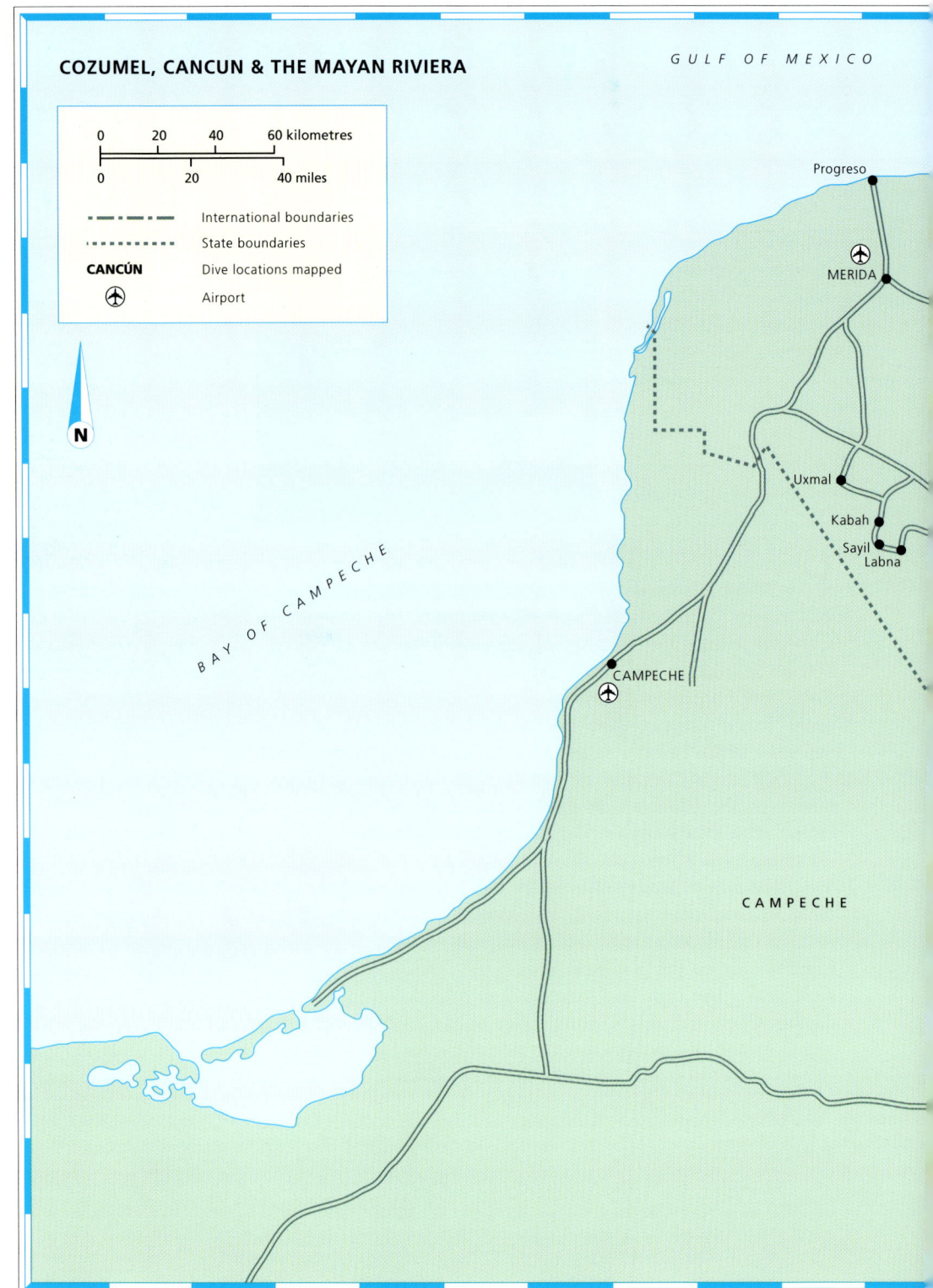

Introduction to Cozumel, Cancún and the Mayan Riviera

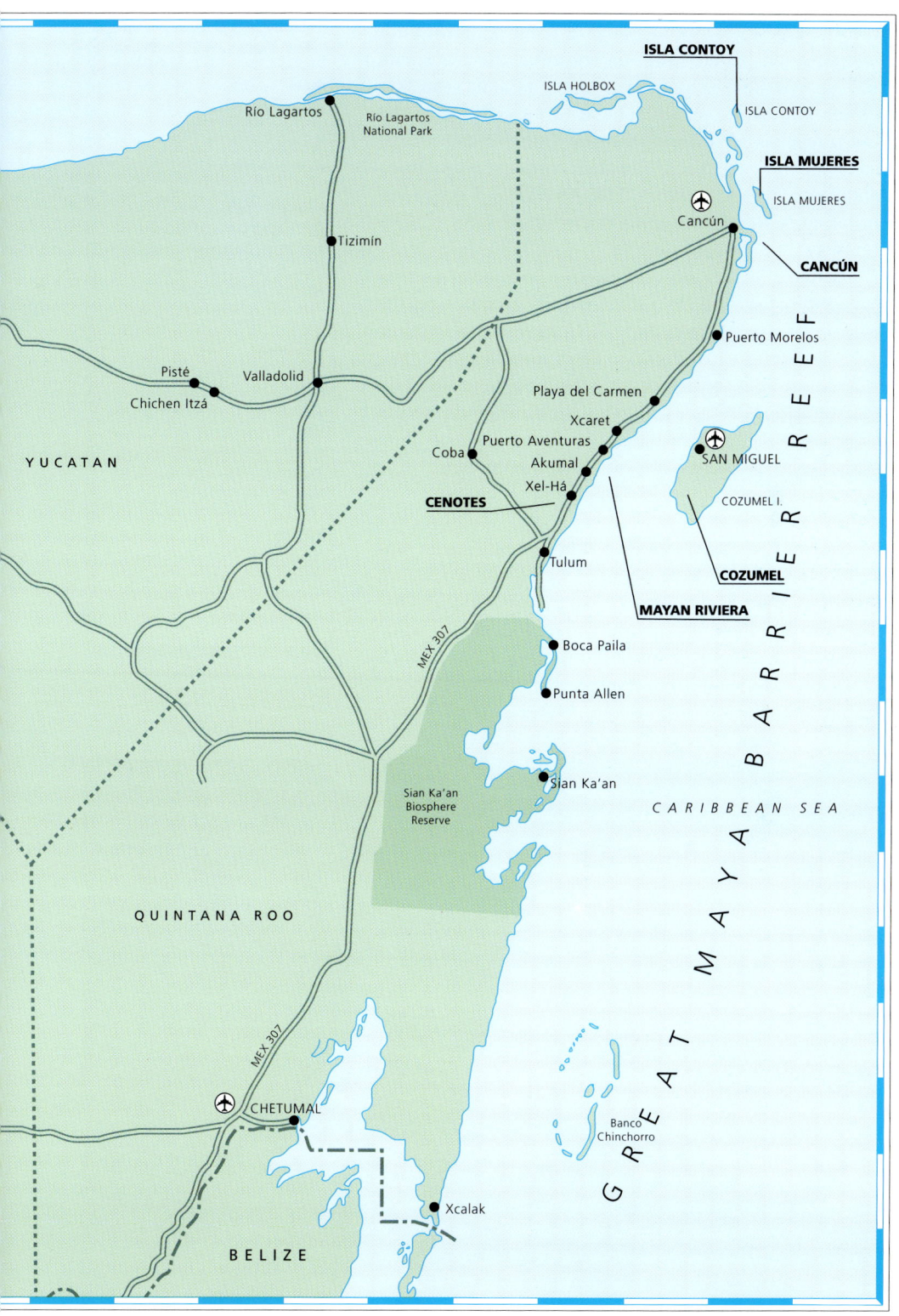

Mexico's largest Caribbean island, a coral platform built on what remains of the tip of an ancient, extinct volcano. North of Cozumel are her two sister islands, the Isla Mujeres and Isla Contoy. These three islands in the western reaches of the nutrient-rich Gulf Stream are all formed in part by the Yucatán's great barrier reef. All three islands have superb beaches, although inland they look uninspiring, with a rather uniform landscape and scrublike vegetation.

These three islands are very close to each other and are influenced by the same tidal streams and currents – yet the northernmost, Isla Mujeres and Isla Contoy, are in the Gulf of Mexico while Cozumel is in the Caribbean Sea. The northernmost limits of the region's coral polyp distribution are around Isla Mujeres, so the occurrence of corals diminishes to the north of the island. There are more fish, though, due to the fast movement of the tidal streams.

THE MAYAN RIVIERA

The coast of Quintana Roo state south from Cancún was once the refuge of Maya people fleeing their Spanish overlords, who were unable to penetrate the vast rainforests that flank its shores. Today, its endless white beaches are accessible from Highway Mex 307, which follows the coast south from Cancún to the diving resort of Akumal and reaches the ancient Maya port of Tulum

THE YUCATÁN PENINSULA

Area
180,000 sq km (70,000 sq miles).

Coastline
9,655 km (5,996 miles).

Political divisions
The Mexican states of Campeche, Yucatán and Quintana Roo cover the north, northwest and northeast of the peninsula. Belize occupies the southeast; and Guatemala the south.

Population
About 1.5 million people live in the Peninsula's Mexican states, of which about 30 per cent are Native Americans, about 60 per cent are mestizos (a mix of Native Americans and Europeans); and perhaps 10 per cent are European, black and East Asian people.

Religion
About 90 per cent of people are Roman Catholics; about 10 per cent are Protestant, Jewish, or follow Native American religions.

A palapa (a café bar with a palm roof) on a Cancún beach.

before turning inland. This developed part of the coast, called the Tourist (or the Cancún–Tulum) Corridor, is punctuated by rapidly growing tourist towns and resorts, but you can still find undeveloped stretches with isolated southern Mexican pueblos, empty sands – and offshore, miles of spectacular coral reefs. It is now recognized by diving clubs and authorities that world-class diving is to be found on the reefs along the Quintana Roo coast, and it is now listed as one of the Caribbean's most important diving destinations.

SOUTH OF TULUM

Extending south from Tulum to just north of Chetumal is the Sian Ka'an Biosphere Reserve (see pages 14–15). This is a UNESCO conservation area of 526,000,100 hectares (3,000 square miles), where diverse ecosystems, from rainforest to reef, are protected. Here, the local communities carry on their traditional ways of life; and they try to develop tourism and create other new industries that utilize natural resources without harming the environment. Sian Ka'an is rapidly becoming the starting point for trips to miles of scarcely dived offshore reefs, principally the huge and spectacular Chinchorro atoll.

Few visitors travel any further south than Tulum, but it is well worth the effort of doing so. Highway Mex 307 runs as far south as Chetumal. This is a small state capital with a population of 100,000 people, located in a beautiful, unspoilt part of the Mayan Riviera. The highway is modern and well maintained, and is being widened. There are huge speed bumps, however, and frequent security checks, so all drivers must carry identification with them if they use this road.

A queen angelfish (Holacanthus ciliaris) *– one of the most beautiful fish on the Caribbean reefs.*

New Frontiers

The Great Maya Barrier Reef along the Quintana Roo coast south of Tulum has exceptional diving potential – yet much of it remains virgin diving territory. Only parts of this long coast have been developed as a holiday destination and few dive boats make trips in this area, so facilities for divers are only just beginning to be developed

SIAN KA'AN
Just south of Tulum is the 526,100-hectare (1,315,250-acre) Sian Ka'an Biosphere Reserve, an ecological park of rainforests, wetlands, lagoons and coral reefs. It is one of the UNESCO's World Network of Biosphere Reserves, in which action is taken to both preserve and develop a region of land, the atmosphere above it, and all their inhabitants.

In the local Mayan dialect *sian ka'an* means 'where the sky is born'. Situated between Boca Paila in the north and Punta Pulticub in the south, Sian Ka'an encompasses two huge natural lagoons, Bahía Ascención and Bahía Espíritu Santo. Here, snorkelling is popular and there may be a chance of seeing manatees or sea cows (see pages 122–23). These creatures are now quite rare along the western Mayan Riviera, but they are protected here and further south, near Chetumal on the Belize border. There are also islands with nesting pink flamingos, brown pelicans, egrets, boobies – and crocodiles.

Scuba-diving – prohibited in the Sian Ka'an lagoons – is popular in the Reserve's offshore areas, where boats travelling along the coast may stop and chance the diving.

THE GREAT MAYA BARRIER REEF
The barrier reef that lies off Sian Ka'an is part of the Great Maya Barrier Reef – one of the world's longest barrier reefs, which stretches 320 km (200 miles) – along the entire length of Quintana Roo state from Cancún and along the Belize coast to the coast of Honduras.

The barrier reef protects the coast from the worst storms and offers innumerable high-quality dives. There can be rough seas on the Sian Ka'an headland, but the corals and fish there are more varied than can be seen within the lagoons, where the visibility rarely exceeds 6 m (20 ft).

Some sections of the reef are protected and they are home to many more fish species than are found in the north. Although the water is not as clear seasonally as along the sheltered west coast of Cozumel, the diving and marine life are spectacular. Turtles can be seen from April until September, and even at other times of the year there is an above-average chance of seeing one on every dive.

The area out beyond the reef is popular for fishing – as a sport and as a commercial activity.

XCALAK
Travelling south from Sian Ka'an toward the border with Belize, before Chetumal, is Xcalak. This resort area is rapidly gaining acceptance as a tourist destination, and it is becoming known as the main staging post for boat trips out to Banco Chinchorro, the largest coral atoll in the northern hemisphere. Chinchorro lies 26 km (16 miles) from the closest point of land and until recently it could be reached only aboard a long-range, live-aboard dive boat from Cozumel over 160 km (100 miles) to the north. Now a few day dive operators will make the trip up to 32 km (20 miles) from Xcalak to Chinchorro's outer reefs – more than two hours' travelling time. It is not always possible to make this journey because the prevailing easterly winds often bring a huge, rolling surge from out in the Caribbean Sea, making the trip dangerous.

SHIPS' GRAVEYARD
Chinchorro atoll is more than 50 km (30 miles) from north to south and covers an area so large that a true perception of its scale can be gauged only from an aircraft flying overhead. Both Cozumel and Isla Mujeres islands could fit inside its lagoon. The reefs have caused countless shipwrecks over the centuries and the southern banks are a graveyard for many hundreds of unfortunate ships and their crews. There are said to be at least 140 recorded wrecks there, including a

New Frontiers

Flamingos fly across the lagoon of Sian Ka'an Biosphere Reserve.

submarine. Much of the southern reef is so beleaguered by adverse weather that no hull of any submerged ship remains intact; all are scattered over the reef and most are now completely overgrown by coral and sponges.

THE SPLENDOURS OF CHINCHORRO ATOLL
Numerous channels cross Chinchorro, cutting through reefs kilometres long, topped by sand bars and scrubby vegetation. On the east side, where the weather tends to be rough, huge spur and groove formations run into the depths. The east side, divided into three sections: Cayo Norte, Cayo Centro and Cayo Lobos, has scarcely been explored. Most diving takes place on the west side, closest to the mainland. Live-aboard dive boats shelter in the lagoons there and venture each day to the outer reefs.

It will take more than a lifetime's work to explore Chincorro's rocky reefs and ridges, coral gardens and sand flats. The reef edge is steeply sloping from 15 to 55 m (50–180 ft) and covered with huge coral growths and sponges. Swept by strong currents from the south, the reefs are festooned in marine life – almost every species of Caribbean marine creature is found among its spires, buttresses, tunnels and canyons. Chinchorro is a protected zone and a favoured 'replenishment area' for many western Caribbean fish and conch stocks.

Only a handful of divers visits Chinchorro every year, so the atoll remains undisturbed by humans. Precisely because it is a new diving frontier, divers who venture to explore its reefs have a responsibility to protect its magnificent natural wonders.

Above: *The Pyramid, the focus of the great temple-city of Chichen Itzá, is one of many well-preserved buildings on the site,* **opposite***, believed to have been built by the Toltecs and the Maya.*

HISTORY AND PEOPLE

By the beginning of the first millennium BC, towns were evolving in the fertile Valley of Mexico – the site of modern Mexico City. They centred on temples to the gods of the rain and the sun built on high, flat-topped pyramids. These presaged the development of the first of a succession of Mesoamerican civilizations which moulded modern Mexico. A large proportion of Mexicans are direct descendants of these ancient peoples and some still speak their languages and follow the customs and religions of their ancestors.

The Olmecs made the first advance toward civilization in the forested region on the western side of the Yucatán Peninsula, overlooking the Gulf of Mexico. They developed the first glyph writing, a counting system, and the Mesoamerican 250-day calendar. From about 900 BC to about 400 BC they planned and built the first large religious and ceremonial centres – most notably at La Venta in the Tonalá river – and developed sculpture: monumental stone heads and jade carvings of gods in the form of jaguars. Their influence extended so widely that they were an formative influence on all subsequent Mesoamerican civilizations.

The Maya first appeared about 1200 BC in the Yucatán Peninsula and modern Guatemala and Honduras. They made great advances in astronomy and mathematics and were the first Mesoamerican culture to develop the concept of zero. By the 4th century AD their civilization had evolved around great city-states, such as Palenque and Tikal. At their heart were great temple-pyramids with richly sculptured walls and roofs supported by corbel vaults. The Maya abandoned these classic temple-cities in the 9th century and built new centres, such as Chichen Itzá, in the northern Yucatán Peninsula. But by AD 1400 the Maya state, infiltrated by groups of Mexicans, had begun to collapse and splinter into warring factions.

The Zapotec civilization appeared in the valley of Oaxaca in southern Mexico before 900 BC. The ceremonial temple-city of Monte Albán, begun in 500 BC on a levelled-off mountain crest, is the greatest Zapotec monument. It has an observatory and a ball-court,

INTRODUCTION TO COZUMEL, CANCÚN AND THE MAYAN RIVIERA

LANGUAGE

The official language in Mexico is Spanish, which is spoken by about 95 per cent of the people. About 3 per cent of the people speak dialects of ancient Indian languages, such as Nahuatl, a Toltec language; Zapotec and, particularly in the Yucatán Peninsula, many Mayan dialects. Mexicans applaud and encourage any attempt by foreigners to speak their language.

English is used commonly in all the tourist resorts and in the cities. All shopkeepers can quote the currency exchange rates in English. However, although many waiters appear to speak good English, most will know only a few key phrases and if you ask for anything beyond the limited scope of their knowledge, they will become confused. It is quite easy to learn a few key phrases in their language.

and temples decorated with frescoes. The Zapotecs also produced decorative pottery and metalwork. They abandoned Monte Albán in the 700s AD and the city was overtaken by the **Mixtecs** (pronounced Mishtecs), also southerners, who built the temple-city of Mitlá, decorated with mosaics of small limestone bricks. The Mixtecs also painted beautiful codices, or narratives, on dried, folded deerskins. By 1400 the Mixtecs had become vassals of the Aztecs.

The Toltecs, a warrior people, won hegemony over a wide area of central and northern Mexico from the 11th century AD. They built their great capital, Tula, north of modern Mexico City, with great columned porticoes, open patios and pyramid-temples to the moon and the morning star. Their frescoes still decorate the walls of some buildings, such as the Jaguar Palace. The Toltecs worshipped the feathered serpent god, Quetzalcóatl (venerated by the Maya as Kukulkán), god of the morning star and creator of people.

The Aztecs – or Mexica, as they called themselves – were displaced by the breakup of the Toltec empire and migrated into Mexico from the north. By the 15th century this warrior people had established an empire over the entire central valley of Mexico and subjugated neighbouring states. The Aztecs are famous for their cult of mass human sacrifice, but they were also notable builders and engineers. They built their capital, Tenochtitlán, on artificial islands in a lake on the site of modern Mexico City. Strongly influenced by the art of the Olmecs, the Maya and the Toltecs, they crafted beautiful artefacts from gold, silver, quetzal feathers, rock crystal, turquoise, and many other precious stones.

> **Día de los Muertos**
>
> On November 2nd each year, Mexicans observe a Roman Catholic festival – All Souls Day – and an ancient tradition of their culture: the celebration of death and rebirth. By mid-October bakeries are piled high with festive sweets and cakes, such as candy skulls engraved with names, which are placed on the graves of dead relatives as gifts from their living family and friends. On the markets toys are displayed with death as their theme.
>
> On November 2nd, the Día de los Muertos (Day of the Dead), families visit graveyards to picnic beside the graves and spend the day with the departed, eating and drinking their dead relatives' favourite food and beverages. They decorate the graves with orange flowers and burn incense.
>
> In the Yucatán, the Maya people invite the spirits of the dead to a whole week of celebration, culminating in a festival designed to entice the spirits back to Earth the following year.

The Spanish Empire

After the Spanish navigator, Christopher Columbus, discovered America in the 1490s, Spain sent soldiers to conquer territories and search for gold and silver and for native populations to work the mines. A conquistador from Spain's colony on Cuba, Francisco Fernández de Córdoba, was the first European to reach Mexico, landing on the Yucatán Peninsula in 1517. In 1519 Hernán Cortés, heading an army of 400 men equipped with horses, armour and gunpowder, defeated the Aztec military and, in 1521, razed their capital, Tenochtitlán.

The Spanish conquistadors claimed territories extending from the Yucatán Peninsula as far north as Oregon and Missouri. Modern Mexico then formed part of one enormous colony, The Viceroyalty of New Spain, which was the world's largest political unit. Colonizers sent from Spain to populate her new territories gradually reorganized them under a feudal system, creating huge agricultural estates and mines in the region that is now Mexico. Spain grew rich on Mexican silver mined by Indians who were forced into bondage. By 1542 a Spanish governor, Francisco de Montijo the Younger, ruled the Yucatán. He established the cities of Campeche and Mérida, and an economy based on plantations of agave cactus or *henequen*, from which rope was made (and from which tequila is made) farmed by enslaved Maya labourers working under appalling conditions and cruelly treated.

Peasant Revolution

In 1808 the French under Napoleon Bonaparte conquered Spain and Portugal. In the colony of New Spain, individuals tried to seize power. On September 15 1810, large numbers supported a call by a Spanish priest, Miguel Hidalgo y Costilla, to rebel against Spanish rule. Hidalgo was captured and executed, but the struggle continued until 1815, when a rebel leader, Vicente Guerrero, overcame the Spanish forces. Independence was declared in 1821 and Spanish troops were expelled the following year. In 1824 Mexico became a republic.

War with America

After independence several military leaders tried to seize power and in 1834 the charismatic General Antonio López de Santa Anna became dictator. In 1835 the United States annexed Texas – then a vast, sparsely populated part of Mexico which was being colonized by homesteaders from Oregon and Missouri. Santa Anna defeated Texan troops in the Battle of the Alamo at San Antonio in 1836, but later that year he was defeated at San Jacinto and forced to sign a treaty recognizing the independent republic of Texas – the Lone Star Republic. The new Mexican government refused to recognize the treaty, and even after Texas joined the United States in 1845, it claimed Texas as Mexican territory.

In May 1846, after a skirmish in Texas, the United States declared war on Mexico. The war ended in 1847 after the Americans captured Mexico City in the Battle of Chapultepec. Under the Treaty of Guadalupe Hidalgo, Mexico recognized Texas as part of the United States of America and ceded the vast territories that are now California, Nevada, Utah, most of Arizona and parts of Colorado, New Mexico and Wyoming.

Introduction to Cozumel, Cancún and the Mayan Riviera

Rebellion and Invasion
The troubled postwar years saw the emergence of liberal government in Mexico under Benito Juárez, a Zapotec Indian, and attempts at reform. But in 1858 conservatives revolted and civil war – the War of the Reform – was the result. Although the liberals won, peace was not established. Mexico was invaded in 1862 by a coalition of France, Great Britain, and Spain; and in 1863 French troops under Emperor Napoleon III occupied Mexico City and turned Mexico into the Mexican Empire, installing the Archduke Maximilian of Austria as emperor. His ineffectual rule was short – he was assassinated in 1867 and Juárez was reinstalled as president. Only five years later Juárez died and one of his generals, Porfirio Díaz, took over, first as president and subsequently as dictator. He initiated 34 years of stability and worked hard to unify and modernize Mexico and to attract foreign investment. But his regime was also characterized by exploitation of the poor, especially the landless peasants, and by rampant corruption.

The Mexican Revolution
Toward the end of the 19th century Mexicans who were concerned about the increasing poverty of the landless peasants and the lack of democracy and press freedom, formed an anti-Díaz movement, led by the son of a rich landowner, Francisco I. Madero. As the movement gained support, leaders emerged in the regions – in the north, a colourful cattle rustler and bandit, Pancho Villa; and in the southern state of Morilos, the charismatic Emiliano Zapata, who battled indefatigably to restore to the peasants the land stolen from them by Spanish settlers. Díaz was forced to resign in 1911 and by 1917 a liberal constitution had been adopted. The struggle for reform continued, however, breaking out as civil war. Successive presidents were assassinated. Eventually, in 1934, Lázaro Cárdenas, a former journalist from a poor background, upheld the 1917 constitution in a series of dynamic reforms, restoring land to Native American communities, and wresting control of Mexico's infant oil industry from the American oil companies.

The Yucatán Today
Since World War II Mexico has proved itself one of the most stable Latin American democracies, despite gigantic social and economic problems – a massive population explosion; a fall in agricultural output, and inflation that has run as high as 160 per cent. Efficient government under a single-party system has succeeded in stabilizing the economy by denationalizing many public utilities and businesses, reducing import duties, attracting foreign investment and reduced the inflation rate to just over one per cent. Mining, manufacturing, oil, electronics, textiles – and tourism – are all major developing industries.

In 2000, 20.6 million people visited Mexico and just over one and a half million visited Cozumel. Mexico now ranks eighth in the world in numbers of annual visitors. American scuba-diving magazines

> **The Yucatán's War of the Castes**
>
> The Maya and other Native Americans of the Yucatán's east coast put up a fierce resistance to the invading Spanish troops, and from the earliest days of settlement right up to the 19th century their culture was brutally suppressed, their lands enclosed and their communities forced into bondage. In the early 19th century their exploitation was intensified by a new wave of Spanish settlers, and in 1841 the Maya retaliated in a bloody uprising called the War of the Castes. Thousands of European settlers were killed. The Maya militia hounded the survivors into the cities, but, at the first signs of the annual rains, returned to their farms. The Spanish raised support and in 1849 took revenge on the Maya, killing and enslaving hundreds of thousands.
>
> The survivors took refuge in the dense rainforests of on the remote eastern seaboard of the Yucatán Peninsula, where they slowly built up economically independent, self-governing communities.
>
> In 1902, however, the Maya again staged a revolt – this time against an assault by the Federal troops of President Díaz, who was determined to overcome their resistance. The Maya fought a dogged guerrilla war until 1920, when the Mexican federal troops pulled out. Eventually, as late as 1935, Maya leaders signed a peace treaty and Quintana Roo became part of the Federal State of Mexico.

> **TIME**
>
> Central Standard Time is observed in Mexico. This is Greenwich mean time minus six hours, so if it is 12:00 hours (12noon) in the UK, it is 18:00 hours (6pm) in the Yucatán.

have rated Cozumel as the most popular scuba-diving destination in the Caribbean; and in polls taken by the American diving industry Cancún and Cozumel have emerged as the top location for value for money and quality of diving. Unfortunately, the growth of tourism has not always enhanced the landscape or the environment – but the major development of Cancún has luckily been confined to one area, the Hotel Zone, and the Cozumel authorities have put the brakes on continuing development. This, however, has motivated time-share operators to develop the coast between Cancún and Tulum and, in consequence, Playa del Carmen has already lost its innocence and old-world charm to high-rise apartment blocks.

CLIMATE

The Yucatán Peninsula is primarily savannah – low scrub on top of an ancient limestone base – and has a pleasant, warm climate, with a wet season from April or May to October and a dry season from November to April. It receives between 100 cm (39 inches) and 200 cm (79 inches) of rain each year. The rainfall is heaviest (and the humidity consequently highest) in May. During the wet season huge, columbiform clouds fill the sky, bringing long periods of rain, stormy showers, and electrical storms in the afternoons. September and October can bring overcast skies and hurricanes.

The temperatures are highest in the Yucatán between September and January, when they soar to 30–40°C (80–90°F) and the humidity level rises to over 90 per cent. In the cooler months – February to August – temperatures are still mild, rarely dropping below 20°C (70°F). However, the temperature and humidity of an area are determined largely by

> **MEXICAN GOVERNMENT TOURISM OFFICES**
>
> **Canada**
> 999 W. Hastings Street, Suite 1610, Vancouver, British Columbia; tel (604) 669 2845; fax (604) 669 3498; email vancouver@visitmexico.com
>
> **Denmark**
> Gammel Vartov Veg 18, 2900 Hellerup; tel (31) 20 8600; fax (31) 20 8248
>
> **Finland**
> Simonkatu 12A, 7th Floor, 00100 Helsinki; tel 0694 9400; fax 0694 9411
>
> **France**
> 4 rue Notre Dames des Victoires, 75002 Paris; tel (01) 40286 9613; fax (01) 4286 0580; email france@visitmexico.com
>
> **Germany**
> Taunusanlage 21, 60325 Frankfurt; tel (69) 253509; fax (69) 253755; email germany@visitmexico.com
>
> **Republic of Ireland**
> 43 Allesbury Road, Dublin 4; tel (01) 2600 699; fax (01) 2600 411
>
> **Italy**
> Via Barberini no.3, 7th Floor, 0187 Rome; tel (06) 4872 182; fax (06) 4201 4293; email italy@visitmexico.com
>
> **Japan**
> Nagata-Cho, Chiyoda-Ku, Tokyo 100; tel (3) 580 2962; fax (3) 581 5539; email japan@visitmexico.com
>
> **Norway**
> Drammensveien 108 B, 0244 Oslo; tel (22) 431 165; fax (22) 444 352
>
> **Spain**
> Calle Velazques no.126, 28006 Madrid; tel (91) 411 0699; fax (91) 411 0759; email spain@visitmexico.com
>
> **Sweden**
> Grevgatan 4, Box 140 58, 104 40 Stockholm; tel (08) 663 5170; fax (08) 663 2420
>
> **UK**
> Wakefield House, 41 Trinity Square, London EC3N 4DJ; tel (020) 7488 9392; fax (020) 7265 0704; email info@mexicotravel.co.uk or uk@visitmexico.com
>
> **USA**
> **California**
> 10100 Santa Monica Blvd., Suite 224, Los Angeles, California 90067; tel (310) 203 8191; fax (310) 203 8316; email losangeles@visitmexico.com
>
> **New York**
> 405 Park Ave., Suite 1401, New York 10022; tel (212) 838 2949; fax (212) 753 2874; email newyork@visitmexico.com

Divers relax in the Caribbean sun beside a pool in Cancún's Hotel Zone – for health reasons divers must stay at sea level for at least 24 hours before an international flight.

its distance from the coast, and during the dry months the coastal areas of the Yucatán are cooled by the eastern trade winds, while the rainforests in the interior are hot and sticky.

The general direction of the winds is from the east to southeast (these winds are called the *alisios*), but occasional winds come from the west and these bring rain showers. Any wind always tails off in the late evening and overnight. Wind speeds average 30 km (19 miles) per hour, but during storms they may rise as high as 160 km (99 miles) per hour. When Hurricane Mitch struck in 1998 a wind speed was recorded in excess of 250km (155 miles) per hour. In past years hurricanes have caused a great deal of damage to the reefs off the Yucatán coasts. As a rule, however, only the exceptional hurricane disturbs visitors' holiday arrangements – usually to make their holiday more exciting.

There is generally very little change in the air or water temperature along the Quintana Roo coast. Its equable temperatures are one of the factors that make the Yucatán such a great attraction for visitors from cold northern countries.

TRAVELLING TO AND IN COZUMEL, CANCUN AND THE MAYAN RIVIERA

This chapter provides a summary of useful travel details to help you plan your trip. For more detailed information – including addresses and telephone numbers of hotels, restaurants and dive facilities, and the numbers of emergency services, please check the regional directory at the end of each regional chapter.

GETTING THERE
Cancún has an influx of more than two million tourists each year, the majority arriving by air into the international airport just a 30-minute drive southwest of Cancún. Over 85 per cent of all visitors are from the USA on regular daily flights with a number of different airlines, all of which offer excellent services. You can now fly from the major hub airports to Cancún or Cozumel in under two hours – British Airways now fly via Houston and Miami into Cancún, the journey from London taking about 12 hours.

Connections to Cozumel are by air and ferry. The size of Cozumel's international airport, northeast of its capital, San Miguel, reflects the fact that over 250,000 air passengers fly into it annually. Cozumel also receives direct flights from Caribbean and North and Central American destinations. Both airports are well designed with lots of space and few delays or hold-ups on international flights in any of the departure lounges. There is a departure tax of US$15 and an arrival tax of US$18, payable in cash. If you have run out of currency, there is an auto-teller machine opposite the payment desk. You will be required to hand over the blue copy of your immigration form when you present your flight tickets and pay the departure tax.

All other flights from North and South American and European destinations are routed through Cancún (these flights also operate daily). From there you can pick up a connecting flight to Cozumel. All connecting flights are scheduled to give a minimum delay between long-distance flights and if a flight is delayed its connecting flight will be kept waiting.

Mexico has an excellent interstate road network and there are good road connections between Mexico City and the states of the Yucatán Peninsula. American tourists drive camper vans from the USA through Mexico to the campsites along the Mayan Riviera.

Opposite: *A dive boat setting out from Cozumel Island.*
Above: *Charter aircraft can use the many small airstrips on the Yucatán Peninsula.*

> **CRUISE LINE STOPOVERS**
>
> Four main operators include Mexico stopovers in their cruise line packages:
> - **Cunard Line**
>   tel: UK (01703) 716 634
>   US (212) 880 7500
> - **Dolphin Cruise Line**
>   tel: UK (0181) 874 1033
>   US (305) 358 5122
> - **Princess Cruises**
>   tel: UK (0171) 800 2468
>   US (310) 553 1770
> - **Royal Caribbean Cruises**
>   tel: UK (01932) 820 230
>   US (305) 539 6000

CUSTOMS AND IMMIGRATION

Visas are not required to enter Mexico but all foreign citizens are required to carry a full passport and, in the case of Americans and Canadians, a tourist card and proof of citizenship (generally either a passport or original birth certificate and photograph ID).

Tourist cards are also required by all people entering the country and these are obtained at the regional embassies, tourist agents or on any of the inbound airlines. The tourist card is a two-part document which allows you to travel anywhere in Mexico. DO NOT LOSE the blue copy which is returned to you after the immigration inspection. It must be returned to Immigration on your departure (generally at the flight check-in desk where you will also pay your departure tax). A good tip is to make a note of the tourist card number and keep it with your travel documents. When approaching Customs, if you have nothing to declare, you press the button on a random selector. If it shows green you can walk straight through, if it shows red, you will be searched.

DEALING WITH OFFICIALDOM

Remember to pack your patience when visiting Mexico. Although people make you very welcome there is a strong feeling that you are only a tourist, with only a tourist's rights. The people in power exercise tight control and like to prove their point. This attitude is true of a few of the dive boat masters and dive shop proprietors.

> **SECURITY**
>
> Never flash or otherwise display valuables or money – carry them in a money belt or, if possible, leave them in a hotel safe. Do not carry money in large-denomination notes – use traveller's cheques instead. If you can, carry your own baggage.
> It is scarcely worth while trying to report a crime to the police unless you speak excellent Spanish and have an infinite amount of patience.

If you get into legal difficulties of any kind, seek the advice of British Embassy officials. Mexico follows the Napoleonic Code, a system in which you can sometimes appear to be treated as if guilty until you are proved innocent. Do not try to get away with something you would not do at home. If you are ever in any situation in which something can go wrong, act with extreme prudence – you can be held for up to 78 hours without being charged.

GETTING AROUND

Taxis charge a fixed rate from the airports to the hotels and condominiums, but taxis from the hotels and condominiums work on a different scale of charges and cost more. In Cancún taxi fares are negotiable – the drivers will always try to charge you more. In Cozumel taxi fares are fixed by local government, and if you think you have been overcharged you can take the driver's number and make a report to the Association. It is always a good idea to ask what the taxi fare will be before you climb into the cab. You can find out from your hotel reception desk the going rates from the hotel into town, the cost of a trip around town, and the fare from the hotel to the airport. If you ask around, you may be able to get a taxi and driver for the day between four people and get the driver to give you an unofficial guided tour. It is an inexpensive sightseeing trip.

To hire a car you must have a valid driver's licence from your country of origin. You must also purchase and carry proof of Mexican car insurance. Rental agencies will take a signed credit card imprint as a deposit. Without a credit card you will not be able to hire a car. Rental prices are in the region of US$55 per day plus US$10 per day for accidental collision insurance. Collect your rental car, jeep or moped early in the day or you may find the better models have been taken. Check the vehicle over before signing for it.

In Mexico you drive on the right-hand side of the road and overtake on the left. All distance markers are in kilometres. Be sure to keep the car filled with fuel as there are very few filling stations. Within the Yucatán, the modern Highway Mex 307 runs from Cancún along the coast to the capital, Chetumal, in the south. It is well maintained and is being widened. There are huge speed bumps, however, and drivers must carry identification because there are frequent security checks on the highway.

Local bus services operate along Highway Mex 307. The services are regular and very cheap (Cancún–Akumal costs as little as US$5). First-class buses run between Cancún and Chetumal and second-class buses operate between Playa del Carmen and Chetumal. Some of them are rather old, however, and do not have air-conditioning.

There are scheduled domestic flights between Cancún, Chetumal and Cozumel. There are often long delays, though, and scuba divers carrying their diving equipment should note that there is a restricted weight allowance.

> **TIPPING**
>
> You will be expected to tip almost everywhere, even when buying petrol. It is common practice to tip baggage handlers up to US$1 per bag, depending on the weight and size of the item. Hotel chambermaids would expect to be tipped US$2 per day, depending on the size of the apartment. (Veteran travellers in Mexico recommend that you tip the hotel chambermaids on arrival to ensure yourself extra-special attention and prompt daily cleaning.) Tipping is also expected on the day dive-boats. Do not over-tip because you have had a great day out, but do tip, or the quality of your next day's diving may be affected.
> Taxi fares are low, so taxi drivers are justified in expecting to be tipped about 10 per cent of the fare.

Opposite: *The jetty on Isla Contoy where the ferry from Isla Mujeres drops and picks up visitors several times a day.*

ELECTRICITY

The power output at most hotels is rated the same as in the USA, which is 110 volts/60 cycles. There are always local differences, however, so if possible use a voltage meter to check the output before you plug in your expensive battery rechargers or strobes. If the charger heats up very quickly you should charge your equipment in short bursts so as not to damage the electronic components.

ACCOMMODATION

There are countless hotels and condominiums along the coast from Cancún to Tulum. On Cozumel the main concentration is to the north and south of the capital, San Miguel, and on Isla Mujeres they are clustered in the capital, Downtown (Isla Contoy is uninhabited). Visitors intending to explore some of the more remote cenotes may find there are no hotels in the vicinity and have to use a hotel in the nearest town or resort as a base from which to drive – or even trek on horseback – to the cenote.

Accommodation in the resorts ranges from basic to luxury, and prices vary accordingly. Many of the newer hotels have full ancillary sports facilities, including their own dive centre, and fast boats to transport guests to and from the dive sites. Hotel rooms are charged per person per night, and condominiums per week for an apartment.

When booking into a hotel you will be asked to sign a blank imprinted credit card slip for incidental charges. This is standard practice and you should not be suspicious.

The local tour operators will advise you where to stay. American dive magazines advertise many hotels offering complete packages, including flights from most major destinations in the USA. Rates are competitive, and it is worth approaching hotels before booking your holiday to see if there are any special offers. Prices rise during Easter and Thanksgiving in response to American demand. The most popular vacation is the three-day/four-night, bed-and-breakfast stay with three two-tank dives plus a night dive.

HYGIENE AND HEALTH

The gastric upset known as 'holiday tummy' in English, *turista* in Spanish, and, facetiously, as 'Montezuma's Revenge' in the Yucatán is a risk to holidaymakers everywhere. Intestinal illnesses such as holiday tummy are usually caused by a combination of factors. Changing time zones, climate, altitude and diet can all affect the normal functioning of the bodily systems. If you do not eat spicy food regularly it is sensible to avoid it for the first few days of your stay. Contaminated water – not just drinking water but water used to make ice cubes, to wash fruit and vegetables, and to clean the teeth – can cause diarrhoea.

The rule is that if you are going to get holiday tummy, symptoms will appear after the first three days. The standard treatment is to rest in bed, eat nothing and drink plenty of water containing 1 teaspoon of salt and 1 teaspoon of sugar per 1 gal (4.5 litres). In very mild cases medications such as Immodium (loperamide) are ideal, and you could also try local remedies: camomile tea (*té de manzanilla*), fresh papaya, and chicken soup (*consomé de pollo*) combined with even more rest.

If the symptoms persist for more than three days you could be suffering from something more serious and you must call a doctor. If they seem very severe, you may have food-poisoning. This is much more serious than holiday tummy and must be treated at a clinic or a hospital.

TELEPHONES

You can make International calls through most hotels, but their taxes and surcharges may add 60 per cent to the cost. Credit card calls from Ladatel phone boxes (on most streets) cost much less. In Cancún, AT&T operators can be reached through international hotels. Freephone 1–800 numbers can only be used from the U.S.A. To make local calls use only the last six digits.

MEDICAL EMERGENCIES

Air Ambulance America of Mexico, tel (from Mexico): (95) [800] 222 3564.
Air Vac (offices in San Diego, U.S.A. and Mexico City);
tel (619) 278 3822.

You can avoid getting holiday tummy if you:
- drink bottled water; do not have ice in your drinking water or other drinks; clean your teeth with bottled water
- wash your hands very thoroughly with soap before eating
- eat only cooked food, testing that it is cooked through and is still hot, unless you are certain that it has been prepared in very hygienic conditions
- ease into eating local food and be careful about buying food from open-air food stalls
- do not let yourself become dehydrated – drink plenty of bottled, non-alcoholic beverages
- give yourself time to acclimatize and take things easy.

Whenever you travel overseas you need a health insurance policy that covers you for treatment for severe illness and serious accidents and emergencies, as well as for minor illnesses. Do not underestimate the cover – you may need an air ambulance or repatriation. You also need insurance against loss of luggage, theft, and cancellations.

> **PURCHASE TAX**
>
> Mexico's VAT charge or *IVA (Impuesto de Valor Agregado)* of 15 per cent is levied on most items. It must be paid by everyone, including tourists, but is sometimes waived (illegally) or hidden in a restaurant bill.
>
> *IVA* has also to be paid on airline tickets for internal flights bought in Mexico; and a 2.5 per cent charge is levied on tickets for international flights bought in Mexico. A departure tax is payable at airports: it is US$12 or £7.50 on flights from Mexico to international destinations and US$7 or £4.50 on domestic flights. If you route your holiday through the USA there may be a departure tax from the USA to Mexico of US$17.

MONEY

The peso has been called the new peso since it was devalued on 1 January, 1993, when three digits were dropped. If you do not understand the face values of the coins, ask at your hotel or a tourist office. US dollars are widely accepted in all tourist resorts and you may

The pools of the Fiesta Americana Cozumel Reef Hotel near Chankanaab National Park.

> **SIESTAS**
>
> Cancún and Cozumel shopkeepers still close for the siesta, between 14:00 and 16:00 hours. Business hours are generally 08:00 or 09:00 to 13:00 or 14:00, reopening until 20:00 or 21:00 each day. Bars, cafés and restaurants remain open all day.

> **HAGGLING**
>
> Haggling over prices is acceptable in open-air stores and markets and with street vendors, but not in resort shops and stores. Prices generally include the 10 per cent *IVA* (VAT) tax, but always check before you settle the bill or hand over your credit card.

find little need to exchange any currency. For one US dollar you will get 13.5 pesos. It is advisable not to trade in sterling as you will lose 30 per cent in the exchange.

Traveller's cheques are perhaps the safest currency and the most widely accepted are American Express Traveller's Cheques. All major credit cards are accepted, but many small shops do not accept credit cards or foreign currency. To avoid the possibility of credit card fraud, retain your credit card counterfoils for every transaction. Currency is fine for tips, taxi fares, etc. Always try to carry at least $20 in $1 bills to use as tips – wages are low and tipping is now expected.

SHOPPING

Mexico is a nation of artists and artisans. Wonderful, old-style wooden chests and boxes are made in Cozumel, and diverse handmade goods can be found in the regions. The work of many artists can be seen in their workshops and studios. Market day in the regional towns should not be missed. Local handicrafts – pottery, ceramics, textiles, woven and leather goods – are cheap, but silverwork is a bargain. Mexico is the world's largest producer of silver. The mark '925' on anything you want to buy indicates that the silver is 92.5 per cent pure – the highest quality.

For those who need the shopping fix only to be found in malls, there are at least a dozen in Cancún. They appear to be clones of each other, but there are shops of local craftsworkers inside. However, the prices of the goods on sale in these workshops are much higher than those of the manufactured goods in the chain stores. There are designer clothes chains in the major beach resorts.

EATING OUT

The cuisine is very hot and spicy. The difference between Mexican food in Mexico and in other countries is that it is the real thing and will be tastier than the food served in Tex-Mex restaurants in your home town. Dining is more expensive in the international hotels, but good, inexpensive food is served at the beachside palapas (open structures with a palm frond roof). Seafood (*mariscos*) is a speciality, but do not order it unless it is thoroughly cooked. Food-poisoning from contaminated shellfish is a hazard. You should also avoid fresh salads or anything served with mayonnaise. Try the regional dishes: *tortas* are the local equivalent of hamburgers and the bread is a delicious, French-style roll called a

> **DINING VOCABULARY**
>
> - a restaurant . . . . . *un restaurante*
> - a table . . . . *una mesa*
> - the menu . . . . *el menú*
> - an order of . . . . . *una ración de*
> - dish, plate . . . . . . *un plato*
> - a snack . . . . *una botana* or *un antojito*
>
> - breakfast . . . . *el desayuno*
> - lunch, meal . . . . *la comida*
> - dinner . . . . *la cena*
> - dessert . . . . *el postre*
> - a drink . . . . *una bebida*
> - a tea . . . . *un té*
> - with/without milk *con/sin leche*
> - a coffee, café . . . *un café*
>
> - a fork . . . . *un tenedor*
> - a knife . . . . *un cuchillo*
> - a spoon . . . . *una cuchara*
> - a cup . . . . *una taza*
> - a glass . . . . *un vaso*
> - wine . . . . *el vino*
> - a tip . . . . *una propina*

Travelling to and in Cozumel, Cancún and the Mayan Riviera

A Tex-Mex/seafood restaurant at Playa del Carmen on the Caribbean coast.

bolillo. Mole is a rich sauce served with chicken or turkey and *tamales* consist of corn meal stuffed with meat, cheese or vegetables steamed in a corn or banana husk.

Sightseeing

Mexico has some 14,000 recorded sites with edifices built by the ancient Maya, who were indigenous to the Yucatán Peninsula and what are now Guatemala and Honduras. Perhaps because it was so remote, the Yucatán has some of the best-preserved Maya ruins in Mexico and these splendid sites should not be missed. Seeing them gives a greater appreciation of the creative work of their descendants – the artisans of the region. On the peninsula are the early ceremonial site of Coba and the great temple-city of Uxmal, which date from the Classic period of Maya civilization (325-925). After about AD 900 the Maya were most active in their northeastern territories, where they built the great temple-city of Chichen Itzá.

> **Street Directions**
>
> Mexican towns and cities are not well supplied with street signs and very few addresses are clearly marked. The locals are unswervingly helpful and friendly. Even if they have no idea about the area or address you are trying to describe, they will direct you to where they think it should be. A few helpful words in local Spanish should alleviate these problems:
> - town square (government buildings, etc.) *zócalo*
> - waterfront (promenade next to beach or harbour) *malecón*
> - market *mercado*
> - downtown or city centre *el centro*.

Tulum in the state of Quintana Roo, south of Akumal on the coast, is the closest site to the resorts and dive centres; and Coba, built during the Classic period, is in the rainforest about 42 km (26 miles) northwest of Tulum. Chichen Itzá, about three hours' drive southwest of Cancún, and Uxmal, 80 km (50 miles) south of Mérida, are in the state of Yucatán, much further inland. There are less impressive Maya remains on Cozumel and Isla Mujeres.

Tulum

The only Maya port to have been discovered and one of the few still occupied when the Spanish arrived early in the 16th century, Tulum is a modest city. It was built during the post-Classic period (AD 1200–1500), 129 km (80 miles) south of Cancún. Within its white walls are two major temples: the Temple of the Frescoes, containing faded murals; and the Temple of the Descending God, which portrays a god tumbling from the heavens. With his hands clasped together in a classic diving pose, this god is often descriptively called the Diving God. There is a temple-pyramid overlooking the sea. Opposite the site, on a cliff on the other side of a small bay, there is what seems to be an early lighthouse. Tulum is easily visited by road and is a major tourist destination, with more than 1.2 million visitors each year. Get there early in the day to enjoy the ruins before the tour buses arrive from Cancún.

Chichen Itzá

The most impressive archaeological site in the Yucatán Peninsula, Chichen Itzá is a temple-city some 10 sq km (6 sq miles). It was founded before the 9th century AD and inhabited until the 13th century, when it was mysteriously abandoned. Some archaeologists believe that it comprises an early city, built perhaps during the 5th century AD by the Toltecs, and a later city built by the Maya. Others believe that the Itzá, a Maya people, settled around the site's sacred well (chichen or cenote) in the 9th century AD, and built a great ceremonial city that later influenced the Toltecs. Toltec culture does seem to be strongly represented in the decoration – there are representations of jaguars, eagles, Tlaloc (the Rain God) and Kukulcán (the Feathered Serpent). Carved representations of elephant trunks and hippopotamuses deepen the mystery.

Excavations which began in the 1920s revealed that the massive temple-pyramid called El Castillo has another pyramid built inside it. It was designed as an astronomical calendar: the outer temple has 365 steps marking the number of days in the solar year; 52 panels for each year of the Maya century; and 18 terraces to mark the months of the Maya year and the celebration of the solstices – the vernal and autumnal equinoxes were celebrated here. At a height of 21 m (70 ft) it must have given the high priests of the time commanding views over their domains. Today spectacular natural light shows are held there, watched by thousands.

An observatory was also built on the site, which is called El Caracol. It has very deep-cut windows through which the stars could be seen even during daylight hours. Other temples include the Templo de los Guerreros (Temple of the Warriors), distinguished by many stone carvings on the façade. The carvings and murals indicate that the Spanish were not the first Europeans to enter the Yucatán, since they include paintings of what look like blond giants.

The largest Mesoamerican ball court found so far (a walled arena in which a ball game was played) was discovered at Chichen Itzá. When one of the site's sacred cenotes (wells) was being excavated, archaeologists found the earliest known example of a vulcanized rubber ball. The Cenote Sagrado or Sacred Well was a place of human sacrifice. From bones recovered from it, the victims appear to have been mainly children (although the ancient Maya were a very small people, so a myth that virgins were cast into the cenote could be true). You can reach Chichen Itzá by air and bus. Count on spending a day there.

Travelling to and in Cozumel, Cancún and the Mayan Riviera

Carvings and sculptures were an important feature of Maya architecture. **Above left:** *the Diving God wall sculpture at Tulum.* **Above right:** *Chac-Mool, the Rain God, overlooking the sea at Cancún.*

COBA

The Coba archaeological site is scattered across an area of rainforest 170 km (105 miles) south of Cancún. These ruins were excavated before Chichen Itzá. There is a 42-m (140-ft) tall temple-pyramid, a ball court, a nine-tiered castle, and the largest section of paved roadway so far uncovered. This road, called a *sacbe*, is built from limestone slabs. There are several lakes and cenotes dotted about the area. Wear hiking boots, and take plenty of water, as you have a 3-km (2-mile) walk to the largest pyramid, then you have to climb it.

SPORTING ACTIVITIES

Although this book is written mainly for scuba divers and snorkellers the Yucatán Peninsula's east coast offers many other sporting opportunities. These may be especially appreciated by non-divers accompanying a partner on a diving holiday.

Golf
There are two championship courses in Quintana Roo. The 18-hole course in Cancún costs approximately US$65 for green fees and the 9-hole course at Puerto Aventuras costs US$30 per day. A new golf club was due to open on Cozumel Island in 2001.

Cancún: Club de Golf Pok-Ta-Pok Apartado Postal 202, Cancún, Mexico 77500; tel (00 52) 988 31230. Mini Golf Palace, Cancún Palace Hotel, bulevar Kukulcán, Zona Hotelera, Cancún, Mexico 77500; tel (00 52) 988 50533 ext. 6635.

Puerto Aventuras: Aventuras Resort Course; tel (00 52) 987 23233.

Tennis
All the large international resort hotels have tennis courts or access to courts nearby. This sport seems to be a very popular option for divers wanting to keep fit between dives.

Hunting
Excellent hunting is centred in three areas in Mexico. Details of the hunting season can be obtained from the Mexican government's department of flora and fauna in Mexico City; tel (00 52) 5 574 5489/fax (00 52) 5 574 4007.

Fishing
The saltwater sport fishing is superb. Licences are available all year round, and an extended season for particular fish species makes the area a very popular destination. Most tour operators can advise on combined fishing packages and the local Mexican tourist offices can offer advice on where and when to go.

Windsurfing
The Yucatán is considered an excellent destination for windsurfing, with above-average facilities and good conditions. Cancún and Cozumel are in relatively exposed locations, so there is always wind and where there is wind you will find windsurfers. All the major international resort hotels have windsurfing boards for hire and many also offer instruction, often at little or no additional cost.

Jetskiing
The jetskiing in Cancún is regarded as world-class, with some of the best facilities and conditions around. The resort's calm, sheltered lagoon is an ideal playground for these otherwise noisy machines.
  Cozumel ranks as excellent for jetskiing, but the open-water conditions are generally more choppy.
  Jetskis can be rented from most of the international hotels in both resorts. The tourist offices will have details.

DIVING AND SNORKELLING IN COZUMEL, CANCUN AND THE MAYAN RIVIERA

The Mayan Riviera – the Yucatán Peninsula's east coast – has emerged in recent years as one of the top diving destinations in the Caribbean, equally popular with American, European and Mexican divers. Isla Mujeres, Isla Contoy and the island of Cozumel mark the northern limit of the second largest barrier reef in the world, and the largest in the northern hemisphere, which extends from Isla Contoy and Isla Mujeres in the north, as far south as the Honduras coast. The reefs are swept by the nutrient-rich waters of a branch of the Gulf Stream called the Yucatán Current, which provides ideal conditions for flourishing marine life. Temperatures in the water rarely fall below 27°C (77°F) during the cooler months of February to August and 28°C (82°F) during the hot, dry season.

Cozumel has long held a reputation as one of the most popular diving destinations in the western Caribbean, but Cancún also has some very interesting dive sites where the concentrations of fish life are at least as high as around Cozumel. Further south along the coast of Quintana Roo state the dive sites are less well explored but just as high in quality. For the adventurous, new territory awaits in the form of the largest atoll in the northern hemisphere – the Chinchorro atoll – offshore from Chetumal (see pages 14–15). In addition to the virgin reefs offshore, there is exciting and challenging cave-diving in the region's spectacular cenotes, or natural wells, and underground rivers.

The prospect of unlimited diving and an unrivalled abundance of marine life draws divers back to the Yucatán coast year after year. The conservation policies that are now being enforced in all locations are helping to ensure that the reefs, walls and shoals (which were in decline during the 1980s, and further damaged by Hurricane Gilbert in 1988) are protected to a much higher level. The Yucatán is in the Hurricane Belt and during the last ten years two major hurricanes have caused considerable damage above and below the sea surface. Before 1988 the regional conservation policy amounted to little more than a voluntary code undertaken by responsible dive shops, but not by the majority of dive operators, who were only interested in making a quick buck. Now, there is a new empathy with marine creatures and an understanding of the need to preserve marine life. Conservation

---

Opposite: *Divers tmay be greeted by schools of fish as they enter the water and when they surface.*
Above: *Dive Paradise dive shop on Cozumel Island.*

> **REEF STRUCTURES**
>
> Although conditions vary all along the east coast of the Yucatán Peninsula, the reefs there are fairly typical of all reefs in the western Caribbean. These are the most commonly seen structures:
> - pinnacle: a large, tower-shaped coral head
> - spur: a narrow ridge of coral separated by a sand channel
> - groove: a sand channel
> - canyon: a slice in the coral reef
> - tunnel: sometimes called a swimthrough, a ravine or a crevice, this is a hole running through the reef
> - chimney: generally a narrow tunnel running vertically up through the edge of the reef
> - shelf: the start of the deep water at the edge of a reef
> - wall or drop-off: the edge of a reef, which forms a shelf
> - sand chute: a deep gully connecting a sand plain above a reef to the depths below it; a sand chute cuts the wall vertically.

policies are now in force, and local people recognize the role of conservation in sustaining future tourism revenue. In 1997, the then President, Ernesto Zedillo (himself a keen diver and conservationist), proclaimed the Cozumel reefs a national park and designated them as protected areas.

PLANNING YOUR DIVING

The on-board dive masters will plan your dive and dive time. A usual day's diving consists of a morning deep dive to approximately 30 m (100 ft), followed within 20 minutes by a much shallower dive on the same reef or on another suitable shallow reef or wreck. It is, however, very important that you do your own pre-dive planning and stick to your plan. If you are diving from a shore location during the day or at night, always leave a message at your hotel or with someone reliable giving details of your dive plan and the approximate time of your planned exit from the water.

Night-diving is always a bonus. There are popular locations fairly close to the hotel centres everywhere except in Cancún, where it will take at least 45 minutes to get to your chosen night-diving location. Unfortunately, most dive centres choose the same location (the one closest to their jetty) and these can be rather crowded. Night-diving from the dive boats is hard work because you spend most of your time following the guide and have little chance to study marine life.

There are over 1,000 recorded dive sites off the Mayan Riviera, Cozumel, Isla Mujeres and Isla Contoy, and there are many offshore reefs. Although the dive sites have been given different names many of them are, in fact, different parts of the same reef. Only the most important have been listed in the following chapters. New sites are discovered each year, so you should check with a dive centre when you arrive to find out about new ones.

WATER VISIBILITY

The water visibility off the Quintana Roo coast is generally excellent and is very rarely influenced by tide or current. However, visibility does vary with location. Cancún has an average visibility of around 10 m (33 ft) between September and April and 25 m (80 ft) from May to August. The water visibility along the Mayan Riviera varies, but broadly speaking, the further you travel south, the better it is. It still hardly ever exceeds 25 m (80 ft) between September and April and 45m (150ft) from May to August.

The water visibility around Cozumel, which is offshore from freshwater run-off, averages 30 m (100 ft) in the winter and well over 60 m (200 ft) between April and September. However, the coastal waters are affected by the long oceanic swell which brings in waves from the central regions of the Caribbean Sea. This swell can make diving along the east coast of Cozumel almost impossible for some of the year, since the shallow, sandy lagoons are often stirred up. Like all island and coastal locations, they are also subject to the April–May and September–October plankton bloom, when reef animals and plants cast their eggs and sperm into the water. The planktonic soup is, however, the lifeblood of the oceans and it soon passes. After particularly heavy rainfall, the islands' water table reaches capacity and the islands seem to flush themselves clean. Every ocean in the world has fluctuations of plankton which clouds the water twice a year. Fortunately the Yucatán is fed by a strong tidal stream from the much deeper, clearer waters of the Caribbean and this tends to keep the water fairly clear.

The freshwater wells or cenotes to the south of the Tourist Corridor are an excellent alternative when the visibility in the coastal waters is poor. These are pools and caves, some filled with fresh, crystal-clear water and some with brackish water (a mixture of fresh and salt water) and a visibility of over 60 m (200 ft), even during the months when the weather is most severe. Several dive operators will lead you on explorations of these amazingly clear cenotes and the caverns and underground rivers leading off them, which are adorned with spectacularly beautiful stalagmites and stalactites.

DIVING CONDITIONS

Dive operators in Cancún, Cozumel and along the Mayan Riviera boast that you can dive every day of the year – even during the worst weather you can always find a lee shore where you can dive relatively safely. Most diving around Cozumel and Cancún is done by boat, and the boat dives are always treated as drift dives. The strongest currents are off Cancún and around the most northerly and southerly points of Cozumel.

TIDAL STREAMS

When the moon is full its gravitational forces exert more pull on the oceans. As a result, tidal movements increase, creating what are called spring tides. During other phases of the moon the tidal streams and currents are slower. These are called neap tides. At the spring and autumn equinoxes, when the sun is closest to the earth, a still greater pull is exerted and the tidal currents are faster and higher than at any other time of year.

Tidal streams cause the twice-daily circulation of water from the Caribbean Sea to the Gulf of Mexico in the north. This accounts for the higher-than-average concentration of marine life to be found in this region and provides a constant supply of fresh, clear water.

A diver explores an underwater cavern on the Mayan Riviera.

> **SURGE**
>
> In winter the oceanic swell rolling in from the mixed waters of the Gulf of Mexico and the Caribbean Sea creates an undertow and surge conditions. The surges make diving difficult for anyone working close to a coral reef; they may be pushed against the corals.
>
> Diving in these conditions can be very tiring. The best way of avoiding this is to swim in the direction of the surge. When the pull is against you, do not fin against it; if you fin when the pull reverses you will cover more ground more safely.

If you are unsure of your ability in strong current, check with the dive master on your dive boat. There have been several scare stories from Cozumel about divers having been pulled down and swept to their deaths. No matter how high the level of training and supervision, divers are killed. Although these deaths are linked to current, the problem occurs when divers go too deep against the flow of current and discover that they have run out of air too quickly at depth. All divers are warned about this during training.

Surge is a problem during the cooler months between February and August, and Cozumel, where most of the diving is along the sheltered west coast, is the preferred location at that time of year. From about October to March or April Cancún and the coast to the south of it are affected by ocean swell. This is caused by periodic storms which, although they occur far out in the southern Caribbean, result in a long, low swell which reaches the coastal regions. It makes boat trips uncomfortable for divers and extends the times between dives. When the sea is too rough for diving and visibility is impaired, diving in the cenotes is an exciting alternative in this part of the world.

DIVE BOATS

There are shallow shore dives off Cozumel, Cancún and the Mayan Riviera, but divers are generally lazy and prefer the personal touch and help offered by dive boat operators. Dive

Holidaymakers can try snorkelling or take a trip in a glass-bottomed boat from the Aquaworld diving platform off Punta Nizúc, Cancún.

boats come in two categories: fast and slow. In Cancún, most are small and fast and reasonably comfortable, working hard to get you out to the site and back to the dive shop as quickly as possible. The slower boats are operated by Aquaworld and are more like ferries, relaying divers out to their platform at Punta Nizúc. In Cozumel a few 'cattle boats' are still used by some of the larger operations.

The fast boats are generally preferred, as there is no hanging about between dives and dive travel time can be halved. Considering that some of the more distant locations are at least a 90-minute trip away, these fast boats are always popular. Slow boats are generally used by more inexperienced divers – or by those who did not get up early enough to book the fast boat. A lunch pack is always included in the slow-boat trips.

Cozumel is popular for night-diving, and taxis or hired cars can be used to reach the favoured locations. However, many night divers find it most convenient to stay only in hotels with shore access to dive sites and they do not venture beyond those sites.

Only fast dive boats operate along the Tourist Corridor. Times to the dive sites are short because the boats only cover an area within a 30-minute radius from their home base. A couple of operators also offer trips across the channel to Cozumel taking about one hour. Most divers prefer to hire cars along this stretch of coast in order to schedule a wide variety of diving, especially if they include cenotes in their itinerary. Divers enter the water from the fast boats by a backward roll or by slipping over the side while keeping one hand on the boat; entry from the slow boats is generally by taking a giant step forward from the rear.

LIVE-ABOARDS

The live-aboard dive boat *MV Oceanus* operates along the Mayan Riviera and the east coast of Cozumel, and takes divers out to the Chinchorro atoll (weather permitting). The boat is

Dive boats often race each other to take their passengers to the best dive sites.

30 m (100 ft) long and can handle 14 guests in seven double state rooms. She has air-conditioning, hot and cold purified water, the latest navigation equipment, two air compressors, two dive-boat tenders, and enough diving equipment and air tanks to give each diver three dives a day. The vessel makes trips to some of the far-flung reefs only when the weather permits – her most active long-haul season is generally in summer when the weather is more stable. Between November and April trips operate daily and overnight, with some excursions lasting three to five days, depending on the charter bookings.

Marine Life

The fish life in the region is astonishingly varied. The largest concentrations are between Cancún and Isla Mujeres, where shallow areas of patch reef are breeding grounds for many species found in the western Caribbean. There are huge schools of snapper, many species of grunt, and one or two especially interesting fish to look – and listen – out for, such as the extraordinary toadfish (see page 100), which, like terrestrial toads, makes a croaking sound.

Learning to dive in the Yucatán

Many thousands of experienced scuba divers visit the Yucatán each year, becoming familiar with the area's dive sites and getting to know certain locations. Many eventually decide to upgrade their diving skills, through the inter-island/mainland dive shop network, which has a reputation for first-class instruction to the highest level.

The waters that wash the eastern side of the Yucatán Peninsula are the perfect location in which to learn to dive. The most important considerations are to choose a diving operation that is affiliated to one of the major schools of instruction and to check that the instructors are qualified by PADI, NAUI or BS-AC. These are the world's leading diver training organizations and all train to the highest standards.

Most of the larger dive operators employ instructors who are qualified with at least two or three different organizations, including PADI (Professional Association of Diving Instructors), which is probably the top-rated association active in the Yucatán. PADI certifies 85 per cent of all scuba divers in the world and is represented in 87 countries. Instructors affiliated to NAUI (National Association of Underwater Instructors) are equally competent, although this organization is less widely known. There are instructors from the BS-AC (British Sub-Aqua Club), which is very strong in Europe and Japan, in several resorts.

Certification

Before you are allowed to rent equipment and go off with a buddy to dive independently, you must be certified as competent. The most popular way is to enrol in the Discover Scuba Programme. Often called a resort course, this crams a lot into two to four hours' instruction: it is designed to give a taste of diving, to fire enthusiasm and to teach basic water safety and preservation of life (not just yours but the lives of people and marine creatures). Resort courses are aimed at prospective divers aged 12 and over (teenagers up to 18 years need parental consent). There is no upper age limit. A resort course is recommended if you have only a few days' vacation. The cost is minimal and includes rental of equipment.

About 25 per cent of all first-timers go on to sit the open-water certification course in the same location. On passing the open-water course you can continue your scuba-diving education by enrolling in many other speciality courses, including wreck-diving, cave- and cavern-diving, underwater photography – and by becoming an instructor and teaching

DIVING AND SNORKELLING IN COZUMEL, CANCÚN AND THE MAYAN RIVIERA

Above: *A first dive usually takes place in a swimming pool, where equipment can be safely tried out.*
Below: *A dive guide leads a group of trainees on their second dive to explore a reef.*

TIPS FOR SAFE SWIMMING
To swim safely, always swim with a buddy, never alone, and:.
1 be cautious when swimming in an area you do not know well.
2 look out for swimming safety flags:
– red means danger;
– yellow means caution;
– blue or green means calm water conditions.
3 do not swim directly after eating or when you are overtired or overheated.
4 supervise children swimming in the surf and when they are utilizing inflatable objects.
5 if you are caught in an undertow do not panic. Do not try to swim directly to the shore; instead, swim parallel to the shore for a few metres. You should soon find you are clear and can swim to shore.
6 keep clear of the corals. They can cause nasty wounds – and they are also extremely fragile.

others this fascinating and rewarding sport. All these courses are available in the Yucatán.

Your certification or 'C' card is recognized worldwide as your qualification to dive. It is valid for life, but if for some reason you are unable to dive more than once a year you should enrol in a refresher course at a dive centre.

DISABLED DIVERS

Several diving operations specialize in instructing disabled divers and organizing diving trips for them. Their boats are specially adapted for wheelchairs. The dive centres can certify people with many different disabilities, including people with poor sight or hearing, paraplegics and quadriplegics. Prospective students must see a physician before enrolling on a course and be pronounced medically fit to dive. Most dive operations that possess a jetty will offer help to disabled divers. Only some some small dive operators are unable to do so (much as they would like to) usually because the dive boat can only be reached by walking down a rocky or sandy beach, followed by wading into chest-deep water.

SNORKELLING

If you are not a qualified diver, snorkelling will give you a thrilling opportunity to see the underwater world at a safe distance. It is a sport for all ages and is best enjoyed with at least one partner or 'buddy' – but it can be a family activity. There is no age limit to snorkelling and it is not dangerous as long as you snorkel in safe protected waters.

Snorkelling combines swimming using arms, legs and fins with breath-hold diving, enabling you to explore a little way below the surface. As a beginner, entering the water for the first time wearing a mask, snorkel and fins can be quite daunting, but with the correct techniques you quickly discover that snorkelling requires little physical effort. Although you must be able to swim, you do not need Olympic stamina. Snorkelling is recommended for gentle exercise and physical and mental stimulation. People with a medical problem who are unsure whether they should snorkel should consult their doctor first. Broadly speaking, snorkelling is not recommended for people who suffer from epilepsy, but asthmatics, who in the past have been banned from diving, may be able to take it up under supervision.

Snorkelling is not expensive. Dive shops and hotels have all the equipment you will need to take a first peek beneath the waves and they offer instruction – often in the centre's swimming pool at first. Once you are hooked (and you will be) you will be able to go off on your own. Then,

DIVING ORGANIZATIONS FOR THE DISABLED
Information on diving for the disabled is available from the tourist offices in Cancún, Playa del Carmen and Cozumel, and from these governing bodies:
British Sub-Aqua Club (BS-AC), Telfords Quay, Ellesmere Port, South Wirral, Cheshire L65 4FY UK; tel (0151) 357 1951/fax (0151) 357 1250.
Handicapped Scuba Assoc. (HSA), 116 West El Portal, Suite 104, San Clemente, California 92672, USA; tel (714) 498 6128.

Opposite: A snorkeller explores a reef in the shallows off the Quintana Roo coast.

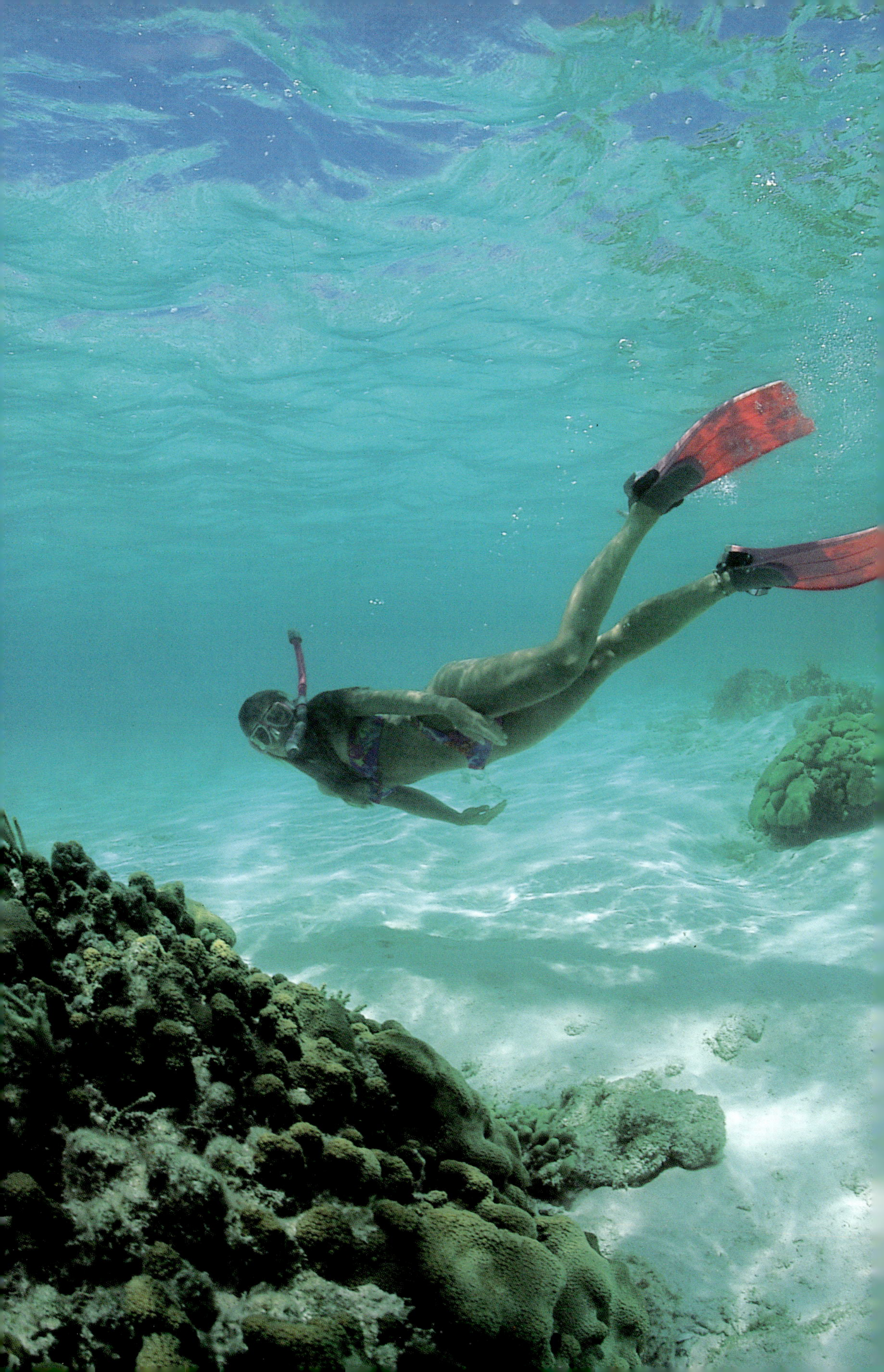

Five Snorkelling Tips

1. Clean your mask before snorkelling by wetting it, then spitting into it and spreading the saliva around with your fingers. Then rinse out the mask. This is a useful tip to prevent the mask from fogging up.
2. Make sure that your hair is not trapped under the seal of the mask.
3. If water gets into the breathing tube, blow sharply through the tube to expel it.
4. If water gets inside the mask, breathe in through the snorkel and out through your nose while pressing the top of the mask against your forehead.
5. Always snorkel with a partner.

Access from the Beach

All beaches in Mexico are open to the public and are free of charge, but charges are made to enter marine parks and biosphere reserves.

Few beaches have lifeguards and many are frequently affected by heavy sea swell and undercurrents, so it is essential to pay attention to the water condition flags at many beaches (see box page 40).

when you realize you are competent, you will feel confident enough to buy some equipment. You will need a mask with an adjustable strap and toughened glass, and an area around the nose to enable you to adjust the air pressure inside. Several makes of mask come with a provision for optical lenses to be installed. If you wear contact lenses, a close-fitting, low-volume mask should be adequate, but you must close your eyes if you have to clear your mask.

The snorkel must not be too long or have too wide a bore because you may need to clear water out of it in one breath if you submerge yourself too far. Modern snorkels have a self-draining device to remove excess water. The snorkel must fit snugly in the mouth, be attachable to the outside of the mask strap, and must not have any restriction that could impair breathing. Fins – flippers – come in a slip-on style with an adjustable ankle strap, often worn over a pair of waterproof pumps or diving bootees; and as a smaller, softer kind that fits snugly around the foot. Buoyancy vests may also be worn as an additional safety measure, but they are rarely used for shallow-water snorkelling.

If the dive centre you have been renting from does not have equipment for sale, they will be able to offer the best advice on where to buy the equipment you need. You find it on sale in the shopping malls of Cancún and in all dive shops. Check with your dive shop whether the area where you are planning to snorkel is safe for you and – if necessary – for your family. If you are in any doubt, do not enter the water. Always seek local advice first.

In addition to basic equipment you should always wear a Lycra swimskin or a thin full wet suit. This will not only protect you against the sun but also against microscopic planktonic creatures which may sting you. However, if you have no other protection, at least wear a T-shirt to protect your from sunburn.

DIVING EQUIPMENT
In addition to basic snorkelling equipment, detailed above, you will need the following equipment for diving:
- an air tank and air
- a regulator or demand valve to breath through
- a contents gauge to show how much air is in your tank
- a depth gauge, clearly readable, to indicate your current depth and maximum depth reached
- a watch with an adjustable bezel or timer device to let you know how long you have been at a specific depth, and the duration of your dive
- a buoyancy compensator or life jacket (to enable you to adjust your buoyancy at depth, to keep yourself off the corals, and to support you on the surface as the need arises)
- a protective suit to guard against abrasions
- a weight belt and weights for neutral buoyancy at depth.

The water temperature drops as low as 24°C (74°F) between November and April and it is advisable to wear a full wet suit instead of the very much thinner swimskin or a Lycra protective suit. The equable year-round water temperature in this area of the western Caribbean means that you will not need more professional equipment, such as dry suits, hoods or gloves, although some people like to wear a hood for night-diving. Some divers carry a small knife in case they become enravelled in fishing line floating loose in the water and need to cut themselves free; the knife must not be used to stab at or kill any marine life. A computer is recommended for experienced divers on an unlimited dive package.

All divers have to learn to limit their time under water. Diving three or more times a day over a sustained period is exhausting and dangerous. It can lead to residual nitrogen in the blood and to the development of the bends.

It is always advisable to dive with a competent partner, (called a 'buddy') and to dive with a recognized dive shop. This is not just for your own safety. The resident dive guides and instructors know the dive location and will guide you to the safest and most scenic part of whichever dive you have chosen.

PREVENTING THE BENDS

Decompression sickness, or 'the bends' occurs when inadequate decompression causes nitrogen bubbles to form in the tissues (see page 170). To prevent it:
Do: – drink plenty of water to prevent dehydration.
  – dive conservatively (do not push the tables or computer).
Don't: – over-exercise before or after diving
  – drink too much alcohol or coffee
  – take hot showers after diving
  – let your body get too cold during or after diving.
If you experience: minor tingling, numbness, extreme fatigue, weakness, dizziness, vertigo, or general health problems, contact the nearest hyperbaric chamber immediately.

NITROX DIVING

Nitrox is air enriched with a higher percentage of oxygen than normal – that is, more than 21 per cent. Using Nitrox for recreational diving is basically much safer than using normal compressed air and it can extend the time of your safe diving limits at depth. However, it does not increase your time for deep diving. Specialized courses in nitrox diving are available at a number of locations in Yucatán. They cost roughly US$250 per person for a minimum of eight people.

Opposite: *A snorkelling boat taking holidaymakers to the Bahía de Mujeres reefs.*

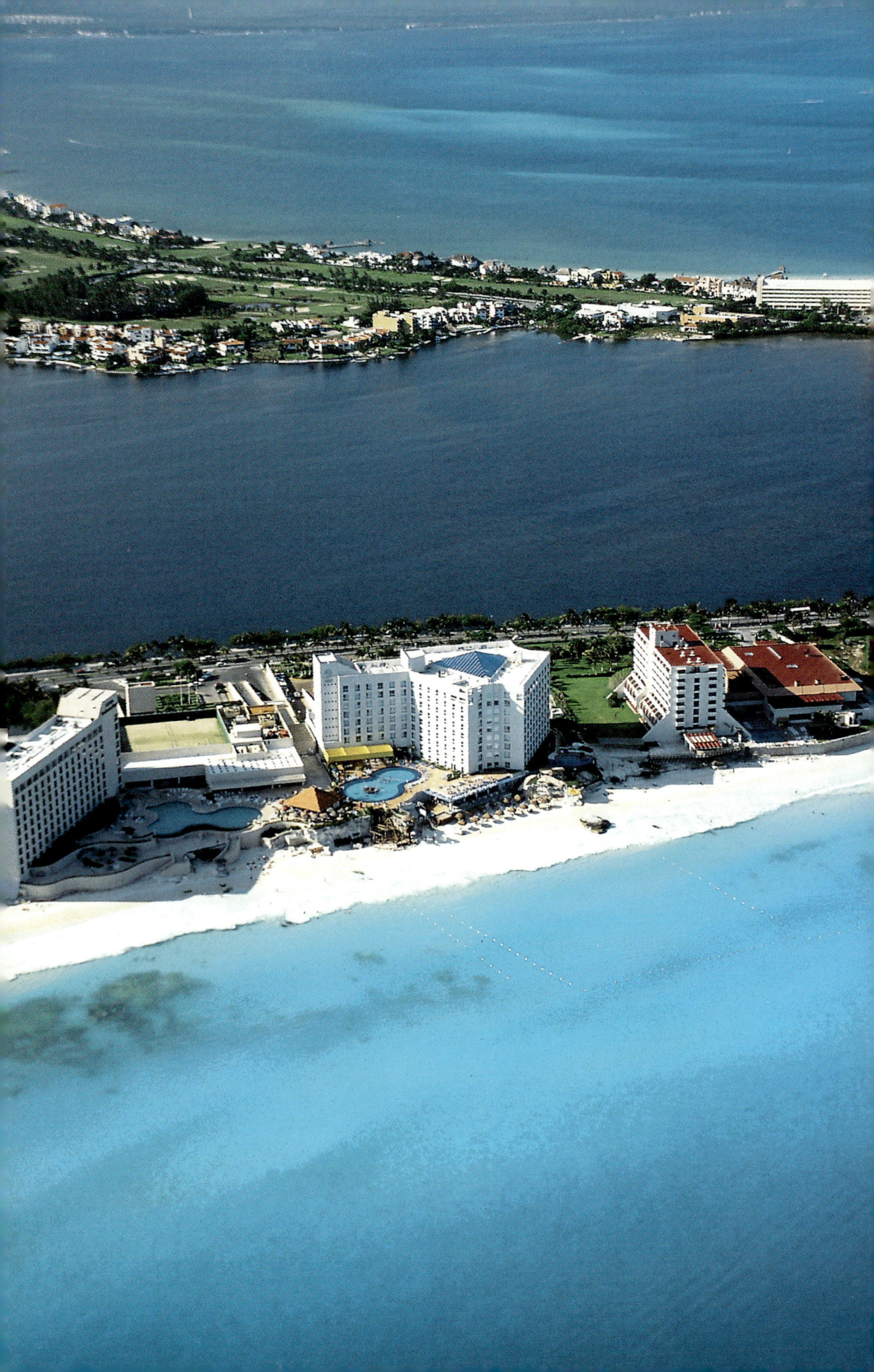

CANCUN

Cancún (pronounced Cahn-koon) was born as a tourist resort only in the 1970s. At that time Mexico had only one coastal area – around Acapulco – designated for tourism, and the Mexican government, recognizing the importance of tourism for the country began a detailed search to pinpoint sites for tourism development. In 1969 a long sandbar on the Caribbean coast emerged as the next area of development, and work first started on the new development – the future Cancún – in 1974. By the early 1980s Cancún was still relatively small and undiscovered, with only a dozen or so hotels, but the mid-1980s brought a building boom. Cancún is beginning to count as one of the Caribbean's top resorts and it is now Mexico's principal source of tourism revenue in terms of foreign exchange.

Cancún has three districts. The first, the City of Cancún, is a boom town of some 300,000 souls, with shopping and dining areas, less expensive accommodation, and a bullring. The second district, the Ecological Reserve, comprises the inner lagoon, the Laguna Nichupté, and the mangrove swamps. The third district, the Resort or Hotel Zone (*Zona Hotelera*) is on an island bordering the Caribbean Sea. Its development has been planned in three stages to minimize its impact on the environment. Stage two, a new marina called Puerto Cancún, and a new residential area, San Buenaventura, is near completion.

CANCÚN'S BEACH RESORTS

The Resort Zone in Cancún runs for 22.5 km (14 miles) along a slender strip of sand shaped like a number 7, and is joined to the mainland by bridges at Playa Linda and Punta Nizúc. The beaches are stunning and clean. The sand, a mixture of limestone, coral and ground shell, is as soft as talcum powder. It never seems to overheat so it is always comfortable to walk on, making Cancún a must for all sun worshippers.

Although it is impressive, the Resort Zone could be anywhere in the modern world – there is nothing of the traditional Mexico in 'Hotel Land'. The hotels are expensive, polished, and international in style. Altogether, the Resort Zone has some 20,000 hotel rooms and over 200 restaurants, catering for all tastes. There are a dozen American-style

Opposite: *Cancún's Hotel Zone stretches along a narrow sandbar reaching out from the mainland.*
Above: *A diving boat from Scuba Cancún.*

> **BAHÍA DE MUJERES**
>
> The sea around Cancún is shallow – the maximum depth of the sea bed in the Bahía de Mujeres is 9 m (30 ft) and the outside reefs bottom out at 17 m (55 ft). The whole area was once dry land. The floor of the bay is old coralline limestone bedrock – an ancient, dead coral reef.
> This bay is at the northern limit of coral growth in the western Caribbean and the Gulf of Mexico, but elkhorn, staghorn, star, brain and other hard corals, including gorgonians, such as the plume-like sea fans, are plentiful, and there are vivid sponges and several species of algae, some a brilliant green.

shopping malls – giant, air-conditioned centres where an atmosphere of unreality seems to prevail.

The beaches at Playa Las Perlas, Playa Langosta and Playa Tortuga are worthy of note as they are fairly sheltered. On the open ocean side of the Hotel Zone, the sea can be rougher, with some strong undertows. While qualified lifeguards patrol the beaches at some of the larger hotels, it is advisable to abide by the flag warnings posted on the beaches. Yellow indicates that precautions should be taken and red signals that it is dangerous to enter the sea. Beaches on this side include Gaviota Azul, Chac Mool, Playa Marlin, Playa Ballenas and Playa Delfines – which is worth a visit for its spectacular view. Cancún is a new city and still growing, but you do not have to travel far to visit the spectacular ruins of the cities of Chichen Itzá and Coba, and the port of Tulum, built by the Toltecs, the Maya and the Aztecs (see pages 16–17). And you do not have to travel a great distance inland to find the colourful culture of traditional Mexico.

THE CANCÚN COAST AND OFFSHORE ISLANDS

The Tourist Corridor – the coastal zone between Cancún and Tulum – is also sometimes called the Costa Turquesa (Turquoise Coast) because of the superb coastal scenery, shallow lagoons and turquoise waters of the Caribbean Sea (in fact the local radio station from Playa del Carmen is called Radio Turquesa).

There are three islands just off the Cancún's north coast, Isla Mujeres and Isla Contoy, the largest and most important (see pages 59–71), and Isla Blanca, which lies between them. They are in the Gulf of Mexico; a few kilometres to the south lies Cozumel (see pages 72–103), Mexico's only Caribbean island.

DIVING FROM CANCÚN

Most of the diving takes place in the sheltered Bahía de Mujeres between Cancún and Isla Mujeres. Much of the diving is done by trainees and first-time visitors to the region, who are intent on exploring a different part of the Caribbean. All dive centres are PADI–certified (see page 38); they offer beginners' courses to a very high standard and they take care of every diving need. Drift-diving predominates and the dive-boat captains keep on station over divers under their charge as they progress along the reef.

Cancún is advertised by tour operators as an all-round vacation resort; its potential as a first-class diving destination is still not widely recognized – despite the fact that there are rarely so many fish in one place as there are among the shallow reefs and mini-walls of the Bahía de Mujeres. Most of the dive centres offer packages: three dives and equipment for US$55; five dives and equipment US$75.

The remote Alacran Banks, 130 km (80 miles) north of Cancún, are offshore, crescent-shaped coral banks, about 16 km (10 miles) long. There are no regular dive charters to these reefs, but a very occasional trip is made by a live-aboard boat based in Cozumel. The reefs are said to have a number of wrecks, and because of their remote location are assumed to be in excellent condition.

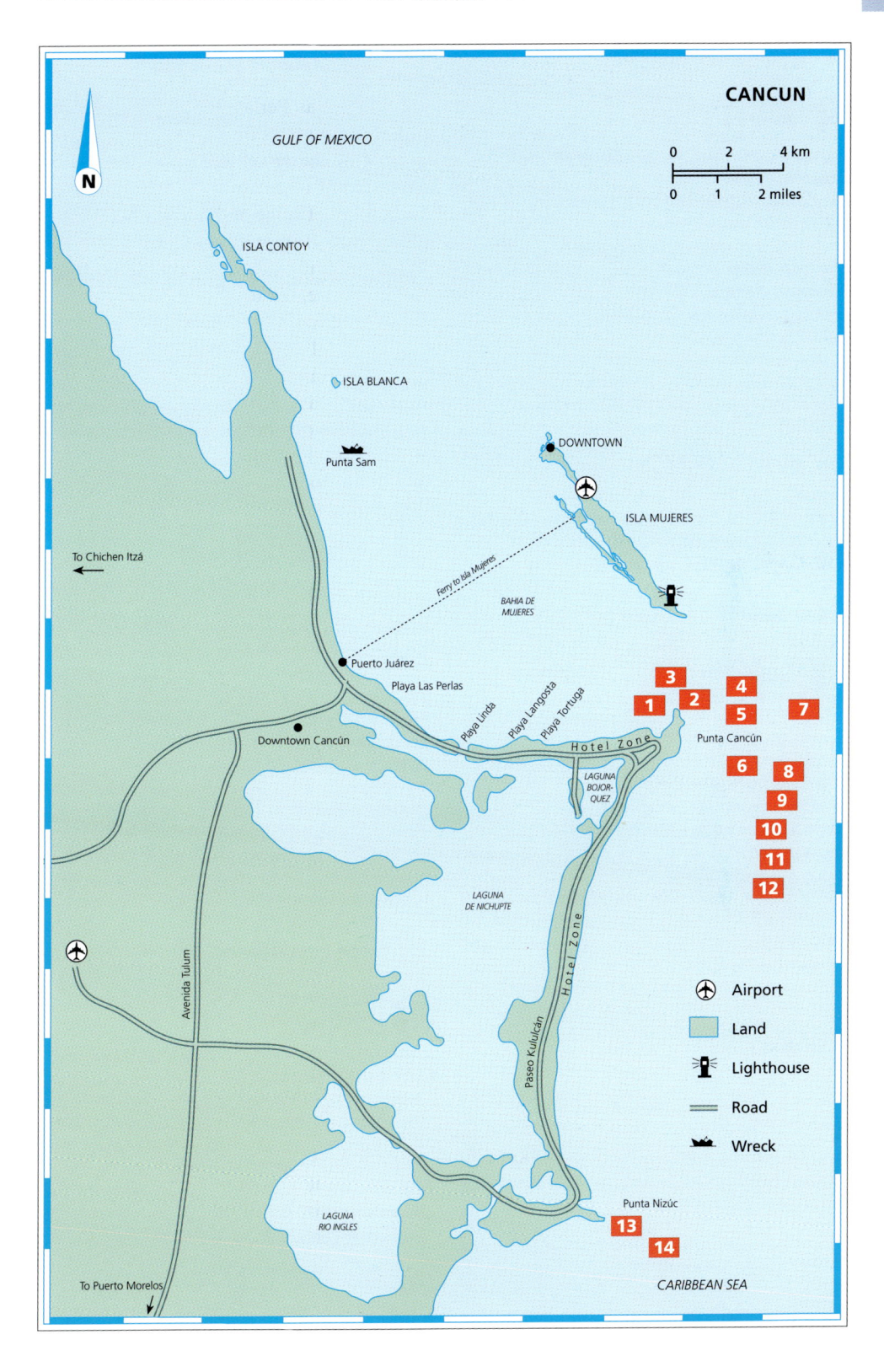

Cancún

47

1 Chintales (Chitales)
★★★★★★

Location: shallow dive, northwest of Punta Cancún.
Access: dive boat.
Conditions: slight-to-moderate current as the tidal stream whips around Punta Cancún. Generally ocean swell creating an underwater surge zone.
Minimum depth: 2 m (6 ft)
Maximum depth: 6 m (20 ft)
Average visibility: over 20 m (66 ft)

A shallow, protected strip reef on the inside, but subject to surge on the more exposed outside. This is essentially a very old, dead reef which is undergoing regeneration. There is new coral growth, with elkhorn coral (*Acropora palmata*) in the shallows and the purple sea fan (*Gorgonia ventalina*) all over. In many places you can find the encrusting gorgonian (*Erythropodium caribaeorum*). The reef is visited every day by the *Nautibus* semi-submersible tourist submarine. Although the corals are not good, there are schools of yellowtail and other snapper, grunts, tangs and other fish.

2 Cueveños
★★★★★★★

Location: shallow dive, northeast of Punta Cancún.
Access: directly from the shore.
Conditions: moderate-to-strong current and swell.
Minimum depth: 5 m (17 ft)
Maximum depth: 9 m (30 ft)
Average visibility: over 20 m (66 ft)

This reef suffered at the hands of Hurricane Roxanne in 1995, but there are good signs of recovery now. *Cueveños* means 'caves', and although there are no true caves there are some very large undercut sections of reef. Huge numbers of juvenile snapper and grunts can be seen, orange filefish (*Cantherhines macroceros*) are evident among some of the larger branches of coral, and blue and grey angelfish can be found under the overhangs. Among some of the coral outcrops there are

---

NAUTIBUS SUBMARINE

The Nautibus Submarine XII is not a real submarine but a boat with a deep, glass-bottomed hull and glassed-in side windows. Through the submerged hull, passengers get a comfortable view of the coral reefs and fishes without having to bend over, as in the old-fashioned glass-bottomed boats. The *Nautibus* operates from the same pier in Cancún as the *Atlantis* and tours the reefs in and around Bahía de Mujeres.

ATLANTIS SUBMARINE

The Atlantis Submarine XII is a fully operational submarine, 20 m (66 ft) long, weighing 80 tons, and licensed to carry 48 passengers. It takes visitors on a one-hour trip round the coral lagoon of Cancún, offering an expert narration in Spanish and English. It explores the coral heads in the area around Manchones Reef (Site 21) and Manchones Xico (Site 22), giving passengers close-ups of snapper, grunt, and other reef inhabitants. The trip costs approximately US$65.

---

channel-clinging crabs (*Mithrax spinosissimus*). This site is a favourite with several dive centres. At night you find green moray eels (*Gymnothorax funebris*) and snowflake morays (*Gymnothorax moringa*) in the larger coral rubble sections. Cleaning shrimps and the occasional nurse shark (*Ginglymostoma cirratum*) are often seen.

3 El Bajito
★★★★★

Location: a shallow dive, directly to the north from Punta Cancún.
Access: by boat or a lengthy swim from the shore.
Conditions: significant surge among the coral rocks. Should only be dived and snorkelled when conditions are perfect.
Minimum depth: 1 m (3 ft)
Maximum depth: 5 m (17 ft)
Average visibility: reduced, due to surge

This is generally a drift dive as the current sweeps round the point rather fiercely. Lobster can be found in the late evening and at night. There is very little coral and the sea fans are rather ragged. This is a very exposed area, but still popular for snorkelling because of the large numbers and varieties of fish.

4 Three Lost Divers
★★★

Location: a shallow dive, southeast of Isla Mujeres and north of Punta Negra (Site 5).
Access: by dive boat only.
Conditions: current is to be expected and it can be quite strong at times. Strong open ocean surface swell makes it difficult to get back into the dive boat safely.
Minimum depth: 12 m (40 ft)
Maximum depth: 17 m (55 ft)
Average visibility: more than 20 m (66 ft)

Opposite: *Silvery shoals of blue-striped grunt* (Haemulon sciurus) *are common around Cancún.*

This site was named after three divers who were swept by a strong current from one of the other low-lying strip reefs and found this reef by accident. The reef is long and narrow and runs for more than 600 m (half a mile) to the north. An old ship's engine block can be seen near the reef's northern end. There are numerous scoured-out sand hollows which seem to be a natural congregation point for several species of fish, especially grunt and snapper. The fish are friendly and they are not fed by the dive guides.

5 Punta Negra
★★★

Location: shallow dive, south of Three Lost Divers (Site 4).
Access: by dive boat only.
Conditions: current to be expected, surge conditions are common.
Minimum depth: 14 m (45 ft)
Maximum depth: 17 m (55 ft)
Average visibility: more than 20 m (66 ft)

This is a flat sea bed with a short mini-wall which rises 1.8 m (6 ft) from the sand. The whole reef is very low-lying and there are numerous small, tall coral heads, as well as the usual strip reef. Large schools of congregating juvenile bluestriped grunt *(Haemulon sciurus)* and cottonwick *(Haemulon melanurum)* can be found among the coral heads.

6 El Tunel
★★★

Location: shallow dive, due east from Punta Cancún.
Access: by boat only.
Conditions: moderate-to-swift current and surface surge make this area uncomfortable between dives.
Minimum depth: 14 m (45 ft)
Maximum depth: 17 m (55 ft)
Average visibility: more than 20 m (66 ft)

This narrow, very low strip reef is in two sections running parallel to the shore and is subject to strong currents on the outward side, but shelter can be found in the lee of the reef. There is some coral damage, but there are many swimthroughs and small tunnels. Two large tunnels run for 6 m (20 ft) through the reef. Instead of the one steady mini-wall, which occurs elsewhere in the bay, this reef is deeply indented. Corals are not plentiful but there are gorgonians and feathery plumes and rods, and an abundance of fish can be found all over this reef section, including pufferfish and filefish.

A sharpnose puffer (Canthigaster rostrata) *peering from inside a pink vase sponge.*

7 Cuevas de Afuera
★★★

Location: a shallow dive, east of Three Lost Divers (Site 4).
Access: by dive boat only.
Conditions: strong currents on this the most northerly strip reef just outside of Bahía de Mujeres. Surface chop and surging are to be expected from November to April.
Minimum depth: 12 m (40 ft)
Maximum depth: 20 m (66 ft)
Average visibility: more than 20 m (66 ft)
A long, thin strip reef, low-lying but with large mounds of star coral (*Monastrea annularis*). Sea fans and various sponges dot this otherwise fairly common reef. Fish are very much in evidence all over: look out for barracuda and numerous blue chromis (*Chromis cyanea*). The yellowtail damselfish (*Microspathodon chrysurus*) is particularly aggressive during the breeding season.

8 San Torbido (San Torino)
★★★

Location: a shallow dive, due east from Punta Cancún but this is the next strip reef further out from Site 7.
Access: by boat only.
Conditions: current is to be expected. All the outside reefs are similar in that the sea bed is at 17 m (55 ft) and all are low-lying.
Minimum depth: 12 m (40 ft)
Maximum depth: 17 m (55 ft)
Average visibility: more than 20 m (66 ft)
This is a low-level strip reef running perpendicular to the shore. There is a short, level mini-wall, slightly undercut, which has numerous sponge growths. Pairs of angelfish can be found dotted around the reef and foureye butterflyfish (*Chaetodon capistratus*) are very evident. Black jacks (*Caranx lugubris*) have been spotted queuing up at cleaning stations, attended by the juvenile Spanish hogfish (*Bodianus rufus*).

9 El Grampin
★★★

Location: a shallow dive. One of the outer reefs south of San Torbido (Site 8), perpendicular to the Cancún shore.
Access: by boat only.
Conditions: current is to be expected running north along this low-lying strip reef.
Minimum depth: 14 m (45 ft)
Maximum depth: 17 m (55 ft)
Average visibility: more than 20 m (66 ft)

This reef is typical of strip reefs along this stretch of the coast. It is low-lying and swept by currents. It is best to dive the site when the wind is blowing from the north as it tends to equalize the current in the water – although it causes rather rough surface conditions. Coral growth includes low fan corals, brain corals and staghorn coral (*Acropora cervicornis*). Blue angelfish, considered rare in this part of the Caribbean, have been seen here.

10 La Herradura
★★★

Location: a shallow dive, south of El Grampín (Site 9) parallel to the shore.
Access: by dive boat only.
Conditions: reef runs south to north and is subject to predictable currents.
Minimum depth: 6 m (20 ft)
Maximum depth: 17 m (55 ft)
Average visibility: over 20 m (66 ft)

The further south these strip reefs are, the better the coral growth. Although the maximum depth is only 17m (55ft) there is great variety and better reef diversity in this location. Between November and April there are many juveniles; a pair of juvenile queen angelfish (*Holacanthus ciliaris*) was spotted by the author, already in their lifelong mating partnership. The juveniles of this magnificent fish are as brightly coloured as the adults.

11 San Miguel
★★★

Location: a shallow dive, continuing south parallel to the Cancún shoreline.
Access: by dive boat only.
Conditions: current is to be expected, running from south to north. Surge on the outside of the reef, but there are numerous sheltered areas on the inside.
Minimum depth: 14 m (45 ft)
Maximum depth: 20 m (66 ft)
Average visibility: over 20 m (66 ft)

San Miguel, an interesting, ancient reef, is a continuation of the strip reef running north to south and parallel to Cancún. You find large rainbow parrotfish (*Scarus guacamaia*) and the stoplight parrotfish (*Sparisoma viride*) blending, with its chequerboard coloration, into the multicoloured shades of the reef. Spotlight gobies (*Gobiosoma louisae*) dart over the sponges and most large brain corals have Christmas tree worms (*Spirobranchus giganteus*) over them.

12 Aristos
★★★

Location: a shallow dive opposite the Aristos Hotel and last section of the same strip reef before Punta Nizúc.
Access: by dive boat only.
Conditions: current is always to be expected, as well as surge on the seabed between November and April.
Minimum depth: 15 m (50 ft)
Maximum depth: 22 m (71 ft)
Average visibility: 20 m (66 ft)

This is as far south as the dive boats travel round the outside of the Cancún lagoon; the exit on this side is at Playa Linda. Several other dive centres at Playa Tortugas, Playa Langosta and Playa Caracol leave directly from the more sheltered northern jetties. This reef is also ancient and is recovering nicely, with some interesting new coral growth and sponges. An excellent night dive.

13 Punta Nizúc
★★★★

Location: a deep dive, southeast from Punta Nizúc opposite Club Med.
Access: by dive boat only.
Conditions: there can be strong currents, but reef is marked with a mooring buoy, so dive tends to be around the reef and back to the line to allow for a safety decompression stop of 3 minutes at 3 m (10 ft).
Minimum depth: 23 m (75 ft)
Maximum depth: 30 m (100 ft)
Average visibility: over 30 m (100 ft)

Any dive boats passing under the bridge from the lagoon at Punta Nizúc must have a special permit from the maritime police. The reef is marked by a mooring buoy, otherwise it would be almost impossible to find the exact location. It is a large patch reef shaped roughly like a doughnut. Current is always to be expected here, but by holding on to and descending down the mooring line, you will reach the shelter of the reef in safety.

Although there are relatively few fish on this reef the marine life that inhabits it is large. Wide-mesh sea fans (*Gorgonia mariae*) and sea whips (*Ellisella elongata*), large arrow crabs (*Stenorhynchus seticornis*), and several species of hermit crab can be found all over the reef. Look out for large specimens of the giant anemone (*Condylactis gigantea*). Big vase sponges dot the reef. If you look closely you may see a colonial zoanthid, looking like a miniature yellow anemone, living in the sponge. Grouper are common and there is a better chance on this reef of seeing larger pelagic fish as they swim with the current searching for prey. Barracuda are always present and large schools of horse-eye jacks (*Caranx latus*) have been seen. Large numbers of the southern sennet (*Sphyraena picudilla*), another member of the barracuda family, can be found closer to the surface.

14 Nizúc Reef
★★★★★★★

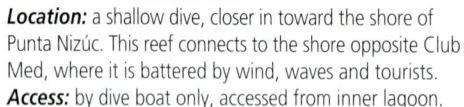

Location: a shallow dive, closer in toward the shore of Punta Nizúc. This reef connects to the shore opposite Club Med, where it is battered by wind, waves and tourists.
Access: by dive boat only, accessed from inner lagoon.
Conditions: current and choppy surface conditions are to be expected.
Minimum depth: 12 m (40 ft)
Maximum depth: 18 m (60 ft)
Average visibility: more than 15 m (50 ft)

An interesting reef with large numbers of grunt and snapper to be seen. There are sponges of every colour and gobies and blennies of various descriptions are everywhere. Coral growth is much better in this area and there are many good examples of hard corals to see. This reef can be snorkelled. In fact a number of the operators like to put snorkellers in deeper water to stop them from holding on to the corals.

Aquaworld of Cancún have installed a floating island where tourists are ferried out to snorkel and ride on the glass-bottomed semi-submersible boats which run regularly every day round these shallow reefs. There are snack bar and toilet facilities. Aquaworld also have a dive centre for visitors who want to see more of the reefs.

The orange tube sponge, Aplysina fistularis, *grows more than 1 m (3–4 ft) long.*

Cancún

How to Get There

Most tourists arrive in Cancún each year by air on regular daily flights operated by a number of international airlines. They fly into **Cancún International Airport**, located 14 km (9 miles) from Downtown Cancún, on the Puerto Morelos highway. Information on airlines flying into Cancún and their schedules is available from travel agents and the information desk at any international airport. For the 24-hour information line at Cancún International Airport: tel: (988) 60049.

Where to Stay

The hotels, condominiums, villas, suites and apartments in Cancún's Hotel Zone and Downtown offer some 25,000 beds. The Cancún Hotel Association has a star-rating system for hotels and a scheme called *Gran Turismo* for large establishments that cater to your every whim. The state tourist office and a free pocket magazine, *Cancún Tips* – available everywhere – give information on hotels. A representative selection of hotels is listed here.

Asociación de Hoteles de Cancún, A.C, Avda Ignacio García de la Torre 6, S.M.1, Apto Postal 1339, Cancún, Q. Roo, Mexico 77500; tel (988) 42853/45895/fax (988) 47115. A full list of the Hotel Association's 73 members is available from this office.
Camara Nacional de Comercio, Servicios and Turismo, Avda López Portillo 11, Downtown, Cancún, Q. Roo, Mexico 77500; tel (988) 44315/fax (988) 41164.
Tourist Information, State Tourist Office, Avda Tulum 29, S.M.5, Downtown, Cancún, Q. Roo, Mexico 77500; tel (988) 48073/ 800-90392 (English-speaking helpline).

Hotel Zone
Expensive
Camino Real Cancún, Punta Cancún, Hotel Zone, Cancún, Q. Roo, Mexico 77500; tel (988) 30100/fax (988) 32965; www.caminoreal.com. Five restaurants, two pools, tennis courts, three beaches, watersports, shopping, a fitness centre, 381 rooms.
Fiesta Americana Cancún, Blvd Kukulcán km 9.5, Hotel Zone, Cancún, Q. Roo, Mexico 77500; tel (988) 31400/fax (988) 32502; www.fiestaamericana.com. Three restaurants, four bars, a pool, 281 rooms.
Fiesta Americana Condessa, Blvd Kukulcán km 16.5, Hotel Zone, Cancún, Q. Roo, Mexico 77500; tel (988) 51000/fax (988) 51800; www.fiestaamericana.com. Four restaurants, two bars, tennis courts, 502 rooms.
Fiesta Americana Coral Beach Cancún, Blvd Kukulcán km 9.5, Hotel Zone, Cancún, Q. Roo, Mexico 77500; tel (988) 32900/fax (988) 33076; www.fiestaamericana.com. Three restaurants, three bars, tennis courts, beauty/health club, 602 suites.
Hotel Presidente Inter-Continental, Blvd Kukulcán km 7.5, Hotel Zone, Cancún, Q. Roo, Mexico 77500; tel (988) 30200/fax (988) 31125; email cancun@interconti.com. Four restaurants, a bar, two pools, five whirlpools, beauty/health clubs, 298 rooms.
Hyatt Cancún Caribe, Blvd Kukulcán km 10.5, Hotel Zone, Cancún, Q. Roo, Mexico 77500; tel (988) 30044/fax (988) 31514; www.hyatt.com. Four restaurants, two bars, tennis courts, three pools, a marina, Jacuzzis, a putting green, 198 rooms and 26 beach-front villas.
Krystal, Blvd Kukulcán km 9, Hotel Zone, Cancún, Q. Roo, Mexico 77500; tel (988) 31133/fax (988) 31790. Four restaurants, three bars, pools, health and beauty salons, 316 rooms.
Ritz Carleton Cancún, Blvd Kukulcán Ret. del Rey, Hotel Zone, Cancún, Q. Roo, Mexico 77500; tel (988) 50180/fax (988) 51015. Three restaurants, two bars, three pools, tennis courts, a spa, health and beauty salons, 370 rooms.
Sierra Cancún, Blvd Kukulcán km 10, Hotel Zone, Cancún, Q. Roo, Mexico 77500; tel (988) 32444/fax (988) 33486. Three restaurants, a bar, tennis courts, three pools, health and beauty salons, 247 rooms.
Westin Regina Resort Cancún, Blvd Kukulcán km 9, Hotel Zone, Cancún, Q. Roo, Mexico 77500; tel (988) 50086/fax (988) 50779; email westin@sybcom.com. Four restaurants, three bars, five pools, tennis courts, fitness rooms, health and beauty salons, 391 rooms.

Moderate
Cancún Marina Club, Blvd Kukulcán km 5.5, Hotel Zone, Cancún, Q. Roo, Mexico 77500; tel (988) 31561/fax (988) 31409. Restaurant, marina, pool, watersports, health and beauty salons, 89 suites.
Holiday Inn Express, Blvd Kukulcán km 4.5, Hotel Zone, Cancún, Q. Roo, Mexico 77500; tel (988) 52200/fax (988) 52532. Two restaurants, two bars, five pools, 119 rooms.
Hoteles Aristos Cancún, Blvd Kukulcán km 9.6, Hotel Zone, Cancún, Q. Roo, Mexico 77500; tel (988) 30800/fax (988) 32087; www.aristoshotels.com. Two restaurants, marina, watersports, health and beauty salons, 250 rooms, all with balconies.
Ocean Club Suites, Pok-Ta-Pok, Hotel Zone, Cancún, Q. Roo, Mexico 77500; tel/fax (988) 832200; email chboyce@mpsnet.mx. Restaurant, pool, 124 self-catering suites.

Inexpensive
Attención a la Juventad, Blvd Kukulcán km 3, Hotel Zone, Cancún, Q. Roo, Mexico 77500; tel/fax (00 52) 988 31337. Government-run Youth Hostel with 33 rooms and 300 beds (shared facilities).

Downtown
Moderate
Antillano, Avda Tulum and Calle Claveles, Downtown, Cancún, Q. Roo, Mexico 77500; tel (988) 41532/ fax (988) 41878. A pool, a bar, a travel agency, a shop, 48 rooms.
Hotel Best Western Plaza Caribe, Calle Pino, between Avdas Tulum and Axmal, Downtown, Cancún, Q. Roo, Mexico 77500; tel (988) 41377/fax (988) 46352; www.bestwestern.com. Restaurant, bars, a pool, 140 rooms.
Hotel Novotel, Avda Tulum 26, Downtown, Cancún, Q. Roo, Mexico 77500; tel (988) 42999/fax (988) 43162. A restaurant, a pool, cabins round poool and on street-side.
Hotel Suites Caribe Internacional, Yaxchilan 36 and Sunyaxchen, Downtown, Cancún, Q. Roo, Mexico 77500; tel (988) 43999/fax (988) 41993. A restaurant, a café, a pool, free beach shuttle, 80 rooms.

Inexpensive
Hotel El Rey del Caribe, Corner of Avdas Uxmal and Nader, Downtown, Cancún, Q. Roo, Mexico 77500; tel (988) 442028/ fax (988) 49857; email reycaribe@cancun.rce.com.mx. Restaurant next door, 25 rooms, some with kitchenette.

Information and Complaints

If you need information or have a complaint or a problem about Cancún or the local services contact these agencies:

State Tourism Information Centre
Avda Tulum 29, S.M.5, Downtown, Cancún, Q. Roo, Mexico 77500 (next to Multibanco Comermex); tel: (988) 48073; freephone Helpline in English: (800) 90892. Open daily 09:00–21:00 hours.

Consumer Protection Agency, (Procuraduría del Consumidor), Avda Coba 10 (altos/upstairs), opposite Social Security Hospital, Downtown; tel: 84 2634; 84 2701, 87 2877/fax: 84 2744. Open Mon–Fri 08:00–14:00 hours; Sat 10:00–13:00 hours.

Restaurant Association, Tulipanes 12, S.M.22, Downtown, Cancún, Q. Roo, Mexico 77500; tel (988) 43315. Contact for information about restaurants.

Cancún

Where to Eat

Eating in Cancún is generally good value. If you are catering for yourself, the food and drinks on sale in local Downtown supermarkets costs about one-third less than in the tourist supermarkets in the Hotel Zone. Most restaurants are typically Tex-Mex, with excellent local seafood and traditional Mexican fare the speciality, but food styles range from bars offering rock music with their barbecues and beer to fine cuisine in the international hotels. 'Turf and Surf' establishments serving the diver's favourite: a combination of fresh lobster, fish or shrimp and steak, are popular everywhere on the Yucatán's east coast. There are excellent Italian restaurants and every major food/club chain has premises in Cancún.

Listed below is a selection of the several hundred restaurants in Cancún's Hotel Zone and a few good-value restaurants Downtown. Personal preferences differ widely, so the choice of restaurants listed is not necessarily a recommendation. Few require advance booking, but if you want to book, several will supply a menu beforehand.

International
Chac-Mool Restaurant & Bar, Playa Chac-Mool; tel (00 52) 988 31107. Traditional English fare, as well as full international, excellent sea views.
Ruth's Chris Steak House, Plaza Kukulcán; tel (00 52) 988 53301. Speciality is imported prime beef.

Mexican
Iguana Wana, Plaza Caracol; tel (988) 30829. Contemporary Mexican, chicken and beef fajitas.
Pericos, Avda Yaxchilan 71; tel (988) 43152/fax (988) 75959. Authentic restaurant and cantina.

Italian
Casa Rolandi, Plaza Caracol; tel (988) 31817. Northern Italian cuisine, romantic Mediterranean atmosphere.
La Dolce Vita, Avda Coba 87; tel (988) 41384. The speciality here is *boquinete* (fish in pastry) – excellent.
Rolandi's Restaurant-Bar, Avda Coba 12; tel (988) 44047. Pizzas, pasta with a northern Swiss/Italian touch.
Savio's, Plaza Caracol; tel (988) 32085.

Seafood
Gypsy's, Paseo Kukulcán; tel (988) 32120.
La Fishería, Plaza Caracol; tel (988) 31395.

Tex-Mex
Carlos N' Charlie's, Hotel Zone; tel (988) 50016/fax (988) 51900.
Mr. Papas, Plaza Caracol; tel (988) 31104/fax (988) 31553.

Señor Frogs, Hotel Zone; tel (988) 32931/fax (988) 32808.
TGI Fridays, Hotel Zone; tel (988) 33542/fax (988) 31466.
Tony Roma's, Hotel Zone; tel (988) 30084/fax (988) 30085.

Chinese
Hong Kong, Plaza Kukulcán; tel (988) 52413.

Dive Facilities

The largest and most well-advertised diving operators are not necessarily the best ones, although these operations are very professional and will try to give the tourist what they are looking for. The author prefers a small operation with a spacious, comfortable boat. It is always recommended to contact the diving operations prior to your trip to check out the facilities and whether they are still prepared to take divers out when there are reduced numbers and whether they have room or facilities for rinsing camera equipment.

Dive Operators
Aquatours, Blvd Kukulcán km 6.25, Cancún, Q. Roo, Mexico 77500; tel (988) 30400/fax (988) 30403; www.aquatours.net.
Aquaworld, Blvd Kukulcán km 15.2, Cancún, Q. Roo, Mexico 77500; tel (988) 52288/fax (988) 52299; www.aquaworld.com.mx.
Blue Peace Diving, Avda Kukulcán km 16.2, Cancún, Q. Roo, Mexico 77500; tel (988) 51447/fax (988) 52179; email bluepeace@caribe.net.mx.

Mr. Papas' Tex-Mex Restaurant on Plaza Caracol, Cancún.

Blue Water Divers, Avda Kukulcán km 15.6, Cancún, Q. Roo, Mexico 77500; tel/fax (988) 50300.
Caribbean Diving Institute, Garcia de la Torre 41, S.M.2-A, Cancún, Q. Roo, Mexico 77500; tel (788) 420 57000/fax(788) 449 67000.
Coral Divers, Plaza Kukulcán L-160, Cancún, Q. Roo, Mexico 77500; tel(988) 50110.
Dolphin Discovery, Centro Commercial Plaza, Quetzal Local 4, Blvd Kulkulcán km 8, Cancún, Q. Roo, Mexico 77500; tel (988) 35710/fax (988) 32617; email splashcn@qroo1.telmex.net.mx.
Krystal Divers, Krystal Hotel, Blvd Kukulcán km 0.9, Cancún, Q. Roo, Mexico 77500; tel (988) 31133/fax (988) 31790.
Manta Divers, Blvd Kukulcán km 6.5, Playa Tortugas, Cancún, Q. Roo, Mexico 77500; tel (988) 34050/fax (988) 09448; email dive@mantadivers.com.
Marina Aqua Bay, Doug Kauffman, Blvd Kukulcán km 10.5, Cancún, Q. Roo, Mexico 77500; tel (988) 31763.
Marina Carrousel, Hotel Carrousel, Blvdo Kukulcán D-6, Cancún, Q. Roo, Mexico 77500; tel (988) 30513/fax (988) 32312.
Mundo Marino Water World, Blvd Kukulcán km 5.5, Cancún, Q. Roo, Mexico 77500; tel/fax (988) 30554.
Nautilus Diving Centre, Marina del Hotel Caribbean Suites, Blvd Kukulcán, Cancún, Q. Roo, Mexico 77500; tel/fax (988) 44967.
Ocean Sports, Calinda Viva Hotel, Blvd Kukulcán km 8.5, Cancún, Q. Roo, Mexico 77500; tel/fax (988) 46034.
Quicksilver Dive, Blvd Kukulcán km 4.5, Playa Linda, Cancún, Q. Roo, Mexico 77500; tel (988) 34632/fax (988) 31228; www.quicksilver.com.
Scuba Cancún, Blvd Kukulcán km 0.5, PO Box 517, Cancún, Q. Roo, Mexico 77500; tel (988) 31011/fax (988) 42336; email scuba@cancun.com.mx.
Scuba Du, Hotel Presidente Inter-Continental, Paseo Kukulcán km 7.5, Cancún, Q., Mexico 77500; tel (988) 30200/fax (988) 32515.
Solo Buceo, Hotel Camino Real, Cancún, Q. Roo, Mexico 77500; tel (988) 30100/fax (988) 32965; www.cancun-webs.com/scuba.htm.

Other Dive Facilities
Aqua II, Terminal Dock, Marina Playa Blanca, Hotel Zone, Cancún, Q. Roo, Mexico 77500; tel (988) 71909/fax (988) 41254. Isla Mujeres cruises, etc.
Aqua Tours Adventures, Blvd Kukulcán km 6.25, Cancún, Q. Roo, Mexico 77500; tel (988) 30400; www.aquatours.com. Snorkelling tours, and self-drive speed boat for a jungle tour of the mangroves.
Aquatec, Bonampak 185L, S.M.4, Cancún, Q. Roo, Mexico 77500; tel/fax (988) 44566.

Cancún

Suppliers of diving equipment to the trade.
Marina Aqua Ray, Blvd Kukulcán km 10.5, Cancún, Q. Roo, Mexico 77500; tel (988) 33007. Small boat, jetski and snorkelling trips.
Marina Jetski, Blvd Kukulcán km 8.5, Cancún, Q. Roo, Mexico 77500; tel (988) 30766. Jetski hire and snorkelling trips.

Marinas
There are 15 marinas in Cancún; all offer private boat charter, diving, snorkelling, deep-sea fishing, jetskiing and windsurfing, as well as private yacht moorings. For details, contact the Tourist Office (see page 53).

EMERGENCY/MEDICAL SERVICES

Recompression Chamber
Most diving operations in Cancún administer a US$1 charge per diver, which goes toward the upkeep of the recompression chamber and the treatment costs of anyone using it. All divers coming should have full holiday and health insurance cover so that treatment costs can be charged against the insurance cover. Divers who need treatment but have inadequate insurance cover will be treated and the extra costs will be met by the fees levied on all the divers who register.

The recompression chamber iis privately owned by Sub-Aquatic Safety Services. It operates on a full 24-hour service, and a a full medical clinic is run alongside it, so that any diving-related incident will be treated by highly trained staff. The facility has a 135-cm (54-in) diameter chamber with a double lock. The medical capabilities in the chamber include the use of IV fluids, EKG machines, ventilators and other emergency equipment, two rooms for patients, a surgery room, an emergency room with X-ray facilities and a closed-circuit television link with the interior of the chamber.
The recommended recompression chamber is on Cozumel Island (see page 103) – flights are always available; tel (987) 20140/22387/21430.
Life Flight (Houston, Texas) for delivery to recompression chamber in the US; tel (800) 392 4357, (713) 797 4357.
Air-Evac (San Diego, California) for delivery to recompression chamber in the US; tel (800) 854 2567, (619) 278 3822.
Radio: La Costera (Coastguard) Channel 16 *(canal numero dieciseis)*.
Belize Link, San Pedro Airstrip; tel (026) 2851/2073.
(DAN) Divers' Alert Network; tel (919) 648 8111.

Clinics
Centro Quirurgica Bonampak, Calle Tierra. 5, Downtown, Cancún, Q. Roo, Mexico 77500; tel (988) 45530.
Clinica Cancún, Calle Tanchacte 1, Downtown, Cancún, Q. Roo, Mexico 77500; tel (988) 41702.
Clinica Victoria, Avda Suntaxchen 59, Downtown, Cancún, Q. Roo, Mexico 77500; tel (988) 42407.
Cruz Roja, Calle Labna 2, Downtown, Cancún, Q. Roo, Mexico 77500; tel (988) 41616/fax (988) 47466.
Hospital Americano, Calle Viento 15, Downtown, Cancún, Q. Roo, Mexico 77500; tel (988) 46133/fax (988) 46425.

Social Services
Mexican Social Security Institute, Avdas Tulum and Coba, Downtown, Cancún, Q. Roo, Mexico 77500; tel (988) 41818/fax (988) 41907.
Segoro Social, Avdas Tulum and Coba, Downtown, Cancún, Q. Roo, Mexico 77500; tel (988) 41820/fax (988) 41907.
Total Assist, Calle Claveles 5, Downtown, Cancún, Q. Roo, Mexico 77500; tel (988) 41058/fax (988) 41092.

Doctors and dentists
English-speaking doctors:
Dr Sergio Galvez, Krystal Hotel, Hotel Zone, Cancún, Q. Roo, Mexico 77500; tel (988) 44754/31374/31133 x387.
Dr Juan Carlos Martínez, Calinda Beach Hotel, Hotel Zone, Cancún, Q. Roo, Mexico 77500; tel (988) 31600 (ask for Doctor's office).
Dr Guido Pinelo, Royal Caribbean & Vacation Clubs International, Hotel Zone, Cancún, Q Roo, Mexico 77500; tel (988) 30855; home surgery (988) 45759.

English-speaking Dentist
Dr Raul Vargas Fonseca, Calle Robalo 39, 1st Floor, S.M.3, Downtown, Cancún, Q. Roo, Mexico 77500; tel (988) 43390/74098.

Pharmacies
Farmacia Canto, Avdas Yaxchilan and Sunyaxchen, Downtown, Cancún, Q. Roo, Mexico 77500; tel (988) 44083.

The Plaza Caracol, Cancún.

Farmacia Extra, Plaza Caracol, Hotel Zone, Cancún, Q. Roo, Mexico 77500; tel (988) 32827.
Farmacia Paris, Avda Yaxchilan, Edificio Marrufo, Downtown, Cancún, Q. Roo, Mexico 77500; tel (988) 40164.
Farmacia Turística, Plaza Caracol, Hotel Zone, Cancún, Q. Roo, Mexico 77500; tel (988) 31894.
Super Gourmet & Deli/Drugstore, Plaza Kukulcán, Hotel Zone, Cancún, Q. Roo, Mexico 77500; tel (988) 53805 (deliveries).

LOCAL HIGHLIGHTS

Numerous tour companies employ touts on the streets to offer tours to local sights. Many also offer introductory discount vouchers to night clubs and restaurants. Prices are negotiable.
The archaeological sites of Coba, Chichen Itzá and Tulum are all in easy reach of Cancún, and there is a fine set of ruins called El Rey in Cancún (see pages 29–31).
Atlantis Submarine, Plaza Quetzal, Local 4, Blvd Kukulcán km 0.8, Hotel Zone, Cancún, Q. Roo, Mexico 77500; tel (988) 33021/fax (988) 34967. A real submarine adventure (see page 48).
Nautibus, Playa Linda Dock, Blvd Kukulcán km 6.5, Cancún, Q. Roo, Mexico 77500; tel (988) 33552/fax (988) 33216. Underwater sightseeing tour in an up-market glass-bottomed boat (see page 48).
Pegaso Air Tours; tel (988) 30879/30880. Flights to all surrounding islands via helicopter.
Ultralight Seaplane Rides, Cancún Avioturismo; tel (988) 830315/fax (988) 831935.

VEHICLE HIRE

A four-wheel-drive jeep or a Volkswagen are the vehicles most commonly available for hire. Blvd Kukulcán – the main coastal road along the Hotel Zone and Downtown – is probably the only road you will need to use. There are numerous car-hire outlets in Cancún. Ask at the airport, your hotel or the tourist office for details of reliable companies. There is only one petrol station in Cancún, situated at the main crossroads in Downtown. Mopeds, bicycles and scooters can also be hired. There is a specified cycle path through the Hotel Zone.

FILM PROCESSING

Cancún Photo Club, tel (988) 70943.
Caribe Film, tel (988) 30770.
Foto Express, tel (988) 33571.
Foto Kabah, tel (988) 74768.
Kodilab, tel (988) 45447.
Magicolor, tel (988) 41348.
Oficentro, tel (988) 40771.
Omega, tel (988) 41679.
Photo Shop, tel (988) 70031.

Angelfish

The fish people associate most closely with coral reefs are the brightly coloured, disc-shaped angelfish. There are five species of angelfish in northern Caribbean waters. The blue angelfish *(Holacanthus bermudensis)* is more commonly found around Bermuda and Florida and is considered rare in the western Caribbean. However, although it is rare in the coastal waters south of Tulum and not seen at all around Cozumel, it is very common around Cancún and Isla Mujeres.

THE QUEEN ANGELFISH

The aptly named queen angelfish *(Holacanthus ciliaris)* is very much the queen of all angelfish species. Its vivid, almost fluorescent blue and yellow markings seem to light up the reef. It is also easily distinguished by the dark blue/black-spotted crown on its forehead, ringed by a brilliant blue. The queen angelfish grows up to 45 cm (18 in).

There appears to be cross-fertilization between blue and queen angelfish, as is evidenced by the variety of colour matches in adults. Juvenile queen angelfish are often mistaken for another species, because their colour formations are so different from adults'.

The descriptively named rock beauty (Holacanthus tricolor) *is a shy, elusive angelfish that tends to hide from photographers.*

THE MOST COLOURFUL ANGELFISH

There are several angelfish species with striking colours. The rock beauty *(Holacanthus tricolor)* has a mainly black body, a brilliant yellow tail, and a yellow head with a blue ring round the eyes and purple lips. The rock beauty is very wary of divers and always hides deep inside the reef when they approach.

French angelfish *(Pomacanthus paru)* are always a delight to see. They are a dark slate grey/blue with a bright yellow pectoral fin and a yellow ring round the eye, and the main body scales are also rimmed with yellow. They are always seen in pairs along the reef, appearing to shadow each others' every move. French angelfish are fairly common along Quintana Roo's southeast coast and are quite easy to approach, so you can take some stunning photographs of them.

The grey angelfish *(Pomacanthus arcuatus)* is one of the larger species, growing up to 60 cm (24 in). They tend to be greyish brown in colour edged with scales of a lighter shade. This fish is fairly common in the northern Caribbean. Like French angelfish, they always swim in lifelong mating pairs. Juvenile grey and French angelfish look very similar and are often mistaken for each other, but grey angelfish young have a brilliant blue flash on their pectoral fins.

Angelfish

Above: *A magnificently coloured queen angelfish* (Holacanthus ciliaris).
Below: *Juvenile queen angelfish are as vividly coloured as their parents.*

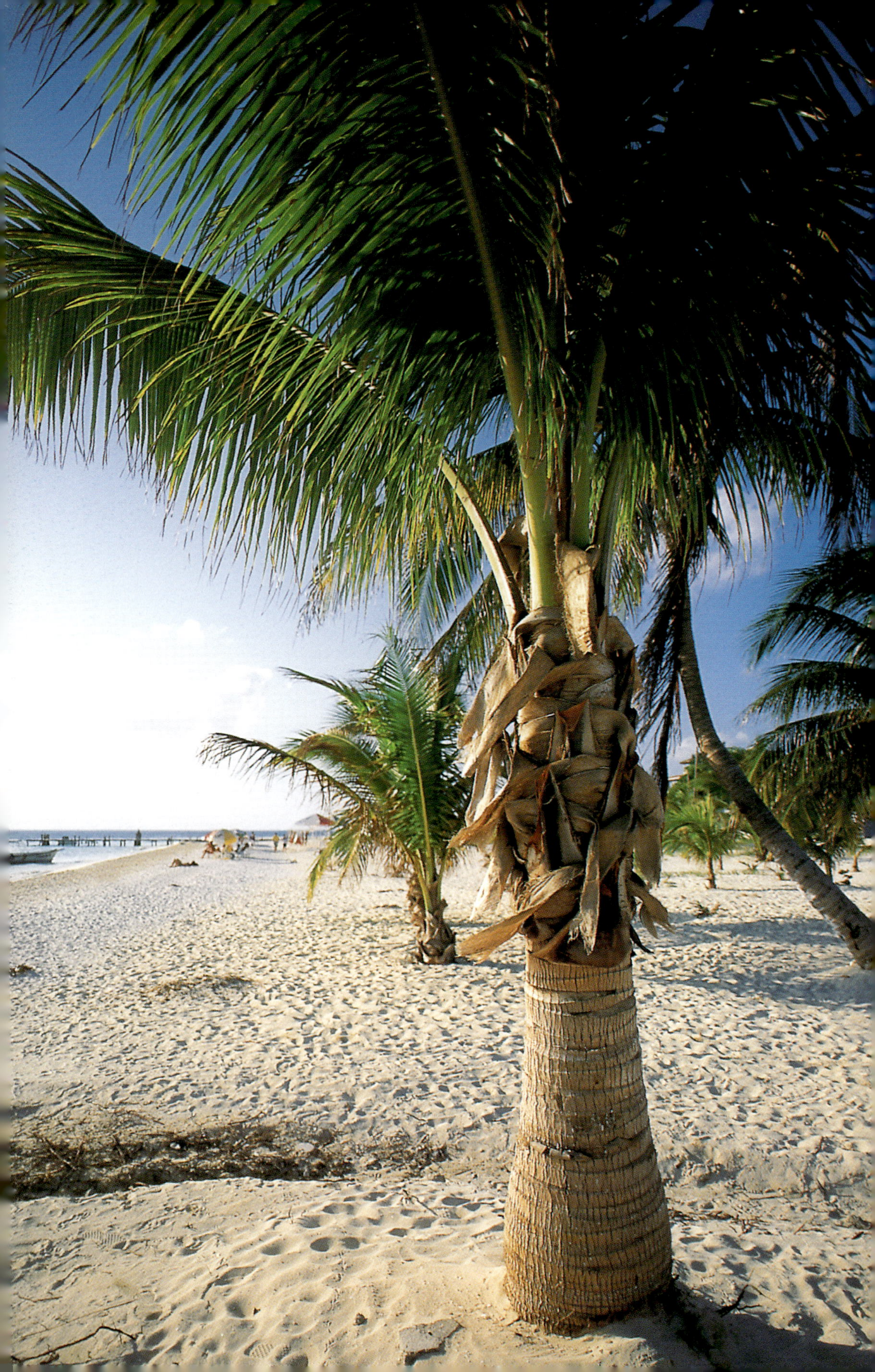

ISLA MUJERES AND ISLA CONTOY

Two major islands lie in the Gulf of Mexico just off Cancún. Isla Mujeres (pronounced Ees-lah Moo-hair-ehs) is a little over 8 km (5 miles) long and 1.6 km (1 mile) wide. It is just 4 km (2.5 miles) offshore north from Cancún and is finger-shaped, lying in a northwest to southeasterly direction. The terrain is flat and the island has beautiful sandy beaches. It also has an equable climate with an average temperature of 26°C (80°F) and a humidity level of 60 per cent. Its population now numbers 11,500, but it was until recently a traditional fishing village and still has a large fleet of shrimp boats which travel far out into the Gulf of Mexico for two weeks or more at a time. Now, daily ferries from Cancún and Cozumel bring boatloads of tourists to sunbathe on the beaches, snorkel and scuba-dive along the coast, and drift-dive out on the reefs.

Isla Contoy is aabout 24 km (15 miles) north of Isla Mujeres and a 45-minute boat trip away. An uninhabited island only 2.5 by 0.5 km (1½ x ½ miles), it is a peaceful State Park and bird sanctuary – and well worth a visit.

ISLAND OF WOMEN

Isla Mujeres has an interesting history. In 1517 an expedition led by a Spanish explorer, Francisco Fernández de Córdoba, landed on the leeward shores of Isla Mujeres during a voyage from Cuba. De Córdoba was looking for new territories where silver and gold might be found, with a local population that could be enslaved to work in the silver mines. But de Córdoba found no inhabitants on the island, only aging clay statues of partly clothed women left by the Maya. Hence the name, Isla Mujeres, 'The Island of Women'. On this sacred island the expedition found many shrines to Ixchel, the Maya goddess of fertility and health. We now know that traders had used the island before the Spanish arrived, because the remains have been found on the southern tip of what could have been a lighthouse.

Following its discovery by the Spanish, the island became a revictualling and safe area for pirates. Among them was Fermín Mundaca de Marechaje – who is said to have fallen in love with a local girl and to have built her a fine hacienda, or ranch, promising that he would give up piracy if she would marry him. This may not be the true story, however,

Opposite: *Palms provide shade along an Isla Mujeres beach.*
Above: *The rare blue angelfish* (Holacanthus bermudensis) *can be seen in the Bahía de Mujeres.*

since another version says that the girl would have nothing to do with Pirate Mundaca because he gained his wealth by running a slave ship from Africa to Cuba to work on the sugar cane plantations. He retired in 1860 when the British Navy made it very uncomfortable for traders in human cargo to continue operating in the Caribbean. He died in Mérida, Mexico. On Isla Mujeres a tiny headstone can be seen in the cemetery near Playa Norte. It has two inscriptions: *Lo que tu eres, yo fuí* ('What you are, I was') on one side; and on the other: *Lo que yo soy, luego seras* ('What I am, you shall be').

DIVING HOLIDAYS ON ISLA MUJERES

Isla Mujeres is a popular island, much visited by locals from Cancún as well as by tourists, and many of the visitors who first come over on a day trip return for a lengthier stay on their next vacation. The island has a relaxed atmosphere, to the extent that even topless sunbathing is allowed on Playa Norte. There is plenty of accommodation in hotels and condominiums in all price ranges. The main (two-lane) road, Avenida Rueda Medina, leads south from the capital, called Downtown, to El Garrafón National Park, the southwestern beach areas and the Maya temples, and on toward the lighthouse, which was partly destroyed by Hurricane Gilbert in 1988.

For scuba-diving and snorkelling fans there are several centres on the island offering instruction and equipment sales and rentals. Some of the better ones are listed on pages 70–71. Fresh water is pumped through a 20-cm (8-in) pipe from the mainland, and a drainage system and a sewage plant have been installed to ensure that the waters round Isla Mujeres remain free from contamination. Some of the dive boats run dives on reefs with fairly strong currents, but the dive centres' experienced boat-handlers will stay on station over the divers just in case anyone gets swept away.

Isla Contoy

An average 1,500 people visit this uninhabited island each month. Beware, this is mosquito territory and visitors should seek medical advice to ensure they take the correct preventive medicines for the region. Isla Contoy is the habitat of more than 100 different bird species and is important as a staging post for migratory birds, particularly between November and April, when double-crested cormorants, frigate birds, snowy egrets, white herons and brown pelicans can be seen nesting. Brown boobies and turkey birds also nest in large numbers. The brown pelicans have two chicks and, if there is little food, the stronger of the chicks kills the other, so making certain that there is enough food for at least one of the hatchlings.There are no breeding birds during the hurricane season (clever birds!).

Isla Contoy is a freshwater emergence zone and the shallow lagoons are infused with fresh water, making a rich planktonic soup. They have become a very important hatchery for the surrounding reefs' fish stocks. Puerto Viejo (Old Harbour) is the largest of the lagoons and is most important to the brown pelican population. Two species of mangrove tree surround the lagoons. Boa constrictors and small crocodiles inhabit the smaller, enclosed and brackish lagoons and ponds.

Facilities

There is no accommodation nor any ancillary services on Isla Contoy. Consequently, all the diving is done by day boats operating out of Isla Mujeres or Cancún. The National Park Service has an interpretive display area, a museum and a high tower with spectacular views of the sea, where the green waters of the Gulf of Mexico mix with the blue waters of the

The uninhabited Isla Contoy is an important sanctuary for waterbirds.

Mexican Caribbean. A guide will accompany visitors to Puerto Viejo and explain how the island's complex ecosystem works.

Marine Life

The reefs round Isla Mujeres teem with life. Although many are in shallows or low-lying, this seems to be no deterrent to fish, judging by the numbers that inhabit them. Huge schools of snapper and grunt and many barracuda are seen on every dive.

East of Isla Mujeres are the Sleeping Shark Caves, where divers may still see sharks. However, the regular appearance of humans on their territory is acting as a deterrent to sharks and the chances of seeing them at this well-known site are lessening rapidly.

Nature is a great threat to the coral reefs in this part of the western Caribbean. On a visit to the reefs in Bahía de Mujeres in November 1995, about one month after the severe Hurricane Roxanne had passed over the area, the author saw that large areas of healthy corals, especially branches of the larger elkhorn coral, had been broken off. There was also sponge debris rolling about the sea bed. Nevertheless, the reefs appear to be recovering well and with reliable water clarity there is much to see.

Isla Contoy is at the limit of the northern coral distribution into the Gulf of Mexico. The long, shallow Ixlache Reef, which stretches north from Isla Mujeres to Isla Contoy, offers an opportunity to see massive brain corals (*Diploria labyrinthiformis*). On the way to it is a shallow reef called Los Galeones Hundidos (The Sunken Galleons), where, in water no deeper than 4 m (13 ft) there are said to be the scattered remains of ancient shipwrecks.

Isla Mujeres

1 El Frío (The Deep Freeze)
★★★★★

Location: deep wreck dive to the northeast of the north of Isla Mujeres.
Access: by boat only, journey time 1-2 hours as it is quite a distance from shore. Satellite navigation equipment is also necessary on the dive boat because the wreck is not marked on any chart or by a marking buoy.
Conditions: Divers should take care as this is a potentially dangerous dive in open ocean. There is generally always a current in this area; the long open ocean swell makes everyone feel queasy.
Minimum depth: 25 m (80 ft)
Maximum depth: 33 m (100 ft)
Average visibility: more than 20 m (66 ft)

This sunken cargo ship rests in 30 m (100 ft) of water and was discovered accidentally by some lobster fishermen. She is thought to have been sunk deliberately because of deterioration, but there is no firm information about her origin or how long she has been under water.

The wreck is 40 km (25 miles) from Cancún and takes between one and two hours to reach, so conditions have to be exceptional before anyone will venture this far. The site has become an artificial reef, and the 60-m (200-ft) long ship is home to a myriad of marine life. Large jewfish *(Epinephelus itajara)* can be found near the bottom, and dog snapper and sergeant majors around the upper areas of the superstructure. The hull is the only part of the ship that remains intact and all the cargo holds are open. There are always barracuda on station above the wreck.

2 Sleeping Shark Caves
★★★★

Location: deep dive to the east of Isla Mujeres.
Access: by day boat only, 5 km (3 miles) northeast of Isla Mujeres.
Conditions: divers should take care entering and exiting the water because of surface swell. Being so far offshore the site is subject to unpredictable currents sweeping through into the Gulf of Mexico from the Caribbean.
Minimum depth: 16 m (52 ft)
Maximum depth: 25 m (80 ft)
Average visibility: more than 20 m (66 ft).

Opposite: *The nurse shark* (Ginglymostoma cirratum) *is one of the most commonly seen sharks in the western Caribbean region.*

Isla Mujeres and Isla Contoy

The caves were discovered by a local lobster fisherman, Carlos García Castilla. While out free-diving on a lobster hunt, he observed that some sharks entered a cave system and that, while some swam out the other side, others did not. His curiosity piqued, he dived down and found several sharks apparently asleep on the sea bed. Until then it was thought that sharks have to swim to stay alive and Castilla's important discovery was later commemorated by Jacques Yves Cousteau, who made a film about the area. Since the caves are now regularly visited by humans, the chances of finding sharks there have fallen to about 30 per cent. This figure is still high, however, as compared with only a 25 per cent chance of seeing a shark anywhere around the Cancún area.

The Sleeping Shark Caves are really just a large jumble of rocks and overhangs, where fresh water emerges. This apparently does two things for the sharks: it has a slight narcotic effect; and it rids them of parasites. The rocky ridges are thickly carpeted with marine life. Some of the caves are quite large. Your exhaled air bubbles will eventually filter through their porous ceilings. Two of the most spectacular of the cave sites are El Arco (The Arch) and El Puente (The Bridge).

3 Barracuda Reef
★★★★

Location: a shallow dive, 1 km (0.6 miles) northeast of Isla Mujeres.
Access: boat dive only.
Conditions: care should be taken as this site is far offshore and subject to unpredictable currents and swell.
Minimum depth: 10 m (33 ft)
Maximum depth: 20 m (66 ft)
Average visibility: more than 20 m (66 ft)

Closer to shore than Site 2, this low-lying strip reef has a mini-wall along one side and overhangs in several areas. These overhangs look like small caves, but do not penetrate far. There are barracuda on this reef and some quite large specimens of *Sphyraena* sp. Small common purple sea fans and large congregations of grunts and snapper are also seen. There appear to be more sponges than hard corals. In fact this whole area has more the appearance of ancient limestone bedrock, indicating that the sea bed was once well above dry land.

4 Tavos Reef
★★★★★★★★

Location: a shallow dive to the east of Isla Mujeres.
Access: by boat.
Conditions: This side of the island is much more prone to open ocean swell conditions and when the wind shifts out of the north diving is virtually impossible. Surge is the main problem.
Minimum depth: 6 m (20 ft)
Maximum depth: 17 m (55 ft)
Average visibility: more than 20 m (66 ft)

A shallow strip reef running pependicular to the shore, with numerous small coral heads dotted about. The channels between these heads have very large schools of juvenile grunt and snapper. This dive is popular with snorkellers because such large numbers of fish are to be seen. Blue angelfish (*Holacanthus bermudensis*), considered rare in this part of the Caribbean, can be seen in a number of locations around Isla Mujeres and in the shallow reefs between the island and Cancún. There is little hard coral growth.

5 El Garrafón
★★★★

Location: a shallow reef to the south of El Garrafón National Park.
Access: directly from the shore.
Conditions: a shallow reef from a beach and ironstone shore. Divers should take care on entering the water, and always wear strong footwear.
Minimum depth: 1 m (3 ft)
Maximum depth: 5 m (17 ft)
Average visibility: under 10 m (33 ft)

A shallow fringing reef and small coral heads. This reef is popular with day-trippers, so there is quite a lot of coral damage, but large parts of the shallow reef areas were also damaged by hurricanes Gilbert and Roxanne. However, thousands of fish throng the site. They are more than friendly and they will accompany you during your snorkelling trip. A safe and easy site.

6 El Jiguero
★★★★★★★

Location: a shallow dive, southeast of the Point of Isla Mujeres and a continuation of El Garrafón (Site 5).
Access: by boat, but can be reached from the shore.
Conditions: choppy surface conditions to be expected and unpredictable currents generally flowing in a northerly direction.
Minimum depth: 6 m (20 ft)
Maximum depth: 11 m (33 ft)
Average visibility: under 10 m (33 ft)

This rather exposed narrow strip and patch reef is teeming with fish. It lies at the point where the Caribbean meets the Gulf of Mexico. This creates an interesting mix, which produces large amounts of plankton and lots of fish to feed on it. French angelfish (*Pomacanthus paru*) and spotfin butterflyfish (*Chaetodon ocellatus*) swim past you in their mating pairs.

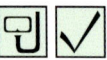

7 Manchones Reef
★★★★★★★

Location: shallow dive, west of Isla Mujeres.
Access: by dive or snorkel boat charter.
Conditions: choppy surface conditions; due to shallow depth; divers can experience surge.
Minimum depth: 4 m (13 ft)
Maximum depth: 8 m (25 ft)
Average visibility: variable

August 17th is celebrated every year as the anniversary of the founding of Isla Mujeres in 1854. A cross of bronze-coloured concrete called the Cruz de la Bahía (Cross of the Bay), 12 m (40 ft) tall and weighing 1 tonne/ton was placed on the sea bed on this reef in 1984, but it was destroyed during Hurricane Roxanne in October 1995. The reef fared better, though. There are good corals and thousands of fish to be seen. This site is popular with operators from Isla Mujeres and Cancún for diving and particularly snorkelling – there is just enough depth for divers to keep their hands off the coral.

8 Manchones Xico
★★★★★★★

Location: a shallow dive beyond Manchones toward Cancún.
Access: by dive or snorkel charter boat.
Conditions: choppy surface conditions and slight-to-moderate current.
Minimum depth: 3 m (10 ft)
Maximum depth: 8 m (25 ft)
Average visibility: in excess of 20 m (66 ft)

This diving and snorkelling site differs from Manchones Reef (Site 21) in that it is primarily a series of coral bommies or patch reef instead of strip reef, which is the main type of reef in this area of Bahía de Mujeres. There appears to be a larger than average number of queen angelfish (*Holacanthus ciliaris*) of all sizes and ages on this reef. The juveniles are just as brilliantly coloured as the adults. Small redspotted hawkfish (*Amblycirrhitus pinos*) dot the reefs, their comical stance attracting the attention of divers. An excellent sight for night-diving.

9 La Bandera
★★★★

Location: a shallow dive in Bahía de Mujeres.
Access: by dive boat only.
Conditions: strong current and choppy surface conditions are to be expected.
Minimum depth: 7 m (23 ft)
Maximum depth: 9 m (30 ft)
Average visibility: variable, often stirred up due to large sandy areas surrounding the reef.

This is a large, convoluted strip reef with a smaller reef on the inside. Although the current is strong there are always lots of sheltered areas where you can rest and watch the fish. Whenever there is a storm out in the Gulf, there are always more fish than usual along these

ISLA MUJERES AND ISLA CONTOY

inner reefs. This is a very nice dive, just an arm's length from thousands of grunt and snapper.

10 Lighthouse
★★★★★★★

Location: a shallow dive, directly off the Lighthouse at the northern point of Isla Tiburón east of Isla Mujeres.
Access: directly from the shore.
Conditions: moderate current but sheltered behind the reef. There can be surge, making underwater photography very difficult.
Minimum depth: 3 m (10 ft)
Maximum depth: 5 m (17 ft)
Average visibility: under 10 m (33 ft)

A popular site because of its close proximity to the local dive centres. The shallow reef extends from the island, but can be swept by the current which passes on this side of the island. A high concentration of algae has seemed to smother some areas of the reef, particularly after the last hurricane. There is always competition for space on these reefs and when coral is damaged, the algae quickly makes a stronghold and can strangle the hard corals. The coral growth is good, however. An excellent sight for night-diving.

The brilliant colours of these sponges on Barracuda Reef (Site 3) can only be seen with the aid of a diver's torch, even in daytime.

Queen Conch

The queen conch *(Strombus gigas)* is the second-largest shell in the conch family and is still relatively common around the northern Caribbean. The other major species is the milk conch *(Strombus costatus)*. In this region conchs are a sustainably managed resource and protected in a number of marine conservation areas.

Conchs (pronounced 'konks') are widely distributed in the Caribbean: their range extends from Bermuda to Florida, the Bahamas, the Turks and Caicos Islands, Mexico and Venezuela. They are social animals, living in groups, and can be found on virtually any flattish area of the sea bed and as deep as 145 m (480 ft). Conchs have no teeth. They feed on algae and detritus, including dead sea grass blades, which they scrape with a rasping motion of their tonguelike radula. They reach sexual maturity at three to four years. Breeding takes place mainly during the warmer months; between March and October a female lays 250,000 to 750,000 eggs, producing as many as six egg masses in a season.

JUVENILE CONCHS

After three days the newly hatched conch, called a veliger, joins the planktonic soup – the life blood of the oceans – for about three weeks. This planktonic stage in the life cycle maximizes the distribution of the species; however, it is also the most vulnerable stage and when you witness the enormous amounts of plankton being scooped up by manta rays and other plankton feeders, you soon realise why so few larvae are able to survive and begin a new life cycle.

Juvenile conchs fall prey to snappers, groupers, stingrays, nurse sharks, wrasse, and many invertebrates, including tulip snails, spiny lobsters, hermit crabs and octopus. A small member of the cardinal fish family often seeks shelter under the shell. To date no diseases have been found in the conch.

PREDATORS

Conchs have few predators once they are three years old, because of the strength of the shell. Their most co(which paralyze the animal with

A queen conch shell in turtle grass looks very like an old coral rock – knobbly and pale in colour.

The conch can retract its light-sensitive eyes, quickly into its body when danger threatens.

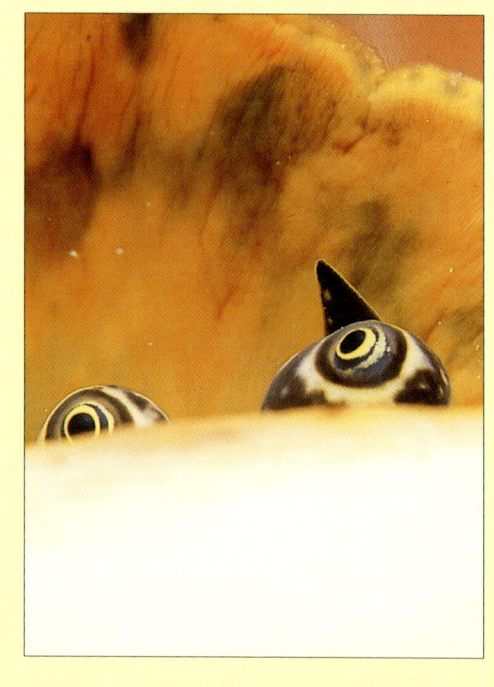

Queen Conch

their bite and then extract it); stingrays (which can flip them over and bite the 'foot' off before they have a chance to retract it); and turtles (whose jaws are strong enough to crush the shell). The older the animal gets, the more worn its shell becomes; a mature adult is easily mistaken for a coral boulder covered in algae.

But nothing has prepared the conch for predation by man. The collection of conchs is permitted from a number of locations in the Caribbean, where restrictions are imposed. However, the author spotted a local snorkeller collecting conch in a conservation area near the Dive Paradise Dive Store at the Barracuda Hotel, but was unable to intervene.

THE CONCH TRADE

The conch has traditionally been harvested for the edible, firm white meat of the foot, which is low in fats and carbohydrates and high in protein. It is considered a delicacy and made into chowder, fritters and cutlets – though some people find it too chewy. In some areas conchs are over-fished and are scarce.

Like oysters, conchs sometimes produce pearls, which can grow up to 3 cm (1 in) in diameter. There is a 10,000:1 chance that a shell may contain one. However, the hunt for pearls is unlikely to be a cause of over-fishing, because conch pearls lose their lustre in time and so they are not considered gem quality and are not very valuable.

Conch shells have always been tradeable. Early Caribbean Indians made tools out of them and made them into horns by drilling a hole in the tip of the spire. They have traditionally been used to decorate pottery and even as a house-building material. Today they are sold worldwide and demand for them increases the strain on populations. It is better to see conchs alive on the sea bed, foraging for algae – their independently moving eyes on eye stalks can be quite comical.

Management of conch-fishing is important – in some areas of the Caribbean it is too late. Collection of conchs is banned in Florida and Bermuda until stocks recover, and most island nations implement strict governmental control to save their remaining fisheries.

Conch shells, cowries and olive shells are sold on street stalls in Isla Mujeres.

Isla Contoy

11 Las Calderas
★★★★

Location: a shallow dive to the northeast of Isla Contoy.
Access: by boat from Isla Mujeres or Cancún.
Conditions: divers should take care as this dive is well offshore and liable to unpredictable currents and ocean surge and swell.
Minimum depth: 6 m (20 ft)
Maximum depth: 17 m (55 ft)
Average visibility: up to 20 m (66 ft)

This northern patch and strip reef has an old, well-broken-up wreck, which is easily explored. There are numerous large brain corals and elkhorn coral, interspersed with patches of turtle grass *(Thalassia testudinum)*. Small schools of grunt and snapper shelter under the coral heads. The surge over the reef and around the wreck makes it difficult to stay in one area and divers should take care not to knock against the coral heads.

12 Ixlache Reef
★★

Location: snorkel dive only to the southeast of Isla Contoy.
Access: by boat.
Conditions: there is almost always surge over the reef,

Above: *Marine life soon encrusts wrecks like this abandoned barge (Site 13).*
Opposite: *The banded coral shrimp (Stenopus hispidus) shelters on pink vase sponges at night.*

PROJECT AWARE

Ten ways a diver can protect the aquatic realm (produced by PADI)
1 Dive carefully in fragile aquatic ecosystems, such as coral reefs.
2 Be aware of your body and equipment placement, and any damage they might cause when diving.
3 Keep your diving skills sharp with continuing education.
4 Consider your impact on aquatic life through your interactions.
5 Understand and respect underwater life.
6 Resist the urge to collect souvenirs.
7 If you hunt and/or gather game, obey all fish and game laws.
8 Report environmental disturbances and any destruction of your dive sites.
9 Be a role model for other divers in your treatment of the environment in and out of the water.
10 Get involved in local environmental activities and issues.

making snorkelling rather difficult in places.
Minimum depth: 3 m (10 ft)
Maximum depth: 5 m (17 ft)
Average visibility: under 10 m (33 ft)

There are some impressive stands of elkhorn coral and some brain corals more than 2 m (6 ft) across. However, in October 1995 Hurricane Roxanne deposited about 5 cm (2 in) of sand over everything and the reef is only now beginning to recover. This site is interesting as a stopover on the way to or returning from Isla Contoy, but it is scarcely worth a special trip.

13 Barge Wreck
★★★★

Location: a shallow dive, due east from Punta Sam ferry terminal.
Access: by boat.
Conditions: a slight-to-moderate current runs past the wreck. There can be surge over the hull.
Minimum depth: the wreck breaks through the surface.
Maximum depth: 5 m (17 ft)
Average visibility: 20 m (66 ft)

This old barge, which used to travel between the islands, is now home to schools of sergeant majors and juvenile snapper. The superstructure is becoming encrusted in fire coral *(Millepora alcicornis)* and small encrusting algae and sea fans. The propeller has been removed, but the rudder and propeller shaft are covered in small corals. The hold is now filled with sand and access can be gained with care. Small plumed scorpionfish *(Scorpaena grandicornis)* shelter against the hull waiting for their next meal to swim by.

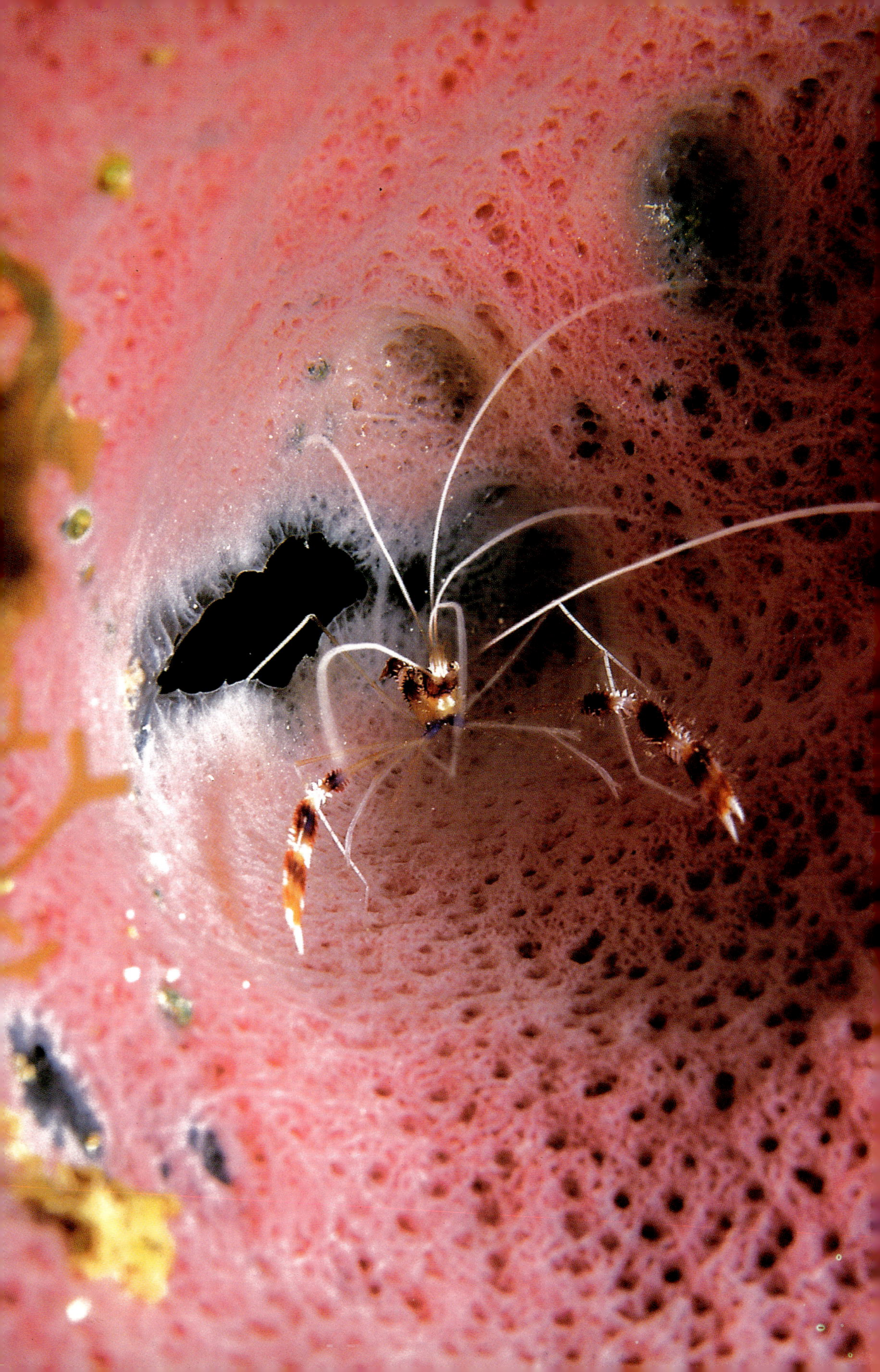

Isla Mujeres

How to Get There

By ferry: from Puerto Juárez, 15 minutes north of Cancún. This ferry, called The People Ferry, takes about one hour to cross. There is a car ferry at Punta Sam, 8 km (5 miles) north of Puerto Juárez, with room for 25 vehicles plus two decks for passengers. Numerous express ferries run regularly from most of the public beaches along Cancún's hotel zone. These take no more than 15 minutes to cross, but they are notorious for leaving ahead of the schedule if they are getting full.

In town you walk everywhere, but to visit the southern beaches, the ruins or the lighthouse, transport is essential. Rental shops Downtown hire mopeds for about N$20.00 an hour and bicycles for N$30.00 for eight hours, basket and lock included. Electric golf carts can be rented from some large hotels. A deposit and a valid driving licence are required.

Where to Stay

Life on Isla Mujeres focuses on Downtown and most of the accommodation is in this area. The more expensive beachside hotels and condominiums have air-conditioning, swimming pools and restaurants. The smaller hotels in town have hot and cold water, and most have ceiling fans. there is no accommodation on Isla Contoy.

It is recommended to telephone or fax the hotels if you are planning to travel to Isla Mujeres for a few days. The island gets very busy during the holiday season , and rooms should always be booked well in advance. It would also be prudent at that time to check on the facilities available, as things do change.

Fast ferry to Isla Mujeres at one of the jetties in Cancún.

Tourist Information Office, Avda Rueda Medina, between Calles Madero and Morelos, Isla Mujeres, Quintana Roo, Mexico 77400; tel (987) 70767.

Belmar Hotel, (above Pizza Rolandi) Avda Hidalgo, Isla Mujeres, Quintana Roo, Mexico 77400; tel (987) 70430/fax (987) 70429. Mexican restaurant and pool.

Hotel Cabañas Del Mar, Avda Arq. Carlos Lazo 1, Isla Mujeres, Quintana Roo, Mexico 77400; tel (987) 70213/fax (987) 70179. On North Beach; cabins; excellent watersports and laid-back tex-Mex restaurant.

Hotel Caracol, Avda Metamoros 5, Isla Mujeres, Quintana Roo, Mexico 77400; tel (987) 70150. Traditional; good restaurant.

Hotel Meson del Bucanero, Calle Hidalgo, Isla Mujeres, Quintana Roo, Mexico 77400; tel (987) 70126/fax (987) 70210. nice air-conditioned rooms above restaurant of same name.

Hotel Na Balam, Calle Zazil Há 118, Isla Mujeres, Quintana Roo, Mexico 77400; tel (987) 70179/fax (987) 70279; www.nabalam.com. On North Beach; moderate; pool and restaurant.

Hotel Perla del Caribe I and II, 1–2 Avdas Madero and Guerrero, Isla Mujeres, Quintana Roo, Mexico 77400; tel (987) 70444/fax (987) 70011. A 91-room beach-front hotel with pool and restaurants.

Hotel Posada del Mar, Avda Rueda Medina 15, Isla Mujeres, Quintana Roo, Mexico 77400; tel (987) 70044/fax (987) 70266; www.mexhotels.com. Beach-front hotel with 30 rooms and 12 bungalows; intimate, with a nice pool and restaurant.

Hotel Rocamar, Eastern end of Calle Guerrero, Isla Mujeres, Quintana Roo, Mexico 77400; tel (987) 70101. This 24-room hotel was the island's first hotel; swimming pool.

Where to Eat

Many hotels have good restaurants and there are many more Downtown. Nearly every menu will include conch, lobster, shrimp, and a choice of fish. Most beach-front bars serve Tex-Mex style food.

Arriba Restaurant & Bar, Avda Hidalgo, (middle of the block, upstairs); tel (987) 70458. International vegetarian and seafood. Fresh, safe vegetables and fruit.

M & J Delicatessen, Avdas Bravo and Guerrero (next to Hotel Rocamar);tel (987) 77400.

Miramar Restaurant & Bar, Avda Rueda Medina (opposite main pier). Tex-Mex and seafood.

Rolandi's, Avda Hidalgo, between Madero and Abasolo; tel (987) 70430/fax (987) 70429. Traditional Italian, excellent pizzas, original wood ovens for extra flavour.

Dive Facilities

Bahia Dive Shop, Avda Rueda Medina 166, Downtown, Isla Mujeres, Quintana Roo, Mexico 77400; tel/fax (987) 7740.

Coral Scuba Dive Centre, Calle Matameros at Avda Rueda Medina, Isla Mujeres, Quintana Roo, Mexico 77400; tel (987) 70763/fax (987) 70371.

Coral Scuba Diving Centre, PO Box 21, Isla Mujeres, Quintana Roo, Mexico 77400; tel (987) 70572/fax (987) 70371; email coral@coralscubadivecenter.com.

Delphin Diving, Plaza Isla Mujeres C-6, Isla Mujeres, Quintana Roo, Mexico 77400; tel(987) 70374; www.delphindiving.com.

Mundaca Divers, Avda Francisco 1, Madero 10, Isla Mujeres, Quintana Roo, Mexico 77400; tel (987) 70607/fax (987) 70601; email mundacadive@hotmail.com.

Scuba Dive Isla Mujeres, Avda Matamoros

Sunwear

Topless sunbathing is permitted only on Playa Norte on Isla Mujeres and on certain Cancún beaches. In other resorts swimwear is de rigueur – topless sunbathing is not accepted in most resort areas. Do not wear tight or flashy clothes – they invite the wrong sort of attention.

Elsewhere in the Yucatán, respect the sensitivities of local people, who are generally much less free in their dress. Swimwear is strictly for the beach or the swimming pool terraces. It is unacceptable for women to wear bikini tops when shopping Downtown, although many foreign tourists do so.

Isla Mujeres

13-a, Isla Mujeres, Quintana Roo, Mexico 77400; tel (987) 70763/fax (987) 70371.
Sea Hawk Divers, Hotel Na Balam, Isla Mujeres, Quintana Roo, Mexico 77400; tel (987) 70279/fax (987) 70593.
Watersports Association, Cooperativa De Servicios Turisticos, Avda Rueda Medina, Isla Mujeres, Quintana Roo, Mexico 77400; tel (987) 70274.

Medical Services

English-speaking doctor: Dr. Antonio E. Salas Torres (general medicine and obstetrics), Calle Hidalgo 8 (next to Farmacia Lily), Isla Mujeres, Quintana Roo, Mexico; tel (987) 70477/70021.
English-speaking dentist: Dr Antonio Rios Chale, Avda Hidalgo Sur 10, Dpto 2, Isla Mujeres, Quintana Roo, Mexico.
Divers' Alert Network (DAN); tel (919) 648 8111.
Recompression chambers:
The nearest recompression chamber is on Cozumel Island; tel 20140.
Air-Evac San Diego, California, USA, for delivery to a recompression chamber in the USA; tel (800) 854 2567 or (619) 278 3822.
Life Flight, Houston, Texas, USA, for delivery to a recompression chamber in the USA; tel (800) 392 4357 or (713) 797 4357.
Radio: La Costera (Coastguard) Channel 16 (canal número dieciseis).

Local Highlights

Beaches
Isla Mujeres is famed locally for its lovely beaches. All the usual services are found at the beaches, including bars, toilets, and showers.
Playa Norte, next to Downtown. Topless sunbathing is allowed on this beach. It was damaged during the hurricane in October 1995 when much of the beach was washed away.
Playa Pares and **Playa Lancheros** are located on the western side of the island.
El Garrafón Beach at the southern end of the island is renowned for its snorkelling, as the reef starts directly adjacent to the shore.

Shopping
The people of **Isla Mujeres** are famous for their work with jewels and precious metals. These and other local handicrafts such as weaving and woodwork are sold locally.

Sights and activities
The lighthouse and the **Maya temple** on the southern point of the island can be reached along a wonderful, scenic drive. Beside the lighthouse are the ruins of a building used by the Maya to honour the goddess Ixchel. The lighthouse keeper may allow you to climb the tower to get some spectacular views of the Caribbean. The temple was also once a lighthouse, used to signal to Cancún, Cozumel and Tulum.
Dolphin Experience at El Garrafón Beach has an enclosure where visitors swim with dolphins. Book well in advance.
Turtle Farm near El Garrafón National Park; check with the tourist office for excact location and opening times. These islands have been used by the green turtle (*Chelonia mydas*) for centuries and many still lay their eggs on the island. The eggs are rescued and the young turtles hatched, raised in captivity, and released into the wild when they are about one year old.
Mundaca Pirate Hacienda was originally built by Fermín Mundaca de Marechaje to woo a local girl (see page 59–60). The impressive stone archway bears the girl's local name, La Trigueña (The Brunette). Transport is needed to reach the hacienda.

Excursions:
Isla Contoy Bird Sanctuary (see page 61) A daily shuttle service runs from the Downtown pier.
Holbox Island, (pronounced 'Hole Boch'), northwest of Isla Mujeres, is devoted exclusively to fishing. There are one or two small hotels and several *palapa* restaurants, which serve fresh seafood. If you enjoy an uncluttered stroll along sandy beaches, and life without any modern trappings, this is your place.

Services

Banks
All banks, including the foreign exchange facility, are open 09:00–14:30 hours Monday–Friday. Money can be exchanged at a number of other locations on the island, so shop around for the best deal. When cashing traveller's cheques, only your passport will be accepted for identification.

Transport
Pepe's Moto Rent, Avda Hidalgo 19, Isla Mujeres, Quintana Roo, Mexico; tel (987) 70019. Mopeds, bicycles and golf carts for hire.
Taxi Services, tel (987) 70066.
Bus Services, for information tel (987) 70529.

Film processing
The nearest E6 film-processing facilities are in Cancún (see page 55). Check with the tourist office – facilities may have opened since this book went to press.

Playa Norte, one of Isla Mujeres' most beautiful beaches.

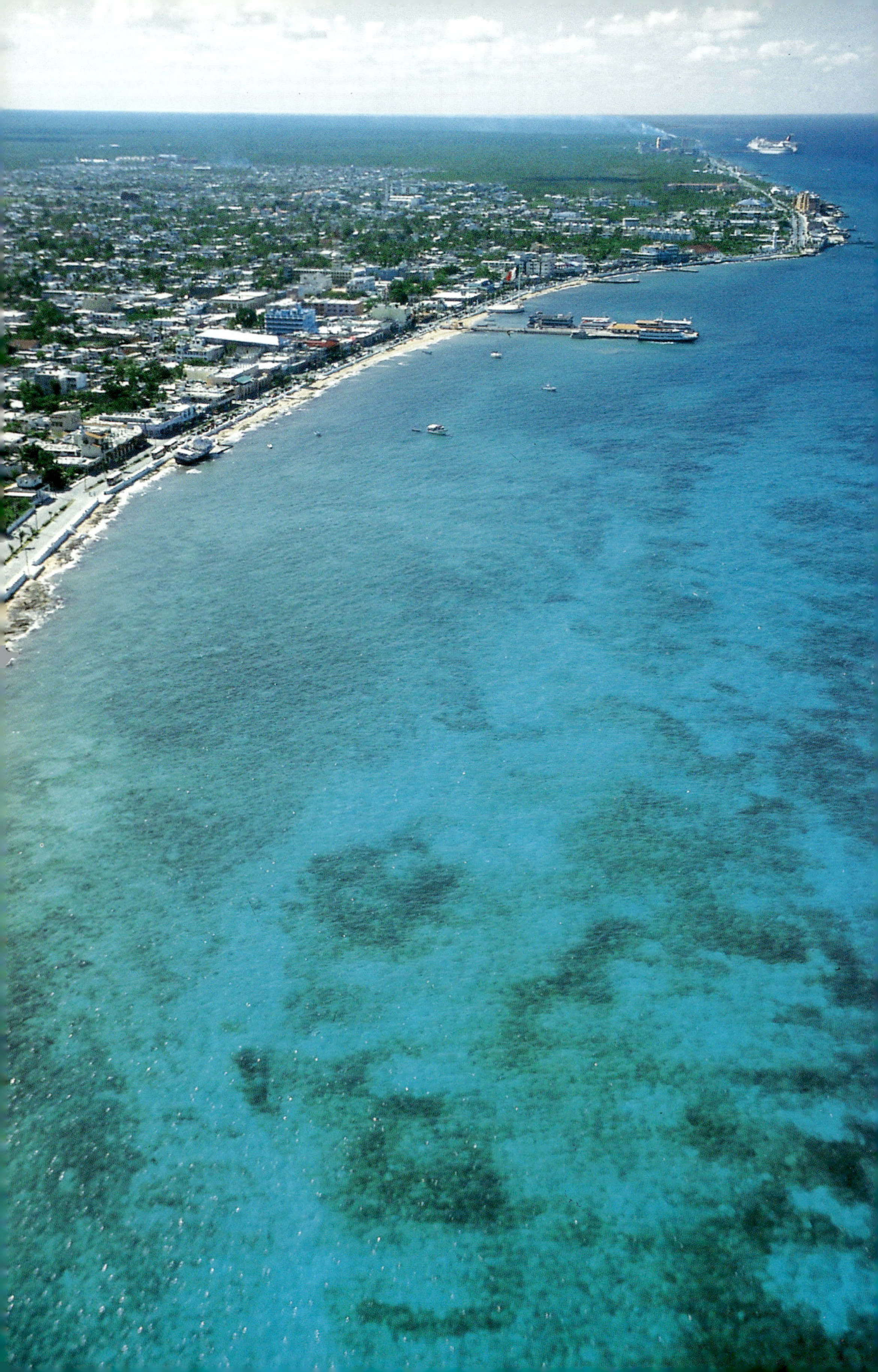

COZUMEL

Mexico's only island in the Caribbean Sea, Cozumel is shaped like a teardrop. It is 47 km (29 miles) long by 15 km (9 miles) wide and is located between parallels 20° 16' and 20° 35' north and meridians 86° 44' and 87° 22' west. Its highest point above sea level is only 14 m (45 ft). Cancún on the mainland is approximately 30 km (19 miles) to the northwest and Cuba is about 95 km (60 miles) to the northeast.

Cozumel is a coral island. It originally grew in the shallows of a submarine plateau that was created by movements of the South American continental plate. At the end of the last Ice Age melting glaciers made the sea level rise approximately 30 m (100 ft), causing the coral reef to grow vertically. The sea level has since lowered, however, and the wind and waves eroded the exposed reef. As a result, much of the coast became petrified, so around Cozumel divers can see a classic example of petrified or ironstone shore and live coral fringing reefs offshore.

THE STORY OF COZUMEL

The Maya, who came into power in the Yucatán between 1200 BC until about AD 1400, considered Cozumel (pronounced Co-zoo-mel) a sacred shrine. It was originally called Ah-Cuzamil-Peten (The Island of Swallows). Maya women would travel by canoe across the narrow strip of water separating Cozumel from the mainland to worship Ixchel, the goddess of fertility and the wife of Itzamna, the supreme lord and sun god. Each woman was expected to make the pilgrimage at least once in her lifetime. Dolls used during the sacred sacrifices to the fertility goddess have been found in at least 40 archaeological sites on the island. There are Maya ruins at a number of sites (see page 103).

The Spanish first set foot on Cozumel early in their conquest of the New World. In 1518 Juan de Grijalva landed with four boats on his way from Cuba. His peaceful visit was soon followed a year later by Hernán Cortés, whose party destroyed the temples and idols they found there. Not only did his men leave the island in ruins but they also left smallpox. This virulent disease reduced the population from about 40,000 in 1519 to 300 by 1570, and by the year 1600 the island was deserted.

Opposite: *San Miguel, Cozumel's coastal capital, facing the blue waters of the Caribbean Sea.*
Above: *A coney, one of the smaller groupers, in its red (juvenile) phase.*

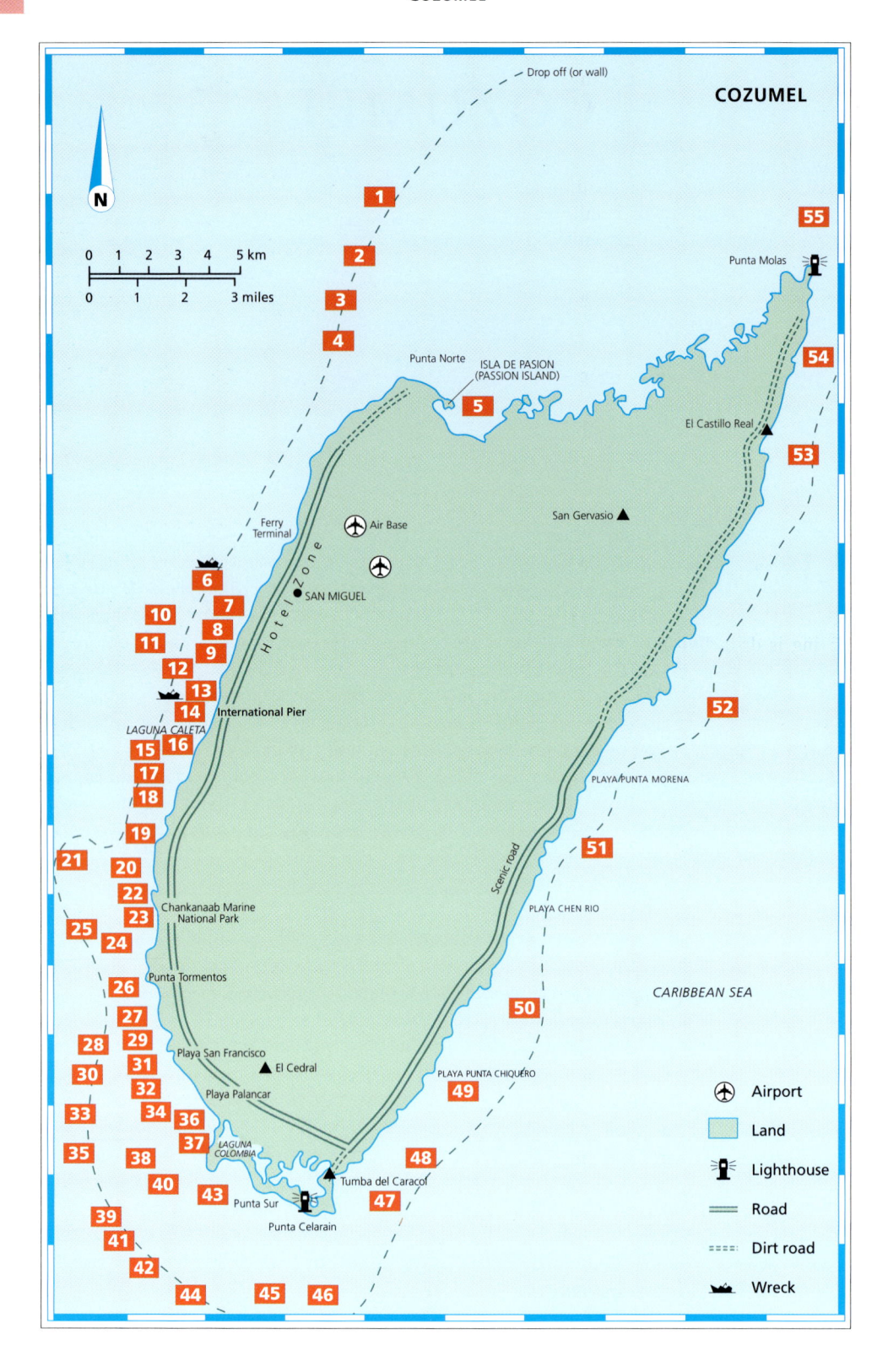

Cozumel

COZUMEL

Drop off (or wall)

Punta Molas

Punta Norte — ISLA DE PASION (PASSION ISLAND)

El Castillo Real

Ferry Terminal

Air Base

San Gervasio

SAN MIGUEL

Hotel Zone

International Pier

LAGUNA CALETA

PLAYA/PUNTA MORENA

Scenic road

PLAYA CHEN RIO

Chankanaab Marine National Park

Punta Tormentos

CARIBBEAN SEA

Playa San Francisco — El Cedral

Playa Palancar

PLAYA PUNTA CHIQUERO

LAGUNA COLOMBIA

Tumba del Caracol

Punta Sur

Punta Celarain

Legend
- Airport
- Land
- Lighthouse
- Road
- Dirt road
- Wreck

During the 17th century Cozumel was used as a base by pirates, including Henry Morgan and Jean Lafitte. It was not settled again until 1848 by people escaping the War of the Castes on the mainland (see page 19). This often violent struggle by the local Maya people was finally settled as late as 1901, when they surrendered to government troops. During the Mexican Revolution of 1910–1921, the Maya were granted important land reforms and freedoms.

By 1970 Cozumel's population had risen to 10,000 and by 2001 it numbered over 60,000. Now, more than 300,000 visitors a year arrive there by air and about 1.3 million day trippers from cruise ships.

Carlos 'n' Charlies Bar in San Miguel serves beer, barbecues, seafood and Tex-Mex.

DIVING AND SNORKELLING IN COZUMEL

The primary purpose of visiting Cozumel is to dive – the island is considered by most to be a diver's paradise – and, in fact, there is little else to do here. The reefs and shoals southwest of Cozumel Island rank among the top dive sites in the world. Almost all the diving is drift-diving to some level, but there are many shallow shore dives close to the major international hotels. This type of boat/drift-diving may not suit divers of all levels, so it is always better to check with the dive store for the details of a dive before travelling for perhaps an hour to the site and back. The waters circulate around Cozumel twice a day, from the Caribbean Sea to the Gulf of Mexico in the north. This accounts for the higher-than-average concentration of marine life to be found in this area and for a constant supply of fresh, clear water.

The prevailing winds are from the east, making the east coast of the island suitable for all water sports. In fact, all the holiday diving takes place off the west coast, mainly because the sea is generally too rough on the exposed eastern shore and it is deemed too far to travel by the local day boats. In exceptional weather conditions one or two of the operators may venture round the southern corner, but almost the whole of the eastern coast is unexplored and still offers great scope. The live-aboard dive boat *MV Oceanus* often makes a trip there during the hotter, less windy months of the year.

There is not enough space in this book to list every dive site, especially since the same short stretch of reef may have three or four location names – many dive operators and boat captains know of at least twice as many dive sites as are listed in this chapter. Nevertheless, so many divers visit the island, particularly during high season from mid-December to May, that there are not enough dive sites to go round.

Some small dive operators give the impression that they do not know where the

---

SAN MIGUEL, COZUMEL

Almost 100 years ago, workers were digging in an area north of the modern capital, San Miguel, when they unearthed a statue of St Michael the Archangel carved in ivory. He was brandishing a sword of pure gold and wearing a golden crown. This event took place on September 29 – the holy day of St Michael – which was considered too much of a coincidence to be dismissed. The predominantly Catholic population decided to give his name to the city. It is common belief that the statue was a gift to the Indians from Juan de Grijalva, who discovered Cozumel in 1518. The statue can be seen on the altar of San Miguel Church at the corner of Avenidas 10 and Benito Juárez.

reefs are: they head for a reef, wait for another dive boat to stop, then make for the same site. However, divers have different reasons for disembarking in a particular place. Some like to start from a certain spot – because of its dramatic archway, for example; others prefer a sand chute, and others the drama of the wall in the hope of encountering large pelagics. Some dive boat captains use a safe anchor drop in a shallow, sheltered lagoon; and most cruise above the divers to avoid anchor damage. Being tailed by smaller dive operators means that no sooner have you arrived than someone else pulls alongside and disembarks their divers in the water. This always leads to confusion on a drift dive and to the very real possibility of diving groups getting mixed up and ending up back on the wrong boat.

When a dive boat leaves the dock, crew members ask their guests where they want to dive. This is democratic, but there are several outstanding dive sites that have become well known and the result is that many dive boats head for the same reef. Ultimately you will enjoy your dives more if you always consider other divers. If the reef you plan to dive on is crowded, wait – or travel to another of Cozumel's superb reefs.

HURRICANE DAMAGE

Cozumel suffered greatly when Hurricane Gilbert struck in 1988; and it was damaged again, although to a lesser degree, by Hurricane Roxanne in 1995. Delicate marine forms, such as some sponges and sea fans, can scarcely withstand such a hammering, and large outcrops of corals are often upturned by wind and waves, but just two weeks after the hurricane there seemed to be little damage to these reefs.

THE WEST COAST

1 Barracuda Wall
★★★★

Location: south of Punta Molas Lighthouse, to the northwest of the island.
Access: by local boat only, limited to six divers per boat, or live-aboard.
Conditions: strong currents expected; windy with surface chop.
Minimum depth: 14 m (45 ft)
Maximum depth: beyond 30 m (100 ft)
Average visibility: over 30 m (100 ft)

This dive, the most northerly reached by any Cozumel dive operator, is visited only rarely. Prior arrangements must be made through the harbour master. Due to the severity of the currents in the area the number of divers per boat that can be carried on one trip is limited to six and all must be experienced open-water drift divers. This is a flat strip reef with sand around, sloping into the depths. The attraction is the above-average chance to see large pelagics, such as barracuda, jacks, rays, and sharks. Very large barrel sponges, rope sponges and elephant's ear sponge can all be found here.

2 San Juan Two
★★★★

Location: south of Punta Molas Lighthouse, to the northwest of the island.
Access: by local boat only, limited to six divers per boat.
Conditions: strong currents always expected; windy with surface chop.
Minimum depth: 16 m (52 ft)
Maximum depth: beyond 30 m (100 ft)
Average visibility: over 30 m (100 ft)

San Juan Two is a continuation of San Juan Reef (Site 3). Because severe currents flow through this area the number of divers per boat is limited to six experienced open-water drift divers. This is a flat strip reef with sand around, sloping into the depths. It is at the northerly range of reef corals in this area of the Caribbean and the few varieties of coral that grow in this area are large, such as *Porites sp*. Large pelagic fish, such as eagle rays and sharks, are sometimes encountered around this site.

Opposite: Santa Rosa Reef off Cozumel is one of the most popular wall dives.

> **SIGNBOARD IN COZUMEL MUSEUM**
>
> 'The destiny of Cozumel – jungle among reefs – rests on its corals and its sand. The sea around it is a road and a barrier; it is its way out and its protection. Below, on the bottom of the sea, life evolves just as it did at the beginning of time, while man admires it and wounds it.'

3 San Juan Reef
★★★★

Location: south of Punta Molas Lighthouse on the same reef as Site 2.
Access: local day boat only and by live-aboard.
Conditions: strong currents expected; windy and only for experienced divers.
Minimum depth: 21 m (69 ft)
Maximum depth: 25 m (80 ft)
Average visibility: in excess of 30 m (100 ft)

Similar to Site 2, but the terrain is more uneven. Permission to dive must be granted by the harbour master. Wire coral and purple sea fans are common, but the large pelagics are the attraction here; the grey reef shark (*Carcharhinus perezi*) is often seen. This dive is not for the faint-hearted. It is a long way to journey just for the chance of seeing big fish, and exploring it is hard work. There is a natural amphitheatre called Pino's Bowl.

4 Barracuda Reef
★★★★

Location: south of Punta Molas Lighthouse, to the northwest of the island.
Access: by local or live-aboard boat only, limited to six divers per boat.
Conditions: a windy site with surface chop and strong currents.
Minimum depth: 21 m (69 ft)
Maximum depth: beyond 30 m (100 ft)
Average visibility: over 30 m (100 ft)

This dive is visited only rarely, and prior arrangements must be made through the harbour master. There are severe currents in this area, so the number of divers per boat is limited to six and all must be experienced open-water drift divers. This is a flat strip reef with sand around, sloping into the depths. The attraction is the above-average chance to see large pelagics, such as barracuda, jacks, rays and sharks. The great barracuda (*Sphyraena barracuda*) is the most common species sighted. Diving here can be exhilarating, but hard work.

5 Passion Island
★★★★

Location: in the lagoon between Passion Island and the shoreline of Cozumel.
Access: by local boat or from the shore.
Conditions: little or no current.
Minimum depth: beach entry
Maximum depth: 6 m (20 ft)
Average visibility: reduced in the lagoon area

A shallow snorkel dive in a sheltered lagoon bordered by mangrove trees. This is a natural hatchery for many of the fish species found on the outer reefs, such as grunt and snapper. There are huge gardens of sea grasses with all manner of invertebrates, including sea hares (*Aplysia dactylomela*).

6 Barge Wreck
★★★★

Location: opposite the Vista Del Mar Hotel.
Access: shore dive primarily, but can be reached by local boat.
Conditions: currents to be expected; windy and surface chop between November and April.
Minimum depth: 9 m (30 ft)
Maximum depth: 12 m (40 ft)
Average visibility: more than 20 m (66 ft)

The barge was sunk in 1976 and is now completely overgrown with marine life. There are many different corals and all manner of sponges. The barge is 30 m (100 ft) long by 9 m (30 ft) wide and 3 m (10 ft) high and sits upright on the sea bed. There are two safe access points to the interior. The barge is a superb night dive and photographers, especially, should not miss it. There are large green moray eels and outstanding numbers of black, Nassau, and other large grouper.

7 Pico's Reef (Barracuda Reef)
★★★★★★

Location: in front of the Barracuda Hotel and the Dive Paradise Pier.
Access: shore dive only.
Conditions: slight currents expected; windy and surface chop.
Minimum depth: shore
Maximum depth: 9 m (30 ft)
Average visibility: more than 15 m (50 ft)

There is an area of artificial reef which is gradually becoming overgrown with algae, sponges and small corals. There are numerous anemones with symbiotic crabs under their tentacles. Conch shells (*Strombus gigas*) can be found all over the reef, and although it is now illegal to fish for them in this reserve area, the author spotted a local person free-diving to collect these delicacies. Pico's Reef is also known for its octopus, which can be seen at any time of day, and – joy of joys – sea horses. This is also an excellent dive at night, when you can always see octopus and small lobster.

8 La Villa Blanca Reef
★★★★★★

Location: offshore from La Villa Blanca Hotel.
Access: from the shore or by local boat.
Conditions: slight-to-moderate currents expected.
Minimum depth: shore
Maximum depth: 6 m (20 ft)
Average visibility: Visibility over 15 m (50 ft)

This is an easy dive for those involved in training and for photographers. Although there is little coral and sponge growth, there is plenty of marine life to occupy you. There are small gorgonians and pencil corals (*Madracis mirabilis*). Fish life includes yellow stingrays (*Urolophus jamaicensis*) and peacock flounder (*Bothus lunatus*).

9 North of International Pier (Gorgonian Flats)
★★★★★★

Location: as the name suggests, this is a shallow reef which runs roughly parallel to the shore to the north of the International Pier, starting at the La Perla Hotel.
Access: from the shore in front of La Perla Hotel.
Conditions: sheltered area, but reduced visibility.
Minimum depth: 3 m (10 ft)
Maximum depth: 8 m (25 ft)
Average visibility: around 10 m (33 ft)

A sheltered, sandy slope leads out to this shallow fringing reef – a scattered string of small coral heads and patch reef – which runs for about 2 km (1¼ miles). The main species to be seen are small clumps of brain coral (*Diplora* sp.), gorgonian sea fans (*Gorgonia ventalina*) and whip corals (*Plexaurella* sp.). This is an easy dive which is often favoured for night trips. The reef can also be accessed from the pier opposite La Villa Blanca Hotel and across the street from the Casa Del Mar Hotel and the Sol Caribe Hotel.

10 La Villa Blanca Drop-Off
★★★

Location: opposite La Villa Blanca Hotel.
Access: mainly from local day boat, but can be reached from the shore (not recommended).
Conditions: strong current expected and surface can be windy and choppy.
Minimum depth: 21 m (69 ft).
Maximum depth: beyond 30 m (100 ft)
Average visibility: more than 30 m (100 ft)

This is a wall dive, but unlike the walls to the southwest of the island, which are vertical, it slopes steeply. This dive is rated as one for experienced divers only. The currents can be quite fierce and you do not get much chance to view the marine life unless it is swimming alongside you. It is only suitable for wide-angle photography. If you dive from the shore, make certain before you start that the current is running from the south to the north; this will give you the chance to make an easier exit if you do get swept away. In summary, however, this dive involves a great deal of work for rather meagre results.

11 La Ceiba Drop-Off
★★★★

Location: directly out from La Ceiba Hotel.
Access: boat dive, day boat or live-aboard.
Conditions: subject to strong currents, 4–5.5 kph (2–3 knots).
Minimum depth: 21 m (69 ft)
Maximum depth: beyond 30 m (100 ft)
Average visibility: more than 30 m (100 ft)

Very similar to Site 10 and should not be tackled by inexperienced divers. The current is quite fierce and therefore unsuitable for most types of underwater photography. The low coral heads on the sand slope have some interesting corals and fish, but generally you are drifting with the current, accompanied by the ubiquitous yellowtail snapper *(Ocyurus chrysurus)* and the white margate *(Haemulon album)*.

12 La Ceiba Reef Preserve
★★★★★★★

Location: directly from the La Ceiba Hotel pier.
Access: swim out from the pier to the Aeroplane Wreck (Site 13) then continue along the reef.
Conditions: shallow, sheltered, good for beginners, photographers and snorkellers.

Longsnout seahorses (Hippocampus reidi) *are rare, but can be seen on Barracuda Reef.*

Minimum depth: 6 m (20 ft)
Maximum depth: 12 m (40 ft)
Average visibility: more than 30m (100ft)

This is a ridge of coral and patch reef interspersed with sandy areas. There are star corals, brain corals, pillar corals and gorgonian sea fans. There is also fire coral *(Millepora sp.)*, which is not a true coral but a member of the hydroid family. It can inflict quite a painful sting if you brush against it with the softer parts of your skin. This dive is very good for fish, such as sergeant majors *(Abudefduf saxatilis)* and the yellowtail damselfish *(Microspathodon chrysurus)*. The coral sea fans look battered in this area, which may well be due to damage by divers.

Coral Replanting

For a number of years now, a few active conservationists around Cozumel have pioneered a replanting scheme for coral. After the last hurricane, large sections of staghorn coral were broken off, and divers, working under strict conservation codes, are now lifting these broken pieces off and replanting them among other live corals. Similarly, a few dive masters and dive guides have begun the practice of following trainee divers so that if any happen to blunder into the coral and break a piece off, the broken sections are immediately replanted in the coral reef. Early indications are that the scheme has a very good chance of success and that more than 70 per cent of coral replanting appears to be effective. It is part of a larger programme which includes lectures on conservation and buoyancy control. The programme is aimed at protecting the reef so that it remains intact for future generations to enjoy.

Fish-Feeding

Fish-feeding is frowned upon by the Mexican Department of the Environment, by the Cozumel Divers Federation – and by the local hospitals. But with no conservation law and only recommendations to go by, it is hardly surprising that the practice is no more controlled on Cozumel Island than in the rest of the Yucatán. And when you consider the thousands of tourists who visit this region's world-famous dive sites, it is not surprising that there is no policy. You cannot condone fish-feeding in one area and ask snorkellers and diving photographers and others not to feed fish elsewhere.

FEEDING AGGRESSION

Despite the official warnings, several unscrupulous dive guides still feed fish in certain popular dive sites, particularly large grouper and moray eels. This would be harmless if the divers who feed the fish were the only ones to visit these locations – as if they were private aquariums. But when the next group of divers approaches this same reef, the fish assume that the group has food for them too and some act aggressively when no food appears. On the author's last visit to Cozumel, a fellow diver received such a nasty bite from an apparently tame, hand-fed moray eel that her hand needed immediate medical treatment, including five stitches, which ruined her holiday.

Some dive operators recommend that divers in their care should never wear gloves; if you, as one of their party, should insist on feeding fish, there is a good chance that the fish may try to feed on you. Such an experience quickly changes people's minds on the issue, especially when they have been bitten by a sergeant major or a yellow-tailed snapper.

UPSETTING THE BALANCE

When food is introduced into the sea it attracts fish to the extent that some areas around the Yucatán, which would not normally sustain a fairly high concentration of fish species, now teem with fish. This is the result of regular feeding on which the fish have learned to depend. The scientific view is that this behaviour is not natural; that it makes the fish species more vulnerable to predation by other species, including people; and that the ecological pattern is being altered.

Ultimately, whether to feed fish or not is your choice. But there is one thing you must NEVER do, and that is kill another marine species, such as a sea urchin, to feed fish – even if you see someone else doing this. The practice has disastrous long-term consequences on the reef ecology, causing increased growth of algae (which sea urchins eat). Algae can smother and kill live corals. If you feed fish, therefore, you risk injuring yourself and the reef environment.

13 Aeroplane Wreck
★★★★★

Location: in front of La Ceiba Hotel.
Access: directly from the pier, either swim along sea bed or swim out to marker buoy.
Conditions: shallow and sheltered, ideal for macro photography.
Minimum depth: 10 m (33 ft)
Maximum depth: 12 m (40 ft)
Average visibility: more than 30 m (100 ft)

This old DC3 40-passenger Convair airliner was sunk deliberately in 1977 as a prop for a Mexican disaster movie. The hull was substantially intact until Hurricane Roxanne passed by in October 1995; she is now well broken up and scattered over the sea bed, resting about 65 m (210 ft) from the pier. The remains of the aircraft are now home to a large assortment of grunts and snapper.

On the shore side of the wreck the sea bed rises rapidly to 5 m (17 ft) and the numerous small coral heads have large numbers of Christmas tree worms (*Spirobranchus giganteus*) and the split-crown featherduster (*Anamobaea orstedii*) on them. Hermit crabs, numerous shrimps and several species of blenny all compete for space among the sea fans and plumes which are a common feature of all Caribbean reefs.

Plans are now being made by the Cozumel Diving Federation to purchase an old seaplane to form an artificial reef in the same location and it is hoped that it will be in place by the time this book appears.

14 International Pier
★★★★★★★★

Location: south of the La Ceiba Hotel pier.
Access: via steps to the south of La Ceiba Hotel pier.
Conditions: there can be a current, but it is generally light to moderate, depending on how far you travel along the pier wall.
Minimum depth: 6 m (20 ft)
Maximum depth: 20 m (66 ft)
Average visibility: generally around 15 m (50 ft), due to shipping traffic

This pier was built in 1978 on a sandy bottom, leading out to the first of the mini-walls which line the western shore of Cozumel. There is considerable concrete rubble and detritus left over from the construction and this offers many interesting nooks and crannies in which various species of marine life install themselves. The pier can only be dived during the weekends, and only after permission has been given by the harbour master. The restrictions are due to the many cruise ships which dock regularly, and the car ferry, which travels between Cozumel and Puerto Morelos on the mainland.

The marine life on the wall is well worth the effort of a visit, particularly at night when the large sheets of encrusting red sponges seem to light up in front of your torches. Divers should, as always, take care with their buoyancy to avoid brushing against the sponges and corals, especially the fire coral, which is everywhere. There are numerous schools of grunts and snapper, and you often see large schools of juvenile barracuda

Opposite: *A school of sergeant majors expecting to be fed by an approaching diver.*
Below: *Social featherduster worms* (Bispira brunnea) *are delicate creatures living around the base of many sponge and coral species.*

sheltering in the canyons created by the columns of the pier. Extra care should be taken when snorkelling because currents push you against the wall.

Plans are now being made for the construction of at least one and possibly two additional cruise ship piers. Jean Michel Cousteau, the eminent marine ecologist, and the Cozumel Dive Federation are very much against such a plan, as it will destroy a large part of Paradise Reef and, after construction, the area between the two piers will be off-limits to divers. It still looks as if the plan might go ahead, as the economics of cruise ship income far outweigh the protection of a small area of reef.

15 Paraíso North
★★★★★★

Location: out from Aeroplane Wreck (Site 13) in front of La Ceiba Hotel to the first section of reef. Approximately five minutes' swim from the wreck.
Access: from steps at La Ceiba Hotel pier.
Conditions: light-to-moderate current usually, but can be stronger during spring tides. (See page 35 for information on tides).
Minimum depth: 12 m (40 ft)
Maximum depth: 15 m (50 ft)
Average visibility: 15 m (50 ft)
All of this section of reef consists of large coral heads and sponges, some of them growing over 1.8 m (6 ft). There are numerous coral heads each with their own groups of molluscs, fish and invertebrates. They look like tiny islands of life in the otherwise fairly uninteresting surrounding sea bed made up primarily of sand and coral rubble. These coral heads are also visited by numerous species of jack which are active predators by day and night. Care should always be taken with the current along this reef as it is quite easy to lose your dive guide if you do not keep up with him or her.

16 Paradise Shallows (Caleta Reef)
★★★★★

Location: continuation of the same reef that runs toward the International Pier to the south. This area is between the shore and Paradise Reef (Site 17).
Access: out from La Perla to sand flats.
Conditions: there can be current. If you are carried north, you can make your exit at the International Pier. If you are carried south, make your way inshore toward the La Perla at Caleta Lagoon and then to the shore.
Minimum depth: 6 m (20 ft)
Maximum depth: 9 m (30 ft)
Average visibility: variable
A fairly easy site for divers and snorkellers of all tastes.

The area is popular with snorkellers and the fish are quite tame, but tend to harass you if there is no food. (see page 80). For diving photographers, this site is best at night. You can find the goldspotted eel *(Myrichthys ocellatus)* and the peacock flounder *(Bothus lunatus)*; numerous sand-dwelling gobies and octopus are common. The use of underwater torches at night seems to make everything so much brighter and more colourful than during the day.

17 Paradise Reef
★★★★

Location: directly out from Caleta Lagoon on the north side of Stouffer El Presidente Hotel.
Access: day boat.
Conditions: light-to-moderate current, generally from a south-to-north direction.
Minimum depth: 7 m (23 ft)
Maximum depth: 12 m (40 ft)
Average visibility: more than 15 m (50 ft)
This stretch of reef is just one of five reefs which form Paradise and Paraíso. It is particularly popular as a night dive because it is near the local dive shop piers.

The coral ridges rise only 2–3 m (7–10 ft) above a sea bed of gently sloping sand dotted with coral blocks. The reef is not espcially interesting, but many species of fish can be seen here. The site is also favoured as a second reef site after a much deeper first dive from one of the outer walls. Dive operators tend to favour these locations as sites where they can easily manage various diving groups of mixed skill and expertise. Here you can expect to find the splendid toadfish *(Sanopus splendidus)* (see page 100), spotted moray eels *(Gymnothorax moringa)* and several species of cleaner shrimp and filefish.

18 Paraíso South
★★★★★

Location: to the north side of El Presidente Hotel.
Access: by local day boat or from the shore to the north of the Caleta Yacht basin.
Conditions: moderate-to-light currents; there can be surface chop.
Minimum depth: 10 m (33 ft)
Maximum depth: 15 m (50 ft)
Average visibility: around 15 m (50 ft)
This dive site is often used by the local day boats as a second shallow site after a deeper first dive (chosen for its close proximity to the dive shop piers). The dive can be just as easily done from the shore and the closest section of the reef is popular with snorkellers, who

Above: *Spanish hogfish* (Bodianus rufus) *range over all areas of the reef.*
Below: *Blue chromis* (Chromis cyanea) *are always seen in large numbers at the top of the reef crest.*

watch the antics of the scuba divers. There is a serious risk with boat traffic in this location, so extra care should be taken when diving or snorkelling from the shore.

There are many different species of tame fish which have been fed on a regular basis by various dive guides. Neither the author, Lawson Wood, nor the conservation services, necessarily condone this practice, but it does make fish photography that little bit easier. The sea grass beds before the reef are important hatcheries, with several fish species and juveniles often to be seen. Spanish hogfish (*Bodianus rufus*) and squirrelfish (*Holocentrus rufus*) can be found. French grunt (*Haemulon flavolineatum*) occupy many of the spaces between the coral heads and sea fans, and sea whips stretch out into the current. This dive is always very photogenic.

19 Las Palmas Shallows
★★★★★★★★

Location: north of the Fiesta Americana Cozumel Reef Hotel.
Access: by day boat. The dive site is approximately 150 m (500 ft) offshore.
Conditions: light-to-moderate current, generally from a south-to-north direction.
Minimum depth: 7 m (23 ft)
Maximum depth: 12 m (40 ft)
Average visibility: more than 15 m (50 ft)

The coral ridges only rise 2–3 m (7–10 ft) above a sea bed of gently sloping sand interspersed with occasional coral blocks. The reef is not especially interesting, but its marine life is abundant, with many species of fish, and is particularly favoured for macro photography. There is an overabundance of invertebrates, including lobster, arrow crabs (*Stenorhynchus seticornis*) and brittle stars (*Ophiothrix suensonii*).

20 Fiesta Americana Cozumel Reef Hotel (Holiday Inn Reef)
★★★★★★★

Location: directly out from the Beach Club across the road from the Fiesta Americana Cozumel Reef Hotel.
Access: from the shore, directly out to the shallow reef.
Conditions: there can be current around the small pier.
Minimum depth: 3 m (10 ft)
Maximum depth: 6 m (20 ft)
Average visibility: 10 m (33 ft)

A gently sloping bottom with a number of tame and well-fed fish species. This site appears over-dived, but this impression is caused by the effects of natural phenomena more than by divers. Hurricanes are a very real hazard to marine ecosystems, as these storm breaks off delicate corals and shifts great quantities of sand. This can smother the coral organisms, damaging the reef.

21 Las Palmas Drop-Off
★★★★

Location: due west of Las Palmas Shallows (Site 19). Named after two lonely palm trees which used to be opposite the site on the beach.
Access: by day boat.
Conditions: moderate current running south to north.
Minimum depth: 15 m (50 ft)
Maximum depth: more than 30 m (100 ft)
Average visibility: More than 30 m (100 ft)

Sand and coral rubble slope gently to the lip of the drop-off. This steeply sloping wall starts at about 21 m (69 ft) and has many large coral sea fans, huge barrel sponges, some more than 2 m (6 ft) across, and bright tube sponges. There is little coral cover on the wall, so that it is sometimes easier to take photographs of queen angelfish (*Holacanthus ciliaris*) and French angelfish (*Pomacanthus paru*). This is an interesting dive, but it is poor in coral growths on the wall.

22 Chankanaab Underwater Park
★★★★★★★

Location: south along highway to the Park (admission $5 for one day).
Access: from any of the sets of steps that lead out from this popular picnic area.
Conditions: very busy, particularly at weekends. Little or no current.
Minimum depth: 3 m (10 ft)
Maximum depth: 11 m (33 ft)
Average visibility: generally less than 15 m (50 ft) due to the volume of divers and snorkellers in the area

Chankanaab is probably the most popular shore-diving and snorkelling location in the whole of Cozumel. The Park has restaurants and palapas, rest rooms, a wildlife preserve with iguanas as a feature of special interest, and a couple of dive shops (see also page 103). It is also used by the cruise ships' passengers, who are disgorged regularly each day and swarm up and down the beach renting snorkelling equipment among other activities.

Chankanaab means 'Little Ocean' and its name refers to the inner lagoon, which is now off-limits to scuba divers and snorkellers. The fish in this natural aquarium can be viewed from a number of wooden platforms that have been built out over the lagoon. The Chankanaab National Park has excellent facilities and is a good place to spend a day. The diving is rather poor for corals, but it is more than made up for by the large variety and numbers of fish. On the bigger coral heads are a large number of Christmas tree worms and horseshoe worms *(Pomatostegus stellatus)*. Look out for the neon goby *(Gobiosoma oceanops)*, which often shelters under these worms. Small schools of grunt and snapper can be found in between the coral heads, and the flamingo tongue mollusc *(Cyphoma gibbosum)* can be seen regularly on the stalks of sea fans.

23 Beachcomber Cavern
★★★★★★

Location: south of Chankanaab Marine National Park.
Access: directly from the shore.
Conditions: care should be taken as this is the entrance to a series of underwater caves which run for an undetermined distance into the interior of the island. Cave-diving should not be undertaken without proper training and the correct equipment.
Minimum depth: 3 m (10 ft)
Maximum depth: 5 m (17 ft)
Average visibility: under 10 m (33 ft)

These caves are famed for the schools of silverside minnows which congregate near the entrance during the warm season. These tiny fish are actually several species of juveniles which school together for additional protection. The openings are large enough to admit several divers at once, and all lead into a larger inner cave. Waves and heavy swell often occur in this area and the caves should be avoided during these times.

24 Chankanaab Reef
★★★★

Location: several hundred yards or metres directly out from Chankanaab Marine National Park at the edge of the main line of strip reef.
Access: by day dive boat.
Conditions: moderate current, can be choppy on the surface.
Minimum depth: 11 m (33 ft)
Maximum depth: 15 m (50 ft)
Average visibility: more than 20 m (66 ft)

This strip reef has a maze of tunnels and fissures which cut through it in many different areas and at varying depths. The surrounding area is fairly flat sand with some coral rubble. This location is popular as a night dive for the abundance of lobster, crabs, toadfish, and octopus that can be seen there. The diamond-backed blenny *(Malacoctenus boehlkei)* can be observed sheltering under the protective reach of the giant anemone *(Condylactis gigantea)*.

25 Bolones de Chankanaab
★★★★

Location: 50 m (160 ft) west of Chankanaab Marine National Park.
Access: by dive boat only.
Conditions: current to be expected, but not strong.
Minimum depth: 15 m (50 ft)
Maximum depth: 17 m (72 ft)
Average visibility: more than 20 m (66 ft)

There are numerous large coral heads covered in many different species of sponge. The reef structure is split into three entirely separate sections, all of which become deeper in steps to the edge of the drop-off. The second section is 50 m (175 ft) further west and the last another 25 m (80 ft) beyond that. All are excellent for marine life, but be careful of your time at these depths: it is very easy to drop several metres without realizing the dangers of the time penalties imposed at depth.

26 Tormentos Reef
★★★★

Location: south of Chankanaab Marine National Park and before Yocab Reef, directly opposite Punta Tormentos.
Access: by day boat.
Conditions: there can be very strong current.
Minimum depth: 9 m (30 ft)
Maximum depth: 21 m (69 ft)
Average visibility: more than 20 m (66 ft)

This is an exposed, widely spread and fairly broken-up patch reef system interspersed with wide, sandy channels. It is quite a popular site for the second dive of the day, since the top of the reef comes to within 9 m (30 ft) of the surface. It drops steeply to 21 m (69 ft) on the outward side of the slope, where there is a secondary reef. The reef consists of around 60 separate coral heads covered in a wide variety of brain corals, sea fans and whip corals. Colourful sponges adorn the canyons and there are many different invertebrates hiding in the rocky crevices. At the end of the dive, as the current takes you gently north, there is a huge underwater formation similar to a terrestrial sand dune, which can be seen quite clearly from the air as you fly into the island.

Although the current can occasionally be strong, the boat-handlers are very experienced along this reef and will drift along with you in the current. Schools of creole wrasse *(Clepticus parrai)* move over the reef crest, Bermuda chub *(Kyphosus sectatrix)* and yellowtail snapper are well used to being fed by a number of the dive guides and they will accompany you on your dive. It was here that the author was shown his first splendid toadfish *(Sanopus splendidus)*.

Arrow crabs (Stenorhynchus seticornis) *are only 6 cm (2½ in) long.*

27 Yocab (Yucab)
★★★★

Location: to the south of Punta Tormentos.
Access: by day boat.
Conditions: there is usually current. The reef is scoured by sand movement and has many archways and overhangs.
Minimum depth: 12 m (40 ft)
Maximum depth: 21 m (69 ft)
Average visibility: more than 20 m (66 ft)

Although all these reefs are essentially drift dives, Yocab, like many of the others, also offers shelter from the current on the outer edges, where underwater photographers can rest up and concentrate on the huge amount of marine life which covers this reef. There are sponges everywhere and of every colour. The sand-scoured overhangs also offer refuge for lobsters, banded coral shrimps *(Stenopus hispidus)* and the arrow crab *(Stenorhynchus seticornis)*. There are also large numbers of squirrelfish and angel and butterflyfish always swimming in pairs. Numerous parrotfish can be found browsing on the live coral and you can quite clearly hear their crunching noises under water.

28 Yocab Wall (Tom's Wall)
★★★★

Location: due west of Yocab (Site 27).
Access: by day boat, because it is too far out to dive from the shore.
Conditions: current is to be expected, but the numerous large overhangs and tunnels across the reef offer plenty of protection for divers wanting to explore its recesses.
Minimum depth: 10 m (33 ft)
Maximum depth: beyond 30 m (100 ft)
Average visibility: more than 20 m (66 ft)

This site is favoured by a number of diving operations and it gets particularly busy along the outer reefs. Large coral buttresses jut out and form a convoluted, scalloped outer reef edge with numerous gullies and swimthroughs. Like most of the outer reefs, San Francisco does not have too many fish, but the fish that inhabit the site are large – such as black grouper *(Mycteroperca bonaci)* and jewfish *(Epinephelus itajara)*. This is a particularly nice dive and its popularity is well deserved.

29 Cardona Reef
★★★★

Location: north of San Francisco Reef (Site 31).
Access: by day boat, because the site is too far out to dive from the shore.
Conditions: current is to be expected, but the numerous large overhangs and tunnels offer plenty of protection for divers wanting to explore the recesses.
Minimum depth: 6 m (20 ft)
Maximum depth: 15 m (50 ft)
Average visibility: more than 20 m (66 ft)

The sand-scoured overhangs and tunnels offer plenty of opportunity to explore and view nocturnal fish, which can be seen in these recesses during the day. Squirrelfish and cardinal fish are the most common, but you can also find the splendid toadfish in this location. Sponges are a predominant feature of the Cozumel reefs and a common species on Cardona Reef is the boring sponge *(Siphonodictyon coralliphagum)*, which is a brilliant yellow colour and bores large holes into live corals.

A brilliantly coloured green algae, common on many different types of reef around Cozumel, inhabits these shady areas of the reef. The hanging vine *(Halimeda goreaui)*, is the main species in this area. It has tiny, rounded, leaflike segments and grows here and there in great profusion. Its calcified leaves are a major contributor of sand to the reef.

30 Punta Tunich Drop-Off (Virgin Wall)
★★★★

Location: opposite Punta Tunich, several hundred yards or metres further out than Yocab, but running parallel with the reef.
Access: by day boat only.
Conditions: generally strong current and choppy surface conditions.
Minimum depth: 15 m (50 ft)
Maximum depth: beyond 30 m (100 ft)
Average visibility: more than 30 m (100 ft)

The northern end of this reef is the most interesting, but it is better to approach it when there is a south-to-north current running. The wall at this end is near-vertical, with numerous caves and crevices which bisect the reef, running from the crest at around 20 m (66 ft) down to much deeper water. Squirrelfish and pairs of angelfish can be approached fairly easily. A number of very large

The hanging vine (Halimeda goreaui), *an algae, has an important role in the reef ecosystem.*

green moray eels *(Gymnothorax funebris)* can be seen along this reef. These eels are used to being handled by a few of the dive guides, but it is not advisable to do this. They are, after all, wild animals with very poor eyesight and they may mistake those waggly bits of pale flesh and bone at the ends of your arms as a probable food source!

31 San Francisco Reef
★★★★

Location: located approximately 1 km (about half a mile) directly offshore from San Francisco Beach.
Access: by day boat only.
Conditions: unpredictable currents can be expected. Perhaps choppy on the surface, which makes boat entry and exit uncomfortable.
Minimum depth: 12 m (40 ft)
Maximum depth: beyond 30 m (100 ft)
Average visibility: more than 30 m (100 ft)
This inclining sand and coral rubble sea bed slopes down over a mini drop-off where the reef crest tops 12 m (40 ft). The steep slope beyond this is strewn with coral rubble and this whole section suffered greatly during Hurricane Gilbert in 1988. The coral reef is made up of large clumps of varieties of brain coral, all topped with sea fans and plumes. Pink vase sponges *(Niphates digitalis)* can be seen all over the reef and small schools of creole wrasse and bluehead wrasse *(Thalassoma bifasciatum)* are abundant in the constantly moving water along this reef.

32 Santa Rosa Shallows
★★★★

Location: east of Santa Rosa Wall (Site 33).
Access: by day boat, because the site is too far out to dive from the shore.
Conditions: current is to be expected, but the numerous large overhangs and tunnels offer plenty of protection for divers wanting to explore the recesses.
Minimum depth: 6 m (20 ft)
Maximum depth: 15 m (50 ft)
Average visibility: more than 20 m (66 ft)
This site is similar to Tormentos Reef (Site 26), in that there is a shallow sandy area on the inside, which folds gently into and through a narrow strip reef. It is topped with numerous purple sea fans and encrusting sponges, and the underhangs and small caves always have large numbers of lobster. Smooth trunkfish *(Lactophrys triqueter)* and trumpetfish *(Aulostomus maculatus)* can always be found here. A very scenic dive.

33 Santa Rosa Wall
★★★★★

Location: next large reef system to the south of Site 32.
Access: by day boat.
Conditions: unpredictable strong currents are to be expected. There is always shelter however, when you reach the reef.
Minimum depth: 10 m (33 ft)
Maximum depth: beyond 30 m (100 ft)
Average visibility: more than 30 m (100 ft)
This is perhaps one of the author's favourite dives in Cozumel. It is not possible to cover all the reef or, indeed, to see all of the wonderful array of marine life in one dive, but the site can easily be split into three separate dives. Its profile becomes larger and more convoluted the further north you travel. As in any exposed area, the southernmost section is low-lying and scoured by currents. The middle section has some very large tunnels which completely cut through the reef crest, and the most northerly section has tunnels, caves, overhangs and underhangs and some sections of wall becoming so steep they are near-vertical.

On the steeper slopes there are numerous rope sponges *(Aplysina cauliformis, Niphates erecta* and *Aplysina fulva)*. File clams *(Lima scabra)* can be seen in the recesses, their orange or white tentacles waving in the current. Many species of hermit crab can be found and there appear to be thousands of tiny gobies and blennies flitting in bursts over the corals and sponges.

Barracuda and large specimens of the black grouper *(Mycteroperca bonaci)*, which shelter under the overhangs above the reef crest, can always be observed here. Stoplight parrotfish seem to blend into the multicoloured reef. Only when you use an underwater torch does the true beauty of the reef reveal itself. One of the most distinctive of the small reef fish is the fairy basslet *(Gramma loreto)*. The front half of its body is a brilliant violet-to-purple and its rear is a deep yellow/gold. These fish are instantly recognizable, but very hard to photograph because of their constant motion.

SEA FANS

Sea fans are fan-shaped corals. They are a feature of almost all the Caribbean reefs and are found as far north as Bermuda. All are located on the top of the reef crest. The fan is quite strong, with a wide, sometimes colourful base of deepest purple. When the fans have been damaged they are often overgrown with fire coral, which follows the existing branches of the fan.

34 Paso del Cedral Reef
★★★★

Location: opposite Punta Cedral to the inside of and running parallel to Santa Rosa Reef.
Access: by day boat.
Conditions: a moderate current runs from south to north. Can be windy on the dive boat.
Minimum depth: 10 m (33 ft)
Maximum depth: 18 m (60 ft)
Average visibility: around 20 m (66 ft)

This a very good photographic dive with lots of opportunities to photograph schooling fish. There are large aggregations of grunt and snapper, particularly the bluestriped grunt *(Haemulon sciurus)* and the schoolmaster *(Lutjanus apodus)*. The corals are fairly low-lying, as you would imagine on this exposed strip reef, but where the reef is cut by sand chutes there are some very interesting small corals, such as disk coral *(Scolymia wellsi)* and cactus coral *(Mycetophyllia lamarckiana)*. The southern stingray *(Dasyatis americana)* feeds in the sandy areas to the inside of the reef. Among numerous molluscs is the occasional the queen conch *(Strombus gigas)*, which is becoming increasingly scarce.

35 Paso del Cedral Wall
★★★★

Location: the next large reef system to the south and west of Paso del Cedral Reef (Site 34).
Access: by day boat.
Conditions: unpredictable strong currents are to be expected. There is always shelter, however, when you reach the reef.
Minimum depth: 12 m (40 ft)
Maximum depth: beyond 30 m (100 ft)
Average visibility: more than 30 m (100 ft)

This site is similar to Santa Rosa Wall (Site 33). It is less convoluted with fewer huge coral buttresses, but still very spectacular. Large grouper hang off the edge and numerous parrotfish are all over the area. Large encrusting and tube sponges, and several species of gorgonian fan corals, are to be seen.

Gorgonian corals, such as this wide-mesh sea fan (Gorgonia mariae), *are a colourful feature of the reefs surrounding Cozumel Island.*

COZUMEL

> ### BLACK CORAL
>
> Conservation laws make it illegal to collect coral from the waters around Cozumel and Cancún. Nevertherless, decorative items made from black coral are on sale in shops in both places. They are made by artisans on Cozumel Island and Isla Mujeres, who import the coral from places with conservation policies that are less strictly applied. The standard of their work is high and black coral products are always popular with tourists. However, environmental groups discourage the trade – all corals are endangered and they are rarely harvested sustainably.

36 Dahlia Reef (Dalila Reef)
★★★★

Location: to the inside and north of Palancar Reef. Named after Dalila Ranch which is located nearby.
Access: by day boat.
Conditions: there can be current and windy conditions on the surface.
Minimum depth: 8 m (25 ft)
Maximum depth: 25 m (80 ft)
Average visibility: more than 20 m (66 ft)

This site consists of a series of strip and patch reefs very similar to La Francesa and Palancar Reefs (Sites 37 and 41). The outer edge is slightly deeper and forms a mini-wall with some very interesting overhangs and crevices. There are lots of tame grouper and green moray eels, plus good coral growth and some spectacular tube sponges. This is an excellent place for photography and many nooks and crannies offer shelter from the current.

37 La Francesa Reef
★★★★

Location: inner strip reef between Palancar Reef and Santa Rosa Reef.
Access: by day boat.
Conditions: moderate current as in most of this location, running from south to north.
Minimum depth: 12 m (40 ft)
Maximum depth: beyond 20 m (66 ft)
Average visibility: more than 20 m (66 ft)

This largely unbroken strip and patch reef is the outer edge of La Francesa (The French Lady). It bottoms out at 20 m (66 ft), but the coral rubble and sand slope continues down to the outer reef edge and drop-off. The inside of the reef has a gradual slope of sand running down to the reef and, in some cases, sand chutes completely dissect the reef. Southern stingrays, peacock flounders and various molluscs are to be found on the sand. There are good-quality corals and an abundance of fish and invertebrates.

PALANCAR REEF

Palancar is one name that is always mentioned when divers talk of Cozumel. The reef is massive, stretching more than 5 km (3 miles) and, for convenience, it is covered here in four entries, which relate to the most popular dives of the Cozumel Diving Association. It is largely undeveloped as a dive site and offers an amazing diversity of marine life and coral formations to suit divers of all tastes and at all levels of diving expertise.

38 Palancar Shallows (Palancar Gardens)
★★★★★★★★★

Location: about 2 km (1 mile) offshore, inside and parallel to the Palancar drop-off and to the north.
Access: by day boat.
Conditions: slight-to-moderate current. Exposed on the surface.
Minimum depth: 5 m (17 ft)
Maximum depth: 21 m (69 ft)
Average visibility: more than 20 m (66 ft)

This is a very interesting reef offering a wealth of diving experiences without the need to travel far. It rises to about 5 m (17 ft) in some places and in others drops in a mini-wall to 18 m (60 ft). The strip reef is more than 20 m (66 ft) wide in much of the area and is cut and dissected by many fissures and caves. There may be current flowing over the reef, but there are so many sheltered areas and shallow water that it never causes problems.

Huge stove-pipe sponges *(Aplysina archeri)* stretch out from the reef and there are black corals, such as *Antipathes pennacea,* in its deeper areas. Bright yellow tube sponges *(Aplysina fistularis)* may be associated with juveniles of the yellowhead wrasse *(Halichoeres garnoti)* and other fish hide in the deep tubes for protection at night. Butterflyfish, angelfish, parrotfish and damselfish can always be seen, To the south, before Palancar Caves, the reef drops much lower and becomes less defined. This dive should not be missed.

39 Palancar Horseshoe
★★★★★

Location: south of Palancar Shallows (Site 38), but before Palancar Caves (Site 40) is reached.
Access: by day boat.
Conditions: windy and exposed on the surface. There can be strong current, but it is sheltered in the 'horseshoe'.

A supermale stoplight parrotfish (Sparisoma viride). *Supermales begin life as females and pass through several colour transformations before they change into males.*

Minimum depth: 9 m (30 ft)
Maximum depth: beyond 30 m (100 ft)
Average visibility: more than 20 m (66 ft)
This is a natural amphitheatre shaped like a giant horseshoe in a stretch of the Palancar Reef. It is always dived separately from the other sites along the coast, which tend to be drift dives. There is enough to delight any diver in just this one spot. The dive is best in the deeper section, which is deeply convoluted. Large gorgonian sea fans stretch out into the current and there is a vast array of fish, corals and invertebrates.

The caves always attract divers, but you must be particularly careful with your buoyancy to be certain that you do not blunder into the minute coral organisms that inhabit these shady areas. Remember always to take a torch with you to pick out the true colours of the animals and corals.

A large bronze statue of Christ (called 'Sacred Protector of the Ocean') was erected in this spot in 1985, but it was knocked over by Hurricane Gilbert in 1988 and has since been relocated at Chankanaab.

40 Palancar Caves
*****

Location: south of The Horseshoe (Site 39).
Access: by day boat.
Conditions: there is generally a current, but you will scarcely feel the effect of it until you emerge through the caves on to the outer wall of the reef.
Minimum depth: 6 m (20 ft)
Maximum depth: beyond 30 m (100 ft)
Average visibility: reduced in the caves, but more than 30 m (100 ft) on the outer wall

Although this is classified as a deep dive, the shallowest part of the reef comes to within 6 m (20 ft) of the surface. The reef slopes outward to the reef edge and deeply convoluted lip. Here, the corals seem to take on a life of their own as they form spires and buttresses, caves, gullies and canyons. Deep fissures run under the corals and sand slopes plummet into the depths. Large sheet corals *(Agaricia grahamae)* jut out from the reef, creating interesting overhangs where squirrelfish and bigeye seek shelter during the day. The brain coral *(Diploria strigosa)* may be found up to 2 m (6 ft) across and there are myriad hermit crabs, blennies and gobies. There are countless caves and canyons along this stretch of reef and you will never be able to see all of them even after several dives. Schooling fish, such as grunts and snapper, constantly appear, and if you take your time as you exit the caves on the outer edge of the reef, you may glimpse a green turtle *(Chelonia mydas)* or a spotted eagle ray *(Aetobatus narinari)* cruising past the wall.

41 Palancar Deep
★★★★★

Location: the outer edge of the reef wall south of the Horshoe and Palancar Caves (Sites 39, 40).
Access: by day boat.
Conditions: exposed on the topside, and current is to be expected. Divers may experience difficulty climbing into the dive boat due to the sea swell.
Minimum depth: 12 m (40 ft)
Maximum depth: beyond 30 m (100 ft)
Average visibility: more than 30 m (100 ft)

This deeply incised wall is an absolute delight. There are so many varied combinations of coral growth that even when repeating the same dive (as may often happen on a dive vacation), you are never bored. Gorgonian sea fans adorn the top of the reef and there is constant competition for space between the corals, sponges and algae; all are brightly coloured and appear to have their own associated fish, crustaceans or invertebrates.

Look out for a number of cleaning stations along this reef. Several different species host these locations, such as juvenile Spanish hogfish *(Bodianus rufus)* on the reef top, the cleaning goby *(Gobiosoma genie)* among the coral heads and the Pederson's cleaning shrimp *(Periclemenes pedersoni)* among the tentacles of various species of anemone in the recesses. (See page 109 for a description of cleaning stations)

42 Colombia Gardens (Colombia Shallows)
★★★★★★★★★★

Location: parallel to the shoreline on the inside of the main reef at the extreme southern end of the island.
Access: by day boat.
Conditions: little-to-moderate current. Can be exposed when the wind is from the south, but when the wind is from the north this reef is almost always calm and clear.
Minimum depth: 2 m (7 ft)
Maximum depth: 10 m (33 ft)
Average visibility: more than 30 m (100 ft)

Colombia reef forms a natural breakwater and protection for the almost flat coast. There are huge coral buttresses covered in many varieties of sponge and some very interesting small – but tall – coral heads. This area is seldom dived, being about as far as any of the day boats will travel, but it is well worth making the effort. It is often done as a second dive after diving the much deeper Colombia Pinnacles (Site 43) or Maracaibo Reef (Site 46), but, like the author, you may find yourself wanting to stay the whole day in this location. The reef is teeming with fish life and every species of tropical fish found around the island seems to be represented here. There is so much nutrient-rich soup passing through here from the depths of the Caribbean and flowing up into the Gulf of Mexico that everything appears that little bit tamer and more colourful and photogenic.

There are extensive meadows of sea grass and turtle grass *(Thalassia testudinum)* between the coral outcrops, which are used as a natural spawning area for many of the island's fish. Dark gullies and canyons between the buttresses (evidence of wind and wave force over many centuries) are inhabited by schools of snapper and grunt. There are elkhorn coral *(Acropora palmata)* and large stands of pillar coral *(Dendrogyra cylindrus)*, beautiful sponges and many anemones.

The snorkelling is among the best on the island due to the rich profusion of corals, but special arrangements have to be made at the dive store for the guides to take you to this site to snorkel. You also have to watch out for boat traffic, as fishing boats pass close to this reef.

43 Colombia Pinnacles
★★★★★★★★

Location: directly south from the island and running parallel to the shore at the edge of the drop-off. Between Palancar Reef and Punta Sur Reef (Site 44).
Access: by day boat.
Conditions: unpredictable current and very exposed on the surface. Not always dived due to the distance from the dive-store jetty.
Minimum depth: 5 m (17 ft)
Maximum depth: beyond 30 m (100 ft)
Average visibility: more than 30 m (100 ft)

Although this reef is shallow at the start it is essentially a potentially very deep dive for very experienced divers only. The snorkelling is delightful among the shallows, but there can be a lot of surface swell, which makes the snorkelling a little more uncomfortable. However, the clear water more than makes up for the discomfort.

The steeply sloping sea bed is littered with coral rubble and large patch reef coral blocks, which become

Opposite: *Corals and sponges on a reef off Cozumel.*

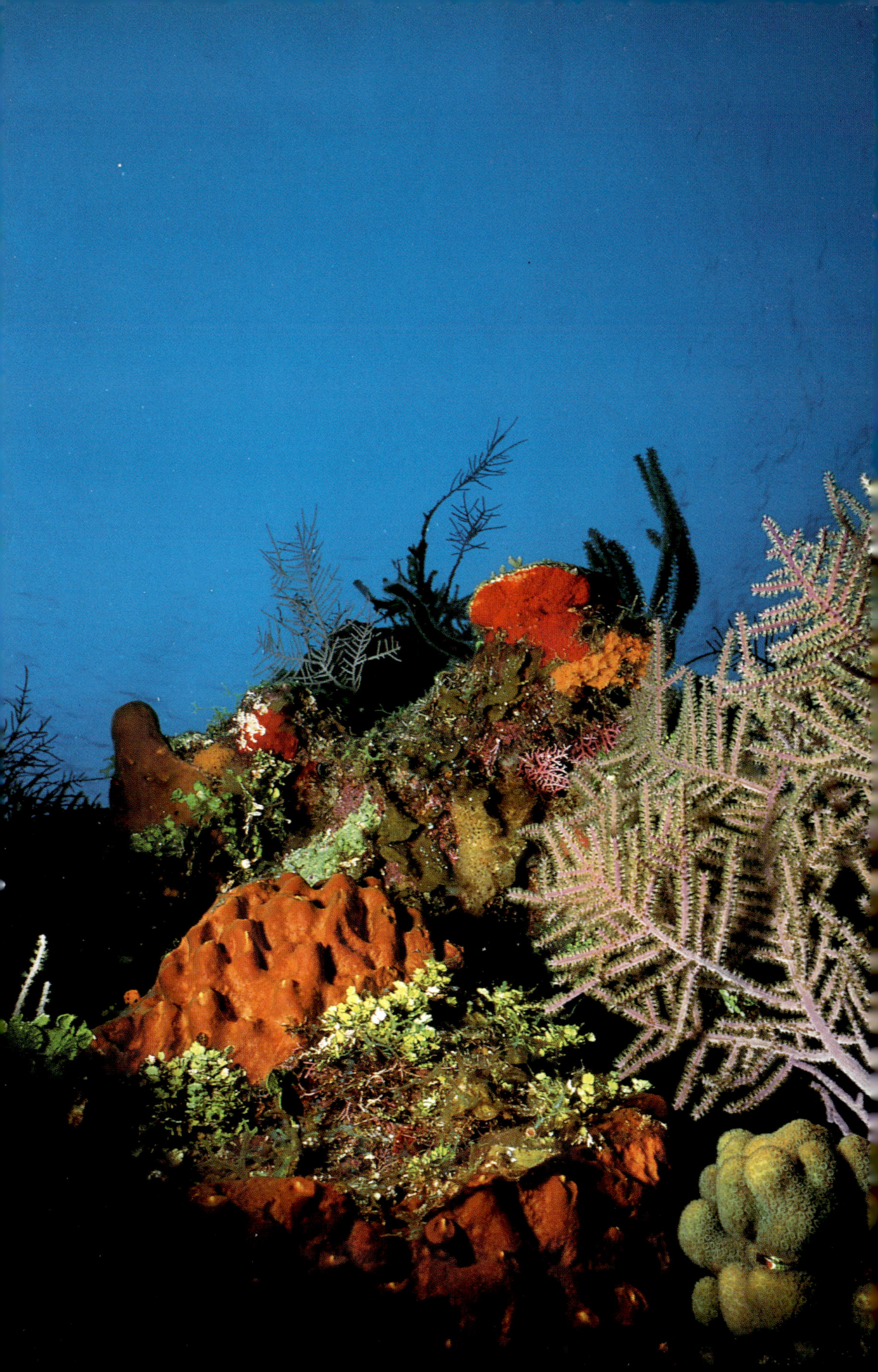

The flamingo tongue (Cyphoma gibbosum) *is a common shell usually seen on sea fans and plumes.*

more pronounced coral buttresses as you swim further out to the edge of the wall. Here there are numerous large coral pinnacles made up of many different varieties of coral, interspersed with vividly colourful sponges. There appear to be two rings of pinnacles. The first starts at about 12 m (40 ft); and the next begins below 30 m (100 ft) and rises to 20 m (66 ft). There are large grouper, turtles can occasionally be seen, and it has been reported that reef sharks regularly cruise the deeper sections of the wall.

This is an excellent location for wide-angle photography – many of the underwater photographers who visit Cozumel want to return to this spot time after time. The clarity of the water and the rich colours make it a very special place and it is justifiably listed as one of the top dive sites in the world.

44 Punta Sur Reef (South Point)
★★★★★

Location: south of Punta Sur at the southern entrance to Laguna Colombia.
Access: by day boat.
Conditions: this site can be very exposed during extreme weather conditions and there is always current. A journey time of over one hour may dissuade some prospective divers from visiting a fascinating dive site.
Minimum depth: 24 m (80 ft)
Maximum depth: beyond 40 m (130 ft)
Average visibility: in excess of 30 m (100 ft)

There is an inner strip reef which rapidly falls away to what is becoming one of the most popular dive locations on the island. Although the site can be visited only when weather permits, the sheer majesty of the deep wall, caves, caverns and fissures put the site at the top of most divers' lists. You enter the larger of the cave systems down a sand chute at 27 m (90 ft), where you enter a superb complex of coral tunnels and caverns which are absolutely bursting with life. One of the larger caves, called The Devil's Throat, opens up into an underwater room with four passageways, one of which leads to The Cathedral, a vast cavern with another three passageways, all interconnecting. Only experienced divers should consider entering these for any distance and any diver intending to explore them should be accompanied by a dive master or instructor.

There are perhaps not as many fish at this site due to the exposed nature of the area, but the usual angelfish and butterflyfish can always be spotted swimming in pairs along the reef edge. The deeper coral walls have whip corals *(Cirrhipathes leutkeni)*, which spiral out into the depths, and large black corals *(Antipathes* sp.). There are also brightly coloured smaller gorgonian sea fans, such as the deep-water fan *(Nicella goreaui)*; and sea whips *(Ellisella elongata)*, including the devil's sea whip *(Ellisella barbadensis)*, are very much in evidence.

This is an excellent dive, but diving time is always limited because of the extreme depth and the complex nature of the site.

45 Chun Chacab Reef
★★★★★

Location: the last deep-water dive site visited by the Cozumel dive operators before the exposed eastern end of the island. Southwest of Punta Celarain.
Access: by day boat only.
Conditions: very exposed to strong surface winds; there is ocean swell and unpredictable currents. Journey time from San Miguel is around 1½–2 hours by boat.
Minimum depth: 3 m (10 ft)
Maximum depth: beyond 30 m (100 ft)
Average visibility: in excess of 30 m (100 ft)
This steeply sloping sand and coral rubble ledge, seldom visited by the Cozumel dive operators, is interspersed with small sections of low patch reef. The sandy areas are typically covered in sea grass and are a natural breeding ground for a number of species of fish native to the island. Molluscs are common in the sandy areas and you are supposed to be able to see dolphins around this point regularly. The lip of the reef starts at 30 m (100 ft) before plunging over the wall, so by the time you reach this area you have usually run out of dive time. There are large canyons and swimthroughs, but you will be well into decompression time if you explore this site further.

46 Maracaibo Reef
★★★★

Location: close to Punta Celarain Lighthouse and south from Colombia Reef.
Access: by day boat only.
Conditions: an exposed location with unpredictable currents. Only the most experienced of divers should consider diving this location.
Minimum depth: 18 m (60 ft)
Maximum depth: beyond 30 m (100 ft)
Average visibility: more than 30 m (100 ft)
This deep reef and steeply inclined wall are subject to unpredictable currents. When descending through open water to reach the descending terraces you must move

The iridescent colours of the blackcap basslet (Gramma melacara) *make it easily recognizable.*

> **RULES FOR DEEP DIVING**
>
> To dive safely at depth:
> - attend a course in deep diving before diving in the ocean
> - increase depth slowly
> - dive only with experienced deep divers
> - do not put yourself or others at risk
> - plan your dive and dive to your plan
> - learn to recognize symptoms of nitrogen narcosis (see page 170) and ascend immediately if symptoms appear.

swiftly and keep close in to the reef or you may be swept away from your planned position on the reef. Wide-angle photography is best, as you keep moving along the reef, the depth is great, and you do not have time to study the reef and its inhabitants. However, you can marvel at the complexity of the old coral limestone structures, caverns, caves and swimthroughs.

Only the most experienced divers should attempt this site and only under the supervision of a very experienced local dive master and boat-handler. Although this is strictly a no-decompression dive with very limited time at depth, groups will be kept together by the dive master and a mid-water decompression safety stop is obligatory on the way to the surface.

THE EAST COAST

The following nine dive sites on Cozumel's east side are rarely dived. The prevailing wind and weather is from the east and this renders the east coast virtually inaccessible to divers. The eastern seaboard is also undived due to the distances the local day boats have to travel to reach the sites. There are enough high-quality dives in the sheltered channel between Cozumel and the mainland to make it hardly worthwhile venturing further.

These dive sites are accessible during the calmer months between April and August. There are classic spur and groove reef formations on the outer crest, with shallower patch and strip reef inside. In common with all areas of the Caribbean, there appear to be three distinct layers of coral reef, which roughly coincide with the ancient climatic changes which have shaped the earth.

The marine life is similar to that of the rest of the island but there are fewer of the more delicate tube sponges and branching corals. There are also fewer pelagic or open-ocean fish, as this area is not a conservation zone and the whole coast is fished commercially.

Opposite Hawksbill turtles (Eretmochelys imbricata) *nest along Cozumel's eastern coast.*
Below: *A swimthrough, formed by freshwater seeping through a reef southwest of Cozumel.*

47 El Islota
★★★★

Location: close to Punta Celarain Lighthouse, travelling north toward the Maya ruins at Tumba del Caracol.
Access: by day boat and live-aboard boat only.
Conditions: an exposed location with unpredictable currents. This site is only accessible during the calmer months between May and September.
Minimum depth: 3 m (10 ft)
Maximum depth: 9 m (30 ft)
Average visibility: more than 30 m (100 ft)
This single large coral 'island' is situated on flat sand and is a natural haven for all manner of marine life. The shallower areas inshore split up into less distinct spur and groove reef formations. An interesting dive site, but there is always surge present. Good for parrotfish.

48 Playa Bush
★★★★

Location: north of Punta Celarain Lighthouse and opposite the next headland beyond the Maya ruins.
Access: by day boat and live-aboard boat only.
Conditions: an exposed location with unpredictable currents. Ocean swell is always a problem here.
Minimum depth: 12 m (40 ft)
Maximum depth: 20 m (66 ft)
Average visibility: more than 30 m (100 ft)
Playa Bush is a simple spur and groove reef which is fairly well broken up on top. There are large numbers of the common sea fan, which bend and sway in the current. Wherever the coral has been broken off you find algae growing and there are numerous species of green algae all over the reef. Angelfish and butterflyfish can be found in their lifelong mating pairs, plus many juvenile wrasse, parrotfish and blennies.

49 El Mirador
★★★★

Location: north to the next set of Maya ruins and directly offshore to the inner spur and groove reef.
Access: by day boat and live-aboard boat only.
Conditions: an exposed location with unpredictable currents. Constant oceanic swell makes things rather uncomfortable in the dive boat and when entering and exiting the water.
Minimum depth: 12 m (40 ft)
Maximum depth: 20 m (66 ft)
Average visibility: more than 30 m (100 ft)
El Mirador is very similar to the rest of the strip, spur and groove reef which runs the entire length of Cozumel Island's eastern coast. There is nothing particularly startling about the dive, except that there is an excellent chance of seeing turtles around this area, which is opposite a nesting site.

Cozumel Marine Communities

In 1988 a marine biologist, E. Martínez, carried out a study entitled, 'The Quantitative and Qualitative Study of the Scleractinians of five reefs of the Island of Cozumel'. The research covered the distribution of reef-building corals, and looked at the structure of the reefs in the popular diving areas. In the north and south of Cozumel are two coastal lagoon systems, the Blind Lagoon and the Silver River to the north, and Colombia Lagoon to the south. It was found that these regions are where most coral reproduction takes place. Unfortunately, little scientific research has taken place since then.

50 Punta Chiqueros
★★★★★★★★

Location: opposite Punta Chiqueros inside the more sheltered lagoon area.
Access: by day boat or from the shore only.
Conditions: This site can be subject to oceanic swell, which not only makes it more hazardous but also stirs up the underwater.
Minimum depth: shoreline
Maximum depth: 6 m (20 ft)
Average visibility: to a little under 9 m (30 ft)

A sheltered lagoon area with few good coral formations. There are large numbers of sergeant majors (*Abudefduf saxatilis*) and the night sergeants (*Abudefduf taurus*), which prefer this more turbulent water. Turtle grass is found in the lagoon and you can always find numerous juvenile species of fish and molluscs, including octopus.

51 Chen Río
★★★★

Location: two-thirds of the way north of the Cozumel east coast before you reach Punta Morena. Inner spur and groove patch reef.
Access: by day boat and live-aboard boat only.
Conditions: a more exposed location with unpredictable currents.
Minimum depth: 9 m (30 ft)
Maximum depth: 15 m (50 ft)
Average visibility: more than 20 m (66 ft)

A shallow and fairly well-battered reef on first appearances. However, there is a wealth of invertebrate life, such as bearded fireworms (*Hermodice carunculata*), which can be found on numerous sponges. The social featherduster worm (*Bispira brunnea*) can also be found in quite large colonies. Fish species include numerous wrasse, parrotfish and small grouper.

52 Punta Morena
★★★★

Location: directly out from Punta Morena to the shallower spur and groove reef.
Access: by day boat and live-aboard boat only.
Conditions: can be subject to unpredictable currents. Reef drops off rapidly so care should be taken with time spent at depth.
Minimum depth: 15 m (50 ft)
Maximum depth: beyond 30 m (100 ft)
Average visibility: more than 30 m (100 ft)

This site is well known for the numbers and different species of moray eel to be found there. The primary reef-builders are star coral and brain coral species. There are also large numbers of anemone, primarily the giant anemone (*Condylactis gigantea*) and the corkscrew anemone (*Bartholomea annulata*). Fish species include blue chromis (*Chromis cyanea*) and the iridescent blackcap basslet (*Gramma melacara*).

53 Los Atolones
★★★★

Location: to the northeast of Cozumel and opposite the Maya ruins of El Castillo Real, along the outer edge of the spur and groove reef.
Access: by day boat and live-aboard boat only.
Conditions: a more exposed location along the northeast coast. Only the most experienced of divers should consider diving this location.
Minimum depth: 9 m (30 ft)
Maximum depth: beyond 30 m (100 ft)
Average visibility: more than 30 m (100 ft)

The spur and groove reef is less defined here and there are large areas of steeply sloping sand and coral rubble. There is always a current in this location and you can drift quite far along the edge of the reef. Occasional barracuda can be seen.

54 Islotes
★★★★★★★★

Location: close to the northwestern point of Cozumel, in the shallows to the east of the shore.
Access: by day boat and live-aboard boat only.
Conditions: an exposed location with unpredictable currents running round the headland.
Minimum depth: 3 m (10 ft)
Maximum depth: 9 m (30 ft)
Average visibility: more than 30 m (100 ft)

There are numerous tiny atoll-like formations called

microatolls on this site. They are created by fresh water percolating through the porous limestone and by the action of tide and currents creating areas of often turbulent and murky water. These coralline formations are unique to the Mexican Caribbean and are so called because of their similarity to the true reef atolls of the South Pacific. They occur as part of the southern Mexican Barrier Reef. Their porous structure allows the surf to flow under and through the microatoll.

55 Punta Molas
★★★★

Location: to the west of Punta Molas.
Access: by day boat only.
Conditions: an exposed location with unpredictable currents. Generally too far for the day boats to travel.
Minimum depth: 12 m (40 ft)
Maximum depth: 20 m (66 ft)
Average visibility: more than 30 m (100 ft)

A shallow patch and strip reef surrounded by wide sandy areas. Coral life is close to the rocky outcrops and consists mainly of encrusting species. Sponges are also of the encrusting kind. Squirrelfish can be seen under the overhangs and there are numerous lobster. However, divers may not consider this dive rewarding enough to merit the long boat trip out to the site.

The bearded fireworm's minute bristles break off in the skin if you brush against them.

UNDERSEA CRATER

In the 1990s, scientists led by Frank Kyte took core samples 1 km (1.6 miles) deep into the floor of a massive subterranean crater found off the north coast of the Yucatán Peninsula. The samples were found to contain the element Iridium, proof that the crater was caused by a meteorite that hit this part of the Earth millions of years ago. The results of this research are important evidence in a debate that has been exercising scientific minds for some years: over 65 million years ago dinosaurs apparently disappeared off the face of the earth, after having dominated it for over 200 million years. Some scientists believe that fragments of a giant comet collided with the earth some 65 million years ago, and that an explosion resulting from the impact threw up so much debris into the thin atmosphere, that the sun was blocked out for over 50 years. This caused the demise of much plant life and some 75% of all living species. The results of their core sample analyses will help understanding of the processes that led eventually to the evolution of many mammals and, ultimately, of humankind.

Toadfish

Toadfish must be among the most bizarre inhabitants of the reefs around the Yucatán coast. There are two distinct species and both are found in the shallower reefs to the south of Cozumel and the shallow waters of Bahía de Mujeres. Toadfish have also been seen in the seas around other Central American countries but little else is known of their distribution.

THE SPLENDID TOADFISH

The splendid toadfish *(Sanopus splendidus)* has a slate grey/blue head striped horizontally with lighter bands, and with 20 or so fleshy, pointed barbels underneath the jaw. The rest of its body is somewhat mottled with patchy grey and slate blue over white, and it has a brilliant yellow fringe on all the fins except the ventral fins, which are completely yellow. This shy, reclusive fish, which grows only up to 20 cm (8 in), hides in dark recesses of the reef and is mainly active at night, when it may venture out of its lair. The much larger large eye toadfish *(Batrachoides gilberti)* – the rather ugly cousin of the splendid toadfish – grows to over 25 cm (10 in).

THE LARGE EYE TOADFISH

The large eye toadfish is a light reddish brown and has diagonal streaks on its dorsal and anal fins. The fleshy barbels under its chin are much thicker than those of its cousin and often branch. As the name suggests, the eyes are large and bulging. These fish are most common in mangrove lagoons, shallow-water harbours and the entrances to creeks, and are not averse to entering fresh water. Relying on camouflage to snare their prey of small fish and crustaceans, they are very wary of divers and retreat into the reef when approached.

TOADS AND TOADFISH

What is most distinctive about toadfish comes from their name. They barely resemble their terrestrial counterparts, but they have one astonishing factor in common: both make croaking noises, which are audible for quite a distance under water. Marine toadfish live beneath coral overhangs, choosing an area where the resonance is amplified by the small coral cave. At night, divers swimming around the reef find them by following the sound. The large eye toadfish is the noisiest and the sound it makes is a tone lower than the croak of the splendid toadfish. Coral reefs are generally noisy, but it is most peculiar to hear a distinctive croaking under water and to trace it to a pair of the more curious of the Yucatán's reef-dwellers.

A splendid toadfish half-concealed beneath a rock overhang.

Cozumel

How to Get There

By air: Cozumel International Airport is five minutes' drive northeast of San Miguel. It handles direct flights from Houston, Miami, California and several Central American countries and Caribbean islands. Many international flights are routed through Cancún, where passengers transfer to a flight to Cozumel. Connecting flights wait for delayed flights.

Small private airlines fly between Cozumel, Cancún, Isla Mujeres, and Chichen Itzá: **Aerobanana Aerotaxi**, tel/fax (987) 25040; **Seaplane Adventures**, tel (988) 71599/fax (988) 72611; **Mayair**, tel (987) 20433/20725/fax (987) 21044.

By ferry: a **car ferry** sails from Puerto Morelos, south of Cancún off Highway Mex 307. The journey takes about four hours, depending on sea conditions. You should be in the queue at least 12 hours in advance to be sure of a place. There is a faster and more expensive **Water Jet ferry** from Playa del Carmen; to book, tel: (987) 21508/21588.

The B/M Mexico II and the B/M Mexico III offer a daily service from Playa del Carmen to Cozumel between 05:15 and 20:45 hours; returning between 04:00 hours and 20:00 hours. Small, slow ferries also operate between the cruise ships and the ports.

Where to Stay

There are 19 hotels/resorts registered with the Cozumel Hotel Association, as well as many more fine resorts on the island. There are also four time share resorts. Prices are dependent on the level of the facilities. Many of the hotels offer special weekend deals where flights, accomodation and diving are all included.

Cozumel Hotel Association PO Box 228, Calle 2 Norte 299C, Cozumel, Quintana Roo, Mexico 77600; tel (987) 23132/fax (987) 22809.

Hotels north of town
You may need to hire a car or taxi to reach the diving operators, which are in town or out to the south, closer to the reefs:
Club Cozumel Caribe, PO Box 43, Cozumel; tel (987) 20100. Pool and restaurant.
Coral Princess Club, North Hotel Zone, Cozumel; tel (987) 23200/fax (987) 22800; email coralprince@cozunet.finred.com.mx. A 48-room beach-front hotel with pool, restaurant and dive shop (Pepe Scuba).
Playa Azul, Carr. A San Juan, km 4 Zona Hotelera Norte, Cozumel; tel (987) 20033/fax (987) 20110; email playaazul@cozumel.com.mx. A 50-room beach-front hotel with pool, restaurant and dive shop (Carlo Scuba).
Sol Cabañas del Caribe, Cozumel; tel (987) 20411/fax (987) 21599. A 321-room beach-front hotel with pool, restaurant and watersports.

Downtown Hotels
These tend to be smaller and older but more intimate and cheaper than those north of town. They are well situated for nightlife and in walking distance of all services.
Bahia Suites, Avda Rafael E. Melgar, Cozumel; tel (987) 29080/fax (987) 29073; email bacocame@dicoz.com. In the centre of Downtown; 27 suites.
Barracuda, San Miguel Hotel Zone, PO Box 163, Cozumel; tel (987) 20002. A 51-room beach-side hotel within walking distance of Downtown, with dive shop (David & Nancy's Sea Scuba).
Canterell, San Miguel Hotel Zone, PO Box 24, Cozumel; tel (987) 20144. Small and traditional.
Casa Mexicana, Avda Rafael E. Melgar No.457, Cozumel; tel (987) 20209/fax (987) 21387. Central location; 90 rooms.
Days Inn, Avda 11 Sur No.460, Cozumel; tel (987) 21600/fax (987) 21692. Adjacent to Downtown; 45 rooms; restaurant and pool.
Hacienda San Miguel Hotel & Suites, Calle 10 Norte no.500, Cozumel; tel (987) 21986/fax (987) 21648; email info@haciendasanmiguel.com. Excellent apartment-hotel, with fully serviced kitchens and breakfast room service.
Mesón San Miguel, PO Box 136, Cozumel; tel (987) 20233/fax 21820. Good location; 97 rooms and restaurant.
Paradisus Cozumel, San Miguel Hotel Zone, Cozumel; email ventas.paradisus.cozumel@solmelia.com. Excellent location; restaurant and dive shop (Sand Dollar Sports).
Suites Colonial, 5a Ave Sur No.9, Cozumel; tel (987) 20211/fax (987) 29080; email bacocame@dicoz.com. Only half a block from Central Plaza; 28 rooms; good restaurant.
Sun Village San Miguel, Avda Juarez 2 Bis, Cozumel; tel (987) 20233/fax (987) 24463. On main boulevard; 90 standard rooms; bar pool and sandwich bar.

South of Town
Hotels in the southern zone spread along the coast past the International Pier:
Allegro Resort, Palancar Beach, Cozumel; email info@divetours.org. Pool, restaurant and dive shop (Dive Palancar); 300 rooms.
Casa del Mar, Cozumel; tel (987) 21900/fax (987) 21855; email delmar@cozumel.com.mx. Pool, restaurant and dive shop (Del Mar Aquatics); 98 rooms and 8 cabanas.
La Ceiba, PO Box 284, Cozumel; tel 1-800-437-9609; tel (987) 20844/fax (987) 20065. A 110-room beach-front hotel with three pools, two restaurants and a dive shop (Del Mar Aquatics).
Costa Club Cozumel Beach Resort, Costera Sur km 1.7, Cozumel; tel (987) 22900/fax (987) 22154; email costaclubczm@cozunet.finred.com.mx. Hacienda-style hotel, with 180 rooms, three resaturants and large pool.
El Cozumeleño Beach Resort, Playa Santa Pilar km 4.5, AP 53, Cozumel; tel (987) 20050/fax (987) 20381; email salescoz@cozumel.com.mx. A 252-room beach-front hotel with pool, restaurant and dive shop (Ocean Tours).
Crown Paradise Club, Sol Caribe Playa Paraiso km 3.5, Cozumel; tel (987) 20700/fax (987) 21301; email cpczm@cozunet.finred.com.mx. Hotel with 355 rooms, 10 restaurants and bars and pools.
Fiesta Americana Dive Resort, Southern Hotel Zone, Cozumel; tel 1-877-FIESTA-8; tel (987) 22622/fax (987) 22666; email resfacdr@fiestaamericana.com.mx. A beach hotel with three restaurants, pools, a dive shop (Dive House), and 172 rooms plus 57 suites.
Fiesta Inn, Cozumel; tel (987) 22811/fax (987) 21855. A 180-room hotel opposite the beach with pool and restaurant.
Iberostar Cozumel, Southern Hotel Zone, Cozumel; tel 1-888-923-2722/fax (987) 29909; email clubbuceo@playadelcarmen.com; www.iberostar.com. A 5-star hotel with 300 bungalow-style rooms, and pools, restaurants and a dive shop (Dressel Divers).
Plaza las Glorias, San Miguel Hotel Zone, Cozumel; tel 1-800-342-AMIGO/fax (987) 21937; email info@bayadventures.com. A beach-front hotel near town, with 154 junior suites, pools, restaurants and a dive shop (Dive Paradise and Bay Adventures).
El Presidente, PO Box 49, Cozumel; tel (987) 20322/fax (987) 23186; email cozumel@interconti.com. A beach-front hotel. Pools, restaurants, a dive shop (Scuba Do), 253 rooms.
Reef Club Isla Cozumel, Carretera Costera Sur, km 12.9, Cozumel; tel (987) 293004/fax (987) 29315; email sisreef@cozumel.com.mx. A 240-room hotel on a superb beach, close to diving reefs.

Where to Eat

The restaurants listed below are a selection of some 60 or so on Cozumel. Advance booking is rarely necessary. Most serve Tex-Mex dishes and specialize in seafood. There are superb Mexican and Italian restaurants in the centre of San Miguel; 'turf and surf' restaurants and music bars prevail outside.

Groceries and drinks for self-catering are cheapest in the supermarkets three blocks back from the waterfront. The mini-markets on Avenida Rafael E. Melgar and

Cozumel

in tourist hotels cost three times as much.
International
Big Julian's Restaurant, Avda Rafael E. Melgar 241; tel (987) 20578. Outdoor tropical garden setting. Mexican and Lebanese.
La Boya, near Casa del Mar Hotel, Avda Rafael E. Melgar; tel (987) 21900. A seafront restaurant, lively and personalized service.
Las Palmeras, Avdas Rafael E. Melgar and Juárez; tel (987) 20532. In the town centre opposite the pier.
Los Arcos, Fiesta Inn; tel (987) 22900/22899. Mexican and international cuisine. Separate bar: The Lobby.
Morgan's Restaurant, on the Plaza; tel (987) 20584. Elegant and memorable.
Pepe's Grill, Avda Rafael E. Melgar and Calle Adolfo Rosada Salas; tel (987) 20213. on the waterfront in San Miguel.
Santiago's Grill, Calle Adolfo Rosada Salas 229 and Avda Sur 15; tel (987) 22137.

Bars/Barbecue
B.B.Qs, Avda Rafael E. Melgar between Avdas 4 and 6.
Carlos 'n' Charlies, Avda Rafael E. Melgar, Downtown; tel (987) 20191. Upstairs, rock music, dive talk, steaks, burgers and buckets of beer.
La Chopa Loca, La Ceiba Hotel, Avda Rafael E. Melgar; tel (987) 20812. Casual, overlooking Caribbean.
The Sports Page Bar and Grill, corner of Avdas 2 and 5; tel (987) 21199. American-style sports bar.

Italian
Il Gatto Pardo, Avda Sur 121. Garden terrace plus waterfall. Italian and Mexican seafood and pizzas.
Pizza Rolandi, Avda Melgar. Pizza (highly recommended) plus home-made wine.

Mexican
Ernesto's Fajitas Factory, Divers Inn Hotel, Avda Rafael E. Melgar; tel (987) 20145. A must when in Cozumel.
La Laguna, Chancanaab Marine National Park. Casual, beachfront, closes at 16:00 hours.
La Mission, Avda Juárez 23; tel (987) 21641. Mexican and seafood, known as the 'Divers' Restaurant'.
Seafood
Acuario Restaurant, Avda Rafael E. Melgar 11; tel (987) 21097.
Café del Puerto, Avda Rafael E. Melgar 2; tel (987) 20316.
Del Museo Restaurant, Avda Rafael E. Melgar 6; tel (987) 20838. Outdoor dining on a second-floor terrace overlooking the sea.

Dive Facilities

The largest diving operators are Downtown and near the Playa del Carmen ferry dock. These operators give a professional service, but tend to cater for day trippers from the mainland. To find a good operator, contact several before your trip to check their facilities. Ask whether they travel only with a full boat or are prepared to take divers out when there are reduced numbers; and whether there is room or facilities on the boat for rinsing camera equipment.

Dive operators
Albatross Charters, Calle 5 Entrada 10–15, Avda 241, Cozumel; tel (987) 23397/fax (987) 24048; email albatrosscharters@hotmail.com.
Aldora Divers, Calle Hidalgo 40–45, Villa Bonita 7, Cozumel; tel.(987) 23397/fax (987) 24048; email jorge@aldora.com.
Aqua Safaris, PO Box 41, Avda Rafael E. Melgar 5–7, Cozumel; tel (987) 20101/fax (987) 20661; email dive@aquasafari.com.mx.
AquaWorld - Cozumel, Carretera Castera Sur Playa Paraiso km 3.7, Cozumel; tel/fax (987) 21210; email aqwssc@cozumel.com.mx.
Black Shark, Avda 5 between Calle Adolfo Rosada Salas and Avda 3 Sur, Cozumel; tel/fax (987) 21451; email blackshark@cozumel.finred.com.mx.
Blue Angel Scuba School, Carretera. A, Chancanaab km 2, Cozumel; tel (987) 21631/fax (987) 20913; email blueangel@cozumel.com.mx.
Blue Bubble Divers, PO Box 334, 5TA Avda Sur 298, between Calle Adolfo Rosada Salas and Avda 3 Sur, Cozumel; tel/fax (987) 21865; email bbubbles@dicoz.com or blubub@aol.com.
Blue Note, Calle 2 Norte, between Avdas 40 and 45, Cozumel; tel (987) 20312; email cozumel@bluenotescuba.com.
Caballito Del Caribbio, Avda Sur 124B X 1RA, Avda Sur and Calle Adolfo Rosada Salas, Cozumel; tel/fax (987) 21449; email cdcaribe@aol.com.
Caribbean Argonauts, Villa Blanca Hotel Beach Club, Cozumel; tel/fax (987) 20312.
Caribbean Divers, Calle 5 Sur (corner of Avda Rafael E. Melgar), Cozumel; tel (987) 21145/fax (987) 21426; email caridive@cozumel.com.mx.
Carlo Scuba, Hotel Playa Azul, Cozumel; tel (987) 20199; email tds@cozumel.com.mx.
Chachacha Dive Shop, Calle 7 Sur between Avdas Rafael E. Melgar and 5, Cozumel; tel/fax (987) 22331; email chacha@cozumel.com.mx.
Chino's Scuba Shop, Calle Adolfo Rosada Salas 16, between Avdas Rafael E. Melgar and 5, Cozumel; tel/fax (987) 24487.
Cozumel Equalisers, Calle Adolfo Rosada Salas between Avdas Rafael E. Melgar and 5, Cozumel; tel/fax (987) 23511; email darwin@cozumel.com.mx.
Cozumel Connection SA, Plaza Villamar Juarez 2, Cozumel; tel (987) 24699/fax (987) 23058.
David & Nancy's Sea Scuba, Avda Juarez, Cozumel; tel (987) 25744/fax (987) 23778; www.cozumel-diving.net/seascuba/.
Deep Blue, Avda 10, Calle Adolfo Rosada Salas, Cozumel; tel/fax (987) 25653; email deepblue@cozumel.com.mx.
Del Mar Aquatics, Carretera A, Chancanaab km4.5, Cozumel; tel (00 52) 987 25949/fax (987) 21900; email delmaraq@cozumel.com.mx.
Dimi Dive & Scuba Tours, Avda 5 and Calle Adolfo Rosada Salas 1a, 109D, Cozumel; tel (987) 22915/fax (987) 23964; email dimidive@cozumel.com.mx.
Dimi Miguel Lopez, Avda Rafael E. Melgar between Calle 5 Sur and Avda 7, Cozumel; tel/fax (987) 22915/fax (987) 23964.
Dive Eco-Cozumel, Calle Adolfo Rosada Sala 16.5 and Avda Rafael E. Melgar, Cozumel; tel/ fax (987) 24187; email roberta@cozumel.com.mx.
Dive House, Main Plaza, PO Box 246, Cozumel; tel (987) 23068; email dive@divehouse.com or resfacdr@fiestaamericana.com.mx.
Dive Palancar, PO Box 488, Carretera SN Fco Palancar km 16.5, Cozumel; tel (987) 23443/fax (987) 25094.
Dive Paradise & Bay Adventures, Avda Rafael E. Melgar 601, PO Box 222, Cozumel; tel (987) 21007/fax (987) 21061; email info@bayadventures.com or appledp@cozumel.com.mx.
Dive With Martin, Avda Norte 50, between Avdas 14 and 16, Cozumel; tel (987) 22610/fax (987) 21340; email dwm@cozumel.com.mx.
Diving Adventures, Calle 5 Sur, between Avdas Rafael E. Melgar and 5, Cozumel; tel (987) 22519/fax (987) 23009; email dive@divingadventures.net.
Emerald Dolphin Dive Services, 19 Sur 1134, between 25 and 25 Bls Gonzalo Guerrero, Cozumel; tel/fax (987) 23270; email castillo@cozumel.com.mx.
Equalisers Scuba Centre, Calle Adolfo Rosada Salas 72, Cozumel; tel (987) 23511; email darwin@cozumel.com.mx.
Fantasia Divers, Carretera Costera Sur, Playa Paraiso, Int. Hotel Sol, Cozumel; tel 800-558-9524.
Manta Ray Divers, Felipe Angeles 273, Cozumel; tel (987) 20684; www.mantaray.com.
Michelle's Dive Shop, Avda 5 Sur 201 and Calle Adolfo Rosada Salas, Cozumel; tel/fax (987) 20947.
Pro Dive SA de CV, Calle Adolfo Rosada Salas 198, Avda 5 Sur, Cozumel; tel/fax

Cozumel

(987) 24123; email prodive@cozumel.com.mx.
Sand Dollar Sports, PO Box 333, Cozumel; tel (987) 20793; email sds@sanddollarsports.com.
Scuba Cozumel, Avda Rafael E. Melgar Prol. Sur 1251, Cozumel; tel (987) 20947/fax (987) 21977; email scubacozumel@cozunet.finred.com.mx.
Scuba Du, Calle 5 Sur between Avdas Rafael E. Melgar and 5, Cozumel; tel (987) 20322/fax (987) 24130; email scubadu@cozumel.net.
Scuba Staff Divers, Calle 1ra 201a, between Avdas 10 and 15, Cozumel; tel (987) 26143/fax (987) 20755; email staffczm@cozumel.com.mx.
Scuba Tours, PO Box 307, Avda 5 between Calle Adolfo Rosada Salas and Avda 3 Sur Cozumel; tel (987) 22915/23656/fax (987) 23964.
Sea-Scuba, Calle Morelos/Avda Sur 2 between nos.15 and 20, Cozumel; tel/fax (987) 25774; email seascuba@cozumel.com.mx.
Snorkel Centre & Diving, 5a Avda 8, between 2 and 4 Nte, Cozumel; tel (987) 26364; email snorkcen@cozumel.com.mx.
Studio Blue, PO Box 473, Calle Adolfo Rosada Salas 21, between Nos. 5 and 10, Cozumel; tel (987) 24414/fax (987) 24330; email studioblue@cozunet.finred.com.mx.
Wildcat Divers, PO Box 85, Cozumel; tel/fax (987) 21928; email wildcatcozumel@hotmail.com.
Yucatech Expeditions, 15 Avda 144, Calle Adolfo Rosada Salas, Cozumel; tel (987) 25659/fax (987) 21417; email tb@tbdiving.com.

Live-aboard:
M/V Oceanus, Club Cozumel Caribe, San Juan Beach, Cozumel, Quintana Roo, Mexico 77600; tel (987) 20100. Operates along Cozumel's east coast and the mainland coast as far as the Chinchorro atoll (weather permitting). The boat is 30 m (100 ft) long and accommodates 14 guests in seven double staterooms. She has air-conditioning, hot and cold purified water, modern navigation equipment, two air compressors, two dive boat tenders, and diving equipment and air tanks for three dives per guest per day. She sails from May to August. From November and April trips are daily or overnight, plus excursions.

Snorkelling tours and trips :
Booking office Calle 5 Sur 25 (Avdas Rafael E. Melgar and 5). A three-hour trip with refreshments and snorkelling equipment departs from Pro Dive pier daily 09:00–13:00.

Emergency Services

Hyperbaric (recompression) chambers:
The Cozumel chamber is privately owned by Sub-Aquatic Safety Services. There is a 135-cm (54-in) diameter chamber with a double lock. Medical facilities include IV fluids, EKG machines, ventilators and other emergency equipment. There are two rooms for patients, a surgery room, an emergency room and X-rays. There is also closed-circuit television inside the chamber.

The hyperbaric (recompression) chamber operates on a 24-hour service. Diving-related injuries and illnesses may be treated in a medical clinic attached to the chamber and staffed by specialists.

All Cozumel diving operators administer a US$1 charge per diver for upkeep of the recompression chamber and the treatment costs of anyone using it who is without the means to pay for it.

Cozumel Recompression Chamber: tel (987) 20140/22387/21430
Life Flight (Houston, Texas) for delivery to a recompression chamber in the USA; tel (800) 392 4357, (713) 797 4357
Air-Evac (San Diego, California) for delivery to a recompression chamber in the USA; tel (800) 854 2567, (619) 278 3822.
Divers' Alert Network (DAN); tel 919 648 8111.

General medical emergencies:
Radio, La Costera (Coastguard) Channel 16 (canal numero dieciseis) Belize Link, San Pedro Airstrip; tel (026) 2851, 2073.
Ambulance, tel (987) 20639.
Hospital, tel (987) 20140.
Private Clinics tel (987) 22919; (987) 2407.
Doctors: Lewis, tel 20912; Segovia, tel (987) 23545; Calderón, tel (987) 21440; Peniche, tel (987) 21419; Ambriz, tel (987) 21671.

Local Highlights

The indispensable free *Blue Guide* to Cozumel is widely available on Cozumel and by subscription to Infotur, Aptdo. Postal 210, Cozumel, Quintana Roo, Mexico 77500; tel/fax (987) 21451.

Cozumel Museum, on the waterfront between Calle 4 Norte and Calle 6 Norte, has a superb display on the complex history of Cozumel and an excellent representation of coral reef ecology. Open 10:00-18:00 hours; tel (987) 21434/21475.

Chancanaab National Park covers an area of 136,000 sq m (162,656 sq yd) of diverse flora and fauna. There is excellent diving and snorkelling from the beach, a restaurant, a gift shop, dive shops and showers. The park is very popular. Open 07:00 to 18:00.

Cozumel Archaeological Park, Avda 65 Sur, five minutes from Downtown and the cruise ship terminal. Exhibits, information and artwork depict the history of the diverse cultures that have shaped Mesoamerica.

Maya ruins are marked on the tourist maps, but only a few are open to the public. **San Gervasio** is probably the most popular; **Santa Rita**, **Ixpal Barco**, **Xhanan** and **Castillo Real** are the best of the larger sites; and **Tumba del Caracol** and **El Cedral** are good smaller sites.

Vehicle Rental

Four-wheel-drive vehicles are the type most commonly hired, and mopeds, scooters and bicycles can also be rented.The main coastal highway will probably be the only road you need to use. If you break down, stay with your vehicle and the Green Angels – local volunteers who patrol the road – will assist any driver able to show a full driving licence and proof of identity. Traffic is light, but beware of potholes – and iguanas.

There is only one petrol station on the island, on the corner of Avenidas Benito Juárez and 30. It is open from 07:00–22:00 or 23:00 hours daily. but it is always busy, especially after the shifts change at 15:00 hours.

Autorent, tel (987) 21900/21922/21944/20844/20812. Safaris, four-wheel-drive vehicles, mopeds, scooters and bicycles, plus free hotel pick-up.
Avis; tel (987) 20099/20322.
Budget, tel/fax (987) 20903.
Fast, Calle 11, 101, Cozumel, Quintana Roo, Mexico 77600; tel (987) 21492.
Fiesta Cozumel Car Rental, tel (00 52) 987 20522. Four-wheel-drive vehicles, mopeds and scooters.
Hertz, Cozumel Airport and Hotel Cozumel Caribe, Cozumel, Quintana Roo, Mexico 77600; tel (987) 20100.
Maya Rent, Airport Blvd, Cozumel, Quintana Roo, Mexico 77600; tel (987) 20655.
National, Avda Rafael E. Melgar and Calle 11, Cozumel, Quintana Roo, Mexico 77600; tel (987) 21515.

Film Processing

Cozumel Images, PO Box 296, Calle 2 Norte, Downtown Cozumel, Quintana Roo, Mexico 77750; tel/fax (987) 22238. Full E6 slide film processing, film sales, underwater photography instruction and rental equipment.
Foto Centro, Calle 4A Sur 5/Avda 10, (centre of town), Cozumel, Quintana Roo, Mexico 77750; tel/fax (987) 23341. Standard holiday instant print services, film sales and so on.

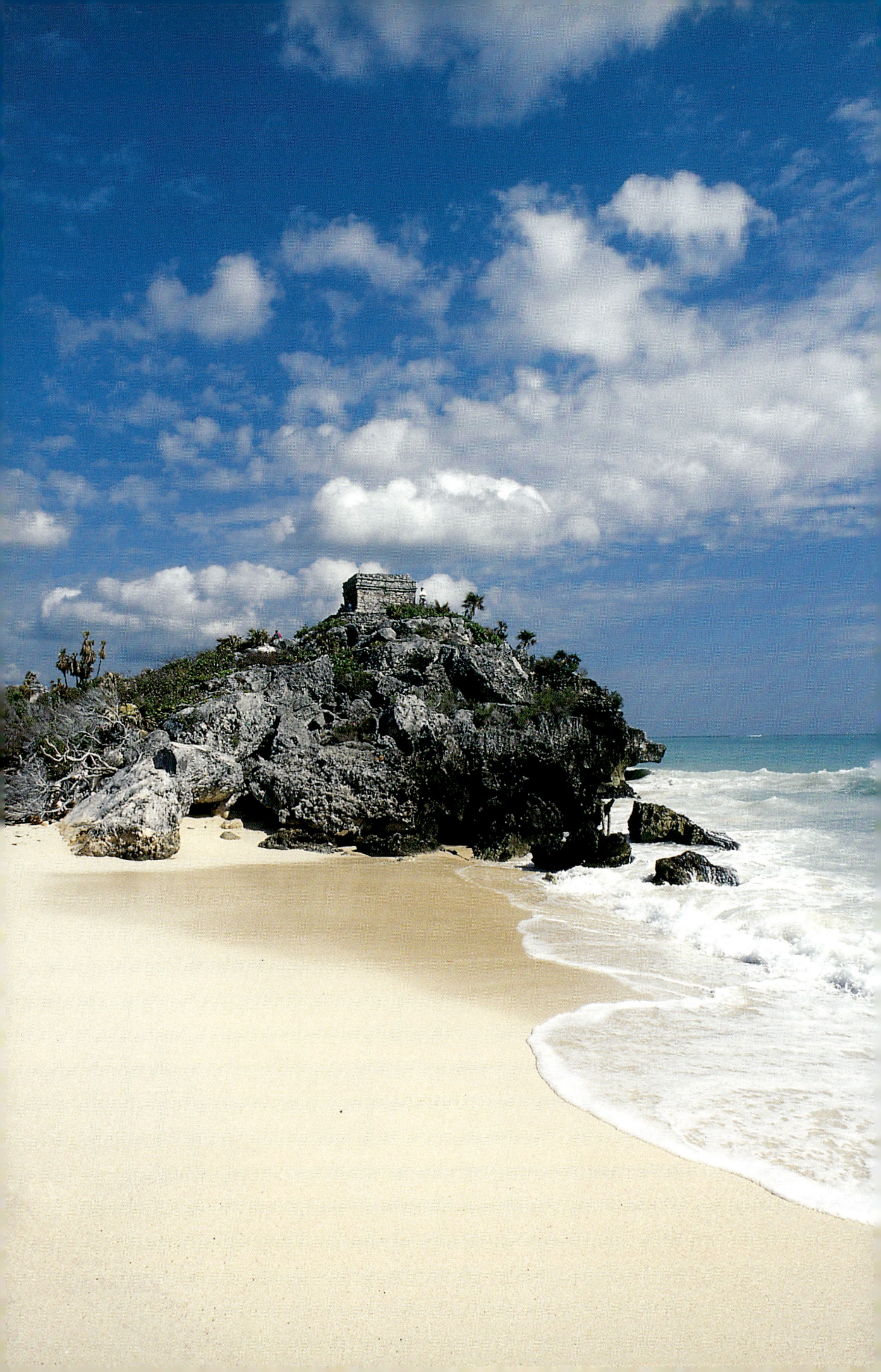

THE MAYAN RIVIERA

The long Mayan Riviera is perhaps the most underrated of all the diving areas of the Yucatán. Most divers head for Cozumel, with Cancún second in line, but some of the best diving of all is to be found along the Great Maya Barrier Reef south from Cancún as far as Chetumal. Because this coast is not yet widely recognized as a top diving destination, the further south you travel, the fewer the numbers of divers thronging the dive sites. Additional attractions of Quintana Roo are the many Maya ruins scattered along it – for centuries this region has been a haven for Maya people escaping repression (see page 19) and the people who live there today follow a traditional way of life. The local bus services are the most inexpensive way to travel down the main highway and to visit all the small coastal towns. But most of the resorts and towns, including Xcalak, have small airstrips.

Diving Along the Mayan Riviera

There seems to be a greater variety of fish along this stretch of the Caribbean coast than there is around Cozumel – in fact the marine life becomes more abundant the further you travel south. However, visibility tends to be much poorer along this stretch of coast than around Cozumel because of the more open conditions. Generally speaking, the further you travel south, the better the visibility, but it hardly ever exceeds 25 m (80 ft) between November and April and 45 m (150 ft) from May to September or October. Some of the dive sites are rather exposed to storms during the wetter months of the year and may be unseasonable. Surge can also be a problem at these times, so that it can be quite dangerous to exit from the water into the dive boat.

The Deep South

If you travel as far south as Xcalak or Xian Ka'an (see pages 14–15), make a diving excursion out to the Chinchorro atoll (located on the map on pages 10–11) – the northern hemisphere's largest coral atoll, which lies 40 km (25 miles) due east into the Caribbean Sea. It is more than 41 km (26 miles) from north to south and 18 km (11 miles) wide. The

---

Opposite: *Ruins of the ancient Maya port of Tulum.*
Above: *A stoplight parrotfish* (Sparisoma viride) *in the red coloration of the initial (pre-adult) phase.*

THE MAYAN RIVIERA

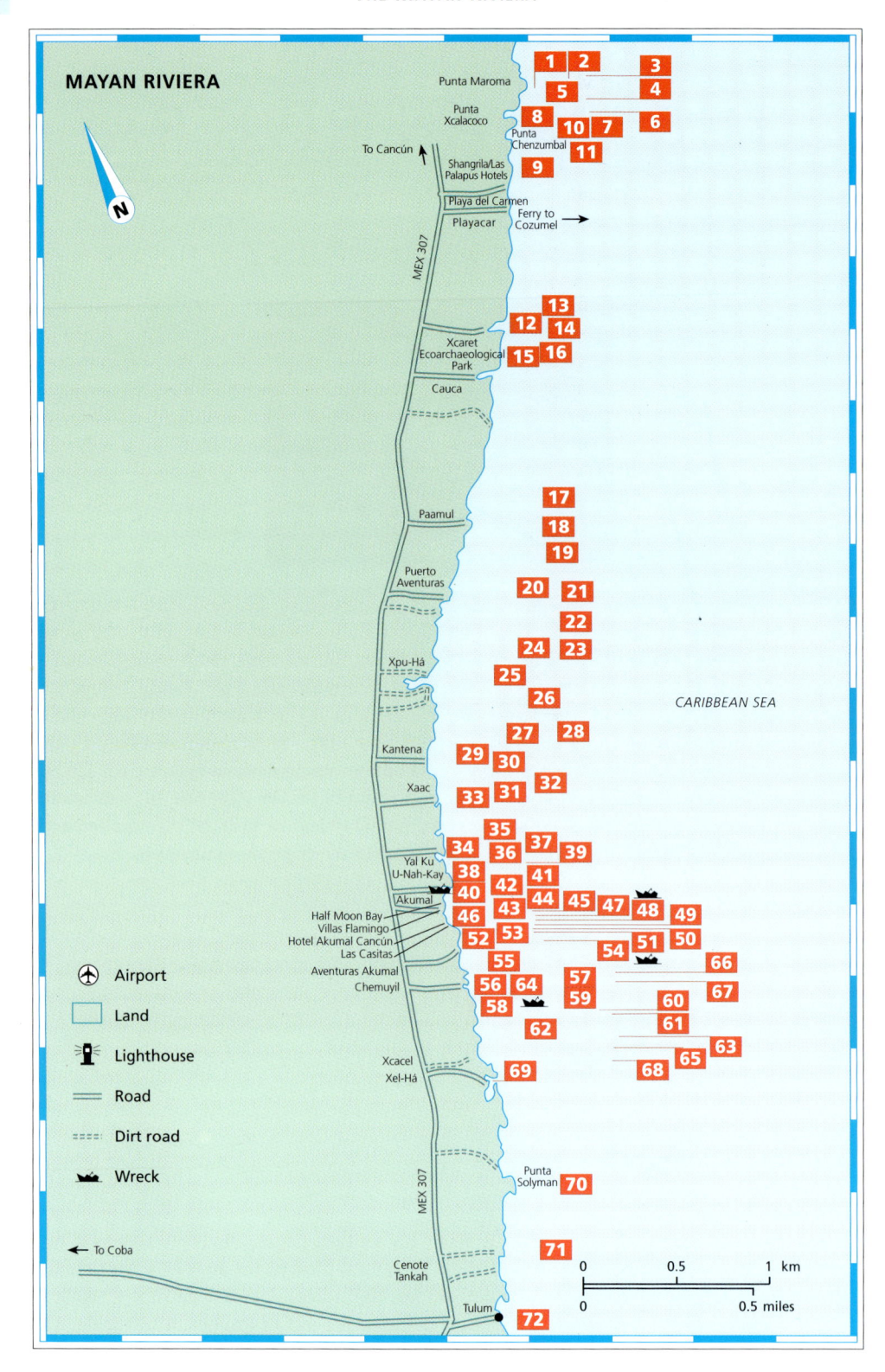

MAYAN RIVIERA

Punta Maroma
Punta Xcalacoco
Punta Chenzumbal
To Cancún
Shangrila/Las Palapus Hotels
Playa del Carmen
Playacar
Ferry to Cozumel
MEX 307
Xcaret Ecoarchaeological Park
Cauca
Paamul
Puerto Aventuras
Xpu-Há
Kantena
Xaac
Yal Ku
U-Nah-Kay
Akumal
Half Moon Bay
Villas Flamingo
Hotel Akumal Cancún
Las Casitas
Aventuras Akumal
Chemuyil
Xcacel
Xel-Há
MEX 307
Punta Solyman
Cenote Tankah
Tulum
To Coba

CARIBBEAN SEA

- ✈ Airport
- ▢ Land
- 🚨 Lighthouse
- ━━ Road
- ═══ Dirt road
- 🚢 Wreck

0   0.5   1 km
0   0.5 miles

average depth in the atoll's lagoon is only 9 m (30 ft). There are said to be more shipwrecks on this reef system than anywhere else in the Caribbean. They date from the earliest vessels that set out to explore these seas to Spanish galleons – and there are some World War II wrecks, including a submarine. Only a handful of divers ever manages to make it out to Chinchorro, yet it probably has the best diving anywhere in the region.

This region of the Yucatán has some of the most spectacular cenotes, natural wells linked by underground rivers, particularly around the Tulum–Coba road. Cenote diving, in which divers follow subterranean river routes through spectacularly beautiful tunnels and caves, is described on pages 143–53.

On the southernmost point of Quintana Roo is its capital, Chetumal (see map pages 10–11), situated on an island in the Milagros Lagoon close to the Belize border. Chetumal is 382 km (237 miles) from Cancún and any travellers seen on the road below Tulum are usually on their way in or out of Belize. The scenery along Highway Mex 307 south of Tulum is fairly monotonous until you reach the massive Laguna Bacalar, just before Chetumal. This area is so stunning that it is amazing so few tourists get this far.

The many dive sites listed on the following pages are all reef-diving locations visited by an increasing number of diving operators, many of whom are attached to resort hotels.

A Maya folk dance troup performing their acrobatic dances at Playa del Carmen.

1 Punta Maroma
★★★★★★★

Location: a headland north of town.
Access: directly from the beach: swim out to the clearly visible, shallow coral reef.
Conditions: shallow and sheltered, ideal for macrophotography.
Minimum depth: shore
Maximum depth: 3 m (10 ft)
Average visibility: about 10 m (33 ft)

These northern shallow sites are perfect for the beginner. The sandy areas have small sections of patch reef with sea fans and other gorgonian corals on the top. Hard corals are reduced in number and the main varieties are *Porites* and brain coral species. This site is ideal for snorkelling and night-diving, but there can be surge between November and April.

2 Maroma
★★★★

Location: east of Punta Maroma (Site 1).
Access: by dive boat only; the closest dive centre is Cyan Há at Las Palapas, too far to swim.
Conditions: shallow and sheltered but there can be surface chop from November to April. Ideal for macro photography.
Minimum depth: 10 m (33 ft)
Maximum depth: 15 m (50 ft)
Average visibility: about 15 m (50 ft)

Maroma is the start of the fringing strip reef which continues in series all the way south along the Quintana Roo coast. Although the site is more exposed, the large coral blocks, wide channels and swimthroughs are encrusted with marine life and have high numbers of fish. There is little current in this area and the diving is good.

3 Maroma Deep
★★★★

Location: due east from Punta Maroma (Site 1) to the edge of the drop-off.
Access: directly from the beach launching site of the local dive boats. Journey time about 20 minutes.
Conditions: moderate current to be expected on the outer mini-wall.
Minimum depth: 25 m (80 ft)
Maximum depth: 30 m (100 ft)
Average visibility: about 25m (80 ft)

Further out to the next ancient strip reef the bottom slopes steeply down to 30 m (100 ft), creating a mini-wall where huge coral limestone blocks are joined together, with numerous swimthroughs. Pairs of angelfish abound and there are some excellent coral and sponge growths. Fortunately these deeper reefs were not harmed by Hurricane Roxanne in 1995 and everything seems in very good order. Little diving is done along this coast and that only from the resort at Shangrila/Las Palapas.

4 Sharkey's Place
★★★★

Location: south of Maroma Deep (Site 3) along the same mini-wall.
Access: by boat only.
Conditions: current to be expected, but only moderate, under 0.9 km (less than half a knot).
Minimum depth: 25 m (80 ft)
Maximum depth: 30 m (100 ft)
Average visibility: rarely more than 30 m (100 ft).

Very similar to Site 3, and when the current is running particularly strongly in a southerly direction you should be able to do both dives at the same time. Large stands of coral, well encrusted with sponges, are everywhere. This site was once noted for large numbers of sharks from about April to November, but they are now rarely found there. Large schools of blue chromis and many species of parrotfish can be seen along the reeftop.

Pinecone algae (Rhipocephalus phoenix)*, one of many species of algae found in the coastal waters of the western Caribbean.*

5 Cabezas
★★★★

Location: opposite Laguna Chuchuben.
Access: by day boat only, too far to swim from the shore.
Conditions: There can be surge conditions and current is to be expected, but it is only moderate at under 1 knot. It is sheltered among coral heads.
Minimum depth: 10 m (33 ft)
Maximum depth: 15 m (50 ft)
Average visibility: 25 m (80 ft)

Out from Laguna Chuchuben the mid spur and groove reef is fairly well protected. There are very good examples of gorgonian sea fans and other delicate corals, and some huge sponges. Green algae can be found under many of the overhangs. There are plenty of fish on the reef at this site – perhaps more than in some of the Cozumel dives. Cabezas is a popular night dive.

6 El Cofre
★★★★

Location: due west of Cabezas (Site 5).
Access: by boat only.
Conditions: moderate current to be expected on outer wall; shelter in the spur and groove reef.
Minimum depth: 25 m (80 ft)
Maximum depth: 30 m (100 ft)
Average visibility: about 25 m (80 ft)

El Cofre, on the outer spur and groove reef, is quite a favourite with the local dive shop. Large black grouper (Mycteroperca bonaci) and yellowmouth grouper (Mycteroperca interstitialis) can often be seen, especially in cleaning stations being attended to by the cleaning goby (Gobiosoma genie). Coral growth is quite good along the top of the reef, and deeper down in the channels you can find species of black coral and other sea fans. The mini-wall is full of live coral and lots of fish.

7 Chimenea
★★★★

Location: along same stretch of reef to the south of El Cofre (Site 6).
Access: by boat only.
Conditions: little or no current. There can be surface chop and surge, making open-water decompression stops uncomfortable.
Minimum depth: 20 m (66 ft)
Maximum depth: 30 m (100 ft)
Average visibility: about 25 m (80 ft)

This intricate and convoluted spur and groove reef could keep you amazed for hours, except that it is all fairly deep and your time is limited. There are some huge tunnels and swimthroughs, many interconnecting and all interesting. Remember to carry a torch, as some of the deeper recesses have lobster, moray eels and octopus, which hide during daylight. Excellent for fish-spotting; many more varieties are found here than off Cancún.

8 Mookche
★★★★★★★

Location: between Punta Xcalacoco and Punta Chenzumbul.
Access: directly from the shore.
Conditions: shallow and sheltered; ideal for macro photography and fish-watching among the shallow coral heads.

CLEANING STATIONS

There are cleaning stations on all reefs – although it takes an experienced eye to spot them. They tend to be located beneath rock overhangs or in coral crevices and they are places where cleaner fish wait to service larger fish that come to be cleaned of parasites, dead skin and diseased scales. Cleaning stations appear to be recognized as neutral territory by the reef population, for predators and prey are commonly seen lining up together, enmity forgotten. This truce is integral to the survival of the fish populations on the reef. The fish are part of a complex integrated community. Our short journeys into their world allow us to see only a small part of this ecosystem at work; even so we are forced to marvel at its complexity.

There are numerous species of cleaners. Many specialize in cleaning certain fish species. Cleaner shrimps are very common – in fact, virtually all the species of shrimp that live along the Yucatán's Caribbean coast act as cleaners. The largest are the **peppermint shrimp** (Lysmata wurdemanni) and the **coral-banded shrimp** (Stenopus hispidus), which clean moray eels, as well as numerous fish. Providing a similar service for moray eels and some of the larger grouper are the **striped cleaner shrimps** (Lysmata grabhami). They are known to climb into the mouths of these fish and clean any debris from the teeth. **Pederson's cleaner shrimp** (Periclimenes pedersoni) lives in association with various anemones and is fairly common.

The **Spanish hogfish** (Bodianus rufus) invites larger fish to come into its cleaning station by a vertical posturing in the water column away from the reef; while some members of the wrasse family act as roving cleaners and will try their luck for a free meal of parasites from any fish they happen to meet. The most common of the cleaners along the western Caribbean coast is the **cleaning goby** (Gobiosoma genie). These tiny fish with their blue and white striped bodies and a yellow 'V' on their heads swarm all over the hard stony corals waiting for fish to approach their protected area of the reef.

Minimum depth: shore
Maximum depth: 3 m (10 ft)
Average visibility: about 7 m (23 ft)
Mookche is an easy, sheltered shore site where you can spend endless hours exploring the shallow coral heads that always have an abundance of fish life. Sergeant majors are the most common species and they will follow you around. Look under the coral heads, because you will always find juvenile angelfish. They are so brightly coloured you cannot fail to notice them.

9 Chenzumbul Shallows
★★★★

Location: opposite Punta Chenzumbul.
Access: directly from the shore, across the beach or by local snorkelling and diving boat.
Conditions: shallow and sheltered, ideal for beginners.
Minimum depth: shore
Maximum depth: 5 m (17 ft)
Average visibility: about 10 m (33 ft)
Nice and easy over a flat sandy area interspersed with patch coral. Sea fans and sea plumes also grow from isolated rocks around the lagoon. There is eel grass and the associated creatures that live among it, such as peacock flounders *(Bothus lunatus)*; bandtail puffers *(Sphoeroides spengleri)* and yellow stingrays *(Urolophus jamaicensis)*. Small families of wrasse congregate around the coral heads.

10 Chenzumbul
★★★

Location: opposite Punta Chenzumbul.
Access: directly from the local dive boat.
Conditions: shallow and sheltered, great for beginners.
Minimum depth: 10 m (33 ft)
Maximum depth: 12 m (40 ft)
Average visibility: about 10 m (30 ft)
A narrow strip reef on the inside of the shallower spur and groove system, with the usual associated fish species, such as blue chromis *(Chromis cyanea)* and barred hamlet *(Hypoplectrus puella)*. The small grouper called the red hind *(Epinephelus guttatus)* seems quite unafraid here and will only move away when you get really close to it. There is also a curious green algae called sea pearls *(Ventricaria ventricosa)*. This is one of the largest single-cell organisms in the plant or animal kingdom. It is dark green in colour, its surface covered in a reflective sheen and small hydroid growths that resemble ornate marbles. This very popular night dive is home to lots of fish and there is much better coral growth than is found in the shallower areas.

Sea pearls (Ventricaria ventricosa) *are fairly common in the Caribbean, but are often passed unnoticed by divers intent on fish-spotting.*

> ### Fire Coral
>
> For many first-time divers and snorkellers an introduction to fire coral *(Millepora alcicornis)* can be a painful and distinctly unforgettable experience. Fire coral is not a true coral but a member of the hydroid family or sea ferns. It has a hard, calcareous (chalky) skeleton, which may be branching or, in the case of *Millepora complanata*, in calcareous plates. The polyps are armed with thousands of stinging cells. These can penetrate human skin, causing a rash that can last for several days. For information on how to treat this painful minor injury see page 173.
>
> Fire coral can be found in most areas of the reef, often completely covering dead sea fans and the upper reaches of ancient coralline limestone.

11 El Jardín
★★★

Location: in front of Shangrila/Las Palapas; the closest reef to the shore.
Access: directly from the shore.
Conditions: shallow and sheltered but much boat traffic.
Minimum depth: 10 m (33 ft)
Maximum depth: 12 m (40 ft)
Average visibility: about 12 m (40 ft)

This section of reef is very popular with local dive stores because it is close to base and is the preferred location for night-diving. The best way to familiarize yourself with the reef is to do the dive in the late afternoon and then continue on through dusk and into the night. Basket stars *(Astrophyton muricatum)* can be found, and the West Indian sea egg *(Tripneustes ventricosus)*, a species of sea urchin with a small shrimp living among its tentacles and spines. There is frequent boat traffic.

12 Xcaret Lagoon
★★★★★

Location: directly out from Xcaret Ecoarchaeological Park.
Access: directly from the pier.
Conditions: shallow and sheltered, great for beginners. Lots of fresh water from the cenote at Xcaret (see page 112) gives this site a mixture of good and bad visibility, as well as warm and cold water.
Minimum depth: 1 m (3 ft)
Maximum depth: 4 m (13 ft)
Average visibility: very variable

French angelfish (Pomacanthus paru) *stay in their bonded mating pairs for life, always patrolling the reefs together.*

An interesting shallow dive round the outer edge of the old pier, which is manufactured from coral limestone blocks. These are now well overgrown with fire coral *(Millepora spp.)*, so divers should take care with buoyancy. The blocks have created hundreds of small recesses where octopus and lobster have made their homes. Sergeant majors are grouped in a large colony and they can be very aggressive toward divers when they are looking after their reddish brown eggs.

13 Xcaret Reef (Xcaret 1)
★★★★

Location: directly out from Xcaret Ecoarchaeological Park.
Access: directly from the pier at Xcaret or by dive boat from further along the coast.
Conditions: shallow and sheltered, great for beginners, very little current.
Minimum depth: 12 m (40 ft)
Maximum depth: 15 m (50 ft)
Average visibility: 20 m (66 ft)

This area is little dived and there is good coral and sponge growth. Surge tends to affect the quality of the dive between April and October. Staghorn coral *(Acropora prolifera)* and small stands of pillar coral *(Dendrogyra cylindrus)* can be seen on the reef top. Blue-striped grunt *(Haemulon sciurus)* and cottonwick *(Haemulon melanurum)* swim together in small schools.

Xcaret

Xcaret is an eco-archaeological theme park carved out of the Yucatán coast 72 km (45 miles) south of Cancún. It covers 80 hectares (200 acres).

Xcaret (pronounced Esh-Ca-Ret) is a Mayan word meaning 'Little Inlet' – many ancient cenotes, or sacred wells on the site feed into an underground river. This meanders into a sheltered rocky inlet of the sea, about 9 m (30 ft) deep. The inlet is home to large schools of snapper, grunt and sergeant majors and is popular with snorkellers. On its seaward side a breakwater has been constructed to protect a small, sandy beach.

ACTIVITY PARK

The owners have linked many parts of the underground river and you can now snorkel down a winding submarine cave system, which is open to the sky through the many cenotes. It is quite interesting – if a little cold – with numerous fish which have made their way up the river.

Visitors can sunbathe on the beach or swim and snorkel in the lagoon created by the breakwater – and in the natural lagoon offshore. They can also learn to scuba dive or take part in a dolphin spectacular, in which individuals are propelled round a sheltered lagoon by a family of tame dolphins. (Incidentally, the dolphins were released into the wild during the last hurricane, in case they came to harm, but after the storm passed they returned once more to Xcaret, where a couple of babies were born.)

The natural inlet has been excavated further inshore toward an ancient Maya temple, at the base of which a huge aquarium has been built and stocked with fish captured from the nearby lagoon.

The sheltered lagoon beside the Caribbean at Xcaret Ecoarchaeological Park.

Xcaret

An Ancient, Sacred Paradise

Xcaret is thought to have been the site of Pole, an ancient Maya port and health spa. The Maya believed that water from the cenote at Xcaret would purify their bodies before they embarked on the crossing to Cozumel Island to worship their goddess of fertility, Ixchel. Maya ruins are scattered across the site. Some have been tastefully restored, and others have been left as they were found – surrounded by rainforest vegetation.

The park, which opened in December 1990, has private owners who have managed to combine the old, the new, the natural and the artificial in sympathetic ways. Subtle landscaping has been blended with natural land features, bringing about a mix of local and exotic flora and fauna. Wild monkeys, native park inhabitants, can be seen, along with birds under protection in a sanctuary.

Facilities and attractions

There is a traditional Mexican hacienda, or farm, in the park, where visitors can watch excellent horsemanship or hire a horse for an excursion along the ocean front. There are beautiful botanical gardens, which still present a riot of colour – despite the fact that the last hurricane clipped and pruned most of the shrubbery.

In the entrance building is an exhibition of scale models of all the major archaeological sites in Yucatán. The models are superbly detailed and they will give you a greater appreciation of the scale of the ruins if you visit any of them.

A regular bus service runs between the park and Xcaret's terminal in Cancún. It is open every day from 09:00 hours to 18:00 hours. For information: tel (00 52) 988 30654/529 883 0743/fax: (00 52) 988 33709.

Tourists swim with dolphins in the lagoon at the Dolphin Experience in Xcaret Park.

> **CENOTE-DIVING**
>
> The Yucatán's Caribbean coast, especially along the Cancún–Tulum corridor, is honeycombed with cenotes – the natural wells unique to Central America – which are entry points to vast networks of underground rivers, some of which flow into the sea, creating areas of halocline – a mix of fresh and salt water. Over centuries, these underground rivers have carved huge caverns and caves from the limestone bedrock, many of which are filled with colourful stalactites and similar rock formations. It has recently been discovered that Quintana Roo province has the two largest underwater cave systems in the world, and the region is fast becoming a new frontier for cave and cavern diving and for training in the special skills needed for this branch of diving. Cave and cavern diving are described and the region's principal cenote dive sites are listed on pages 143–53.

14 Xcaret 2
★★★★

Location: east of Xcaret 1.
Access: by boat only; too far from shore to swim.
Conditions: there can be slight-to-moderate current in exposed areas of reef flat. Choppy surface conditions.
Minimum depth: 18 m (60 ft)
Maximum depth: 25 m (80 ft)
Average visibility: about 20 m (66 ft)

A deeper dive on the outer spur and groove reef. The coral structures, falling in steps down to the sandy sea bed, are interesting in shape and yield all manner of marine life. There appear to be more fish here than around the west coast of Cozumel. There is slight current off the outer wall, but it is always sheltered in the various swimthroughs and gullies. Queen angelfish (*Holacanthus ciliaris*) are common in this area and you may get as many as six or seven all feeding around the same coral head.

15 Inna
★★★★★★★

Location: between Xcaret and Cauca.
Access: from the shore or by local small snorkelling and diving boat.
Conditions: shallow and sheltered.
Minimum depth: shore
Maximum depth: 3 m (10 ft)
Average visibility: about 3 m (10 ft)

A nice easy shore and snorkel dive in this natural lagoon near Xcaret Ecoarchaeological Park. The visibility is always reduced because of freshwater outpourings from the cenote at Xcaret. This causes a rippling effect in the water. Fresh water travels on the sea surface and salt water underneath and as you pass through it you get a strange feeling of disorientation. The fresh water is also much colder than the salt water. These differences in water salinity and temperature – called halocline – affect corals and sponges but appear to have no effect upon the local fish populations.

16 Inna Reef
★★★

Location: west of the lagoon.
Access: by boat only.
Conditions: there can be choppy surface conditions and surge.
Minimum depth: 18 m (60 ft)
Maximum depth: 25 m (80 ft)
Average visibility: 15 m (50 ft)

The spur and groove outer reef system is a little closer in to the shore in this area and it is cut in several places by fairly wide sand chutes which pass through into the depths. There are always sand tilefish (*Malancanthus plumieri*) among the coral rubble; they are rather skittish and always retreat into their protective burrows when you approach them. Sand divers (*Synodus intermedius*) are also notable in this area. The coral platform is topped by sea fans and plumes, some overgrown by fire coral. Large sponges of many different colours are also found around this site.

17 Paamul Wall
★★★★

Location: opposite Paamul to the edge of the drop-off.
Access: by boat only. Approximately 15 minutes' journey time by boat from Puerto Aventuras.
Conditions: moderate current can be expected.
Minimum depth: 22 m (71 ft)
Maximum depth: 40 m (130 ft)
Average visibility: over 25 m (80 ft)

This spur and groove reef – a potentially serious deep dive – is now becoming much more convoluted in shape, with many interesting gullies and canyons. Large green moray eels (*Gymnothorax funebris*) can be seen being cleaned by the banded coral shrimp (*Stenopus hispidus*), the largest of the cleaning shrimps. Small schools of glassy sweepers (*Pempheris schomburgki*) and numerous lobster can be seen deep under the reef.

Opposite: *A banded coral shrimp* (Stenopus hispidus) *busily cleaning a green moray eel of parasites, which provide its food.*

18 Junland Wastes
★★★★

Location: south of Paamul.
Access: by boat only.
Conditions: water very clear.
Minimum depth: 25 m (80 ft)
Maximum depth: 36 m (120 ft)
Average visibility: over 25 m (80 ft)

This site is a deep drift dive along a deep spur and groove reef. It is named after the snowy waste area from one of the *Star Wars* films, and it is a huge sand chute falling into the depths. There are garden eels (*Heteroconger halis*) and snake eels (*Myrichthys breviceps*). Yellowfin majorra (*Gerres cinereus*) also common in the area and there is a good chance of seeing southern stingrays. There are patches of coral which are islands of marine life with a high concentration of everything.

19 Chaumanjun
★★★★

Location: south along the same section of deep spur and groove reef as Site 18.
Access: by boat only.
Conditions: current to be expected on outer wall, but it is sheltered in the canyons.
Minimum depth: 20 m (66 ft)
Maximum depth: 36 m (120 ft)
Average visibility: over 25 m (80 ft)

This reef is fairly similar all the way along, but it can open up in some areas and become much more dense in others. Here, it is a standard spur and groove reef, with large vaulted columns of corals and sponges. There are large gorgonian sea fans on the lower walls, surrounded by bluehead wrasse (*Thalassoma bifasciatum*) of various colours depending on age and sex.

20 Vero's Garden
★★★★

Location: south along spur and groove reef.
Access: by boat only and generally from Puerto Aventuras.
Conditions: sheltered in gullies and swimthroughs.
Minimum depth: 18 m (60 ft)
Maximum depth: 22 m (71 ft)
Average visibility: 20 m (66 ft)

There are very good coral formations and sponges here, including stovepipe sponges (*Aplysina archeri*) and yellow tube sponges (*Aplysina fistularis*), which stretch out into the current. French angelfish (*Pomacanthus paru*) swim by in their lifelong mating pairs, and grouper hide in the recesses. Queen parrotfish (*Scarus vetula*) are quite common. They produce a mucus cocoon when they sleep at night to protect them from moray eels on hunting expeditions.

> ### Buoyancy Control
>
> His work as an underwater photographer makes Lawson Wood constantly aware of the contact divers sometimes make with the coral reef. It is essential that all divers master the art of buoyancy control. The basic need is to be able to hover both horizontally and vertically close to the reef or the bottom without having to touch either. Buoyancy is controlled by inflating or deflating the buoyancy compensator at various depths. Once you have achieved expert buoyancy, your pleasure in diving is bound to increase. You will notice a drastic reduction in your air consumption, you will see more marine life on each dive, and you will cut down on accidental environmental damage dramatically.
>
> Photographers are advised not to use extension tubes with attached framers on the lens, as this necessitates touching the reef to take a photograph. Why not switch to a single lens reflex camera in a waterproof housing, using an appropriate lens to allow you to take close-up photographs of the creatures on the reef? If you have to touch the reef, use only one finger for leverage to hold you still or to push you off from an area of dead coral only. NEVER touch live coral.

21 Chalulal Wall
★★★★

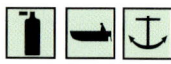

Location: south of Puerto Aventuras along the same deep stretch of spur and groove reef.
Access: by boat only.
Conditions: there can be mild current on the outer reef. Surge and surface between November and April.
Minimum depth: 22 m (71 ft)
Maximum depth: 40 m (130 ft)
Average visibility: 25 m (80 ft)

Here the spur and groove reef is much more in the shape of a mini-wall in which the 'grooves' are more overgrown and with some narrow and interesting swimthroughs. Blue tangs (*Acanthurus coeruleus*) are common on the reef top and black jacks (*Caranx lugubris*) seem to dive-bomb the reef in their constant hunt for smaller fish prey.

22 Paradise Deep
★★★★★

Location: next section of large spur and groove reef south from Chalulal Wall (Site 21).
Access: by boat only.
Conditions: sheltered in gullies and canyons; ideal for photography.
Minimum depth: 25 m (80 ft)
Maximum depth: 42 m (140 ft)
Average visibility: 25 m (80 ft)

The reef once more starts to open out in this area and it is absolutely superb. The coral growth is excellent and there are brightly coloured sponges everywhere. This dive is a particular favourite with a number of the dive shops, especially when underwater photographers are present. There is so much to see that there is never enough time and the site is always well worth a repeat visit. It is a very convoluted reef, with tremendous interest.

23 Canyonlands
★★★★★

Location: continuing south along the same deep reef system as Sites 21 and 22.
Access: by boat only.
Conditions: it can be exposed on the outer reef. There is usually a long journey to reach this reef, which can be rather rough at times.
Minimum depth: 21 m (69 ft)
Maximum depth: 33 m (110 ft)
Average visibility: 25 m (80 ft)

As the name suggests, the reef has formed many canyons which cut through, creating passageways, caves and gullies. Every part of the reef seems to be alive with fresh growth, and even the fish seem friendly. Arrow crabs (*Stenorhynchus seticornis*) and the large channel crab (*Mithrax spinosissimus*), which always seems to challenge your presence in its domain, are commonly seen around this site.

24 Cedam Caves
★★★★★★★

Location: inshore from Canyonlands (Site 23).
Access: by boat only.
Conditions: shallow and sheltered; ideal for fish photography.
Minimum depth: 10 m (33 ft)
Maximum depth: 12 m (40 ft)
Average visibility: 15 m (50 ft)

This inner spur and groove reef is famous for its numerous narrow caves and swimthroughs which are a delight. Remember to hold your breath in some of the caverns in case your air bubbles dislodge some of the more delicate marine life forms. Sea plumes and fans adorn the reef top. The concentrations of fish are high and they include Bermuda chub (*Kyphosus sectatrix*) and

---

Opposite: *A diver approaching a wall must maintain correct buoyancy and ensure that no equipment works loose. A trailing regulator may damage corals and other marine creatures.*

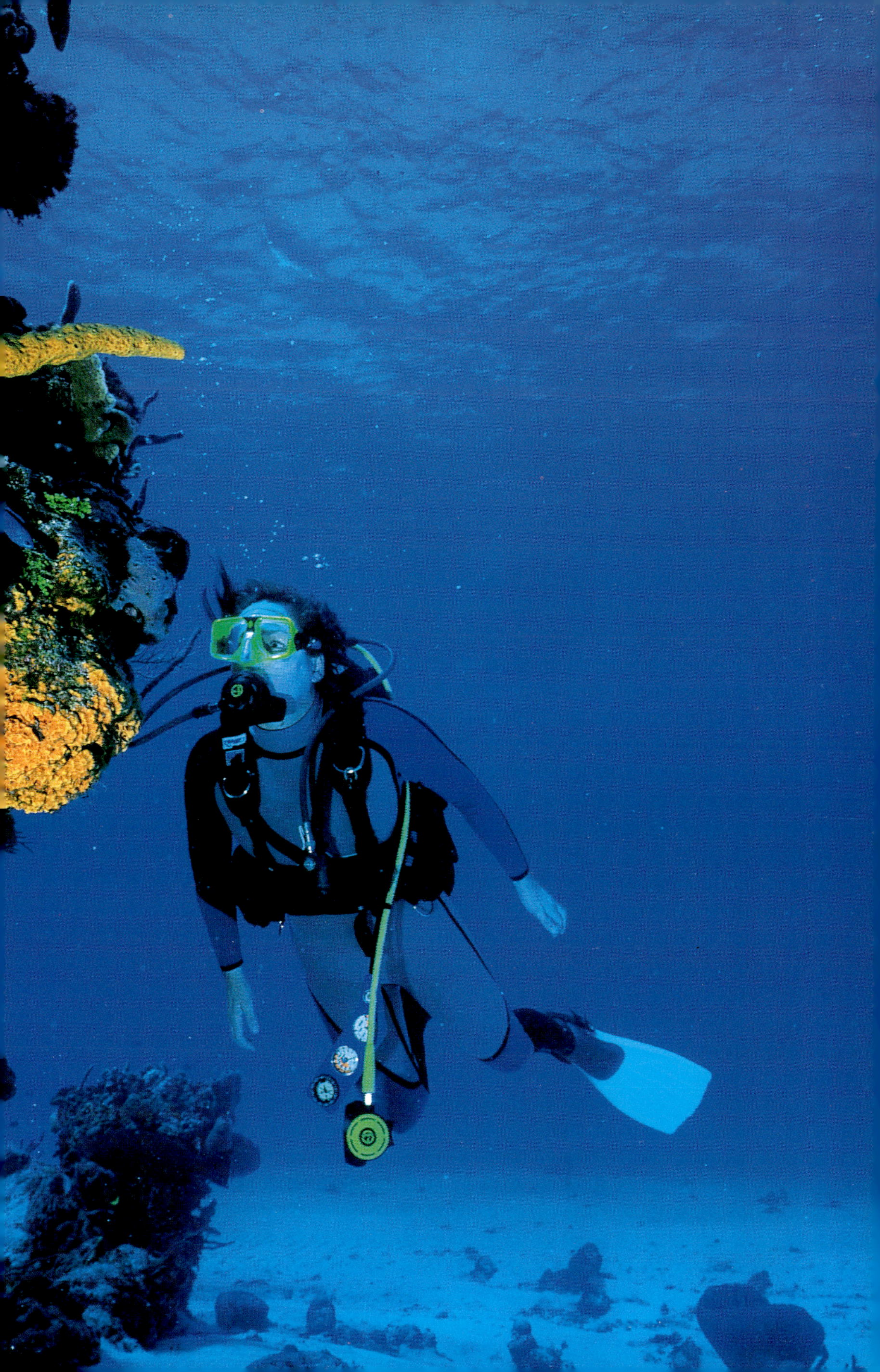

small barracuda (*Sphyraena barracuda*). The usual snapper and grunts are found in small schools and parrotfish seem to be everywhere.

25 Aquario
★★★★★★★

Location: south of Cedam Caves (Site 24) opposite the inlet at Xpu-Há along the same inner strip reef.
Access: by boat only.
Conditions: shallow and sheltered; there can be surge conditions, which can be dangerous among the shallower reefs.
Minimum depth: 10 m (33 ft)
Maximum depth: 12 m (40 ft)
Average visibility: 15 m (50 ft)

Aquario, or the Aquarium, is well named. The further you travel south along this series of three widely spaced reefs the higher the concentration of fish life and the better formed the coral growth. Although the inner reefs have fewer large coral formations, they are always interesting. Smooth trunkfish (*Lactophrys triqueter*) are common and the plumed scorpionfish (*Scorpaena grandicornis*) can be found among the algal growths, blending into its surroundings.

26 Maya Ruina
★★★★

Location: south of Xpu-Há on mid-reef section of large coral blocks.
Access: by boat only.
Conditions: there can be current and patches of fresh water which affect visibility and salinity.
Minimum depth: 18 m (60 ft)
Maximum depth: 28 m (90 ft)
Average visibility: 28 m (90 ft)

This site consists of a large series of huge coral blocks, widely spaced and interesting: you could quite easily spend the time of a dive on each coral block. Sponges and sea fans are profuse in the deeper areas, and goatfish (*Mulloidichthys martinicus*) can be seen excavating in the sandy areas between the coral blocks. The site lies opposite some Maya ruins on the shore.

27 Troy's Reef
★★★★

Location: south along the same secondary reef system as Site 26.
Access: by boat only.
Conditions: sheltered around coral blocks.
Minimum depth: 14 m (40 ft)
Maximum depth: 18 m (60 ft)
Average visibility: about 15 m (50 ft)

The inner spur and groove reef here is not so defined; the sand slope appears to fold over into the reef in some areas and in others cut through it, creating mini-walls in the canyons. These are always undercut and there is a chance of seeing lobster and moray eels. Splendid toadfish (*Sanopus splendidus*) are also known in this area of reef.

28 Las Gorgonas
★★★★

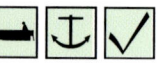

Location: due east from Troy's Reef (Site 27).
Access: by boat only.
Conditions: moderate current on outside of mini-wall.

The spotted scorpionfish (Scorpaena plumieri) *is perfectly camouflaged against its background.*

THE MAYAN RIVIERA

The redspotted hawkfish (Amblycirrhitus pinos) is the only hawkfish found in the Caribbean, and is quite rare. It makes an excellent subject for the marine photographer.

Minimum depth: 18 m (60 ft)
Maximum depth: 27 m (90 ft)
Average visibility: about 25 m (80 ft)

The name is apt, in that there appears to be a larger than usual number of species of gorgonian sea fans. Some are tightly packed in the narrow canyons, while others are more solitary. Some species, such as *Erythropodium caribaeorum*, are encrusting and others, such as the sea whip (*Nicella schmitti*) seem to stretch out into the current with fine, delicate fingers. The reef is a classic spur and groove formation, with some interesting, brightly coloured corals, sponges and fish. Look out for the redspotted hawkfish (*Amblycirrhitus pinos*); it is very shy and makes a difficult but very photogenic subject.

29 Umbrella Reef
★★★

Location: northeast from Kantena.
Access: by boat only.
Conditions: sheltered area away from currents, but surge conditions between November and April can affect the quality of the dive.
Minimum depth: 12 m (40 ft)
Maximum depth: 18 m (60 ft)
Average visibility: about 15 m (50 ft)

The reef is more widely spaced in this area and is fairly average. There are always plenty of fish, however, and the reef top has nice sea fans and plumes. During a storm the surrounding sand tends to be swept over the reef, suffocating isolated areas. It takes another storm to shift this sand, which may again be deposited on live coral.

30 Elkhorn
★★★★★

Location: southeast from Kantena along inner strip reef.
Access: by boat only.
Conditions: shallow and sheltered, great for beginners. There can be surge. This reef is a long journey by boat, but a nice, easy dive and generally worth the effort.
Minimum depth: 8 m (25 ft)
Maximum depth: 10 m (30 ft)
Average visibility: 15 m (50 ft)

Large stands of elkhorn coral (*Acropora palmata*) thrust upward and there are always associated snapper and grunt, such as schoolmastesr (*Lutjanus apodus*), French grunt (*Haemulon flavolineatum*) and white margate (*Haemulon album*). Grouper are common and there are always hundreds of cleaning gobies and other species swimming on the coral heads. Divers should take advantage of the maximum time allowable to enjoy this reef, which is also popular with snorkellers.

Golden Rules

Divers often unintentionally cause serious damage to coral reefs. The following list gives a few golden rules divers should observe to ensure that they do no accidental damage:
1 Avoid touching coral with your hands or any other part of your body, or with your fins, tanks, or other equipment.
2 Do not wear gloves.
3 Never stand on coral.
4 Avoid overweighting and become expert at buoyancy control.
5 Do not collect any marine life.
6 Do not feed wild fish.
7 Do not let your equipment consoles drag on the coral.
8 Do not use spear guns.
9 Do not molest marine life.
10 Avoid creatures that sting and bite (see pages 172–73).
11 Do not climb inside barrel sponges.

31 Palmera
★★★

Location: south of Elkhorn (Site 30).
Access: by boat only.
Conditions: shallow and sheltered.
Minimum depth: 10 m (33 ft)
Maximum depth: 12 m (40 ft)
Average visibility: can be variable

Similar to Elkhorn (Site 30), this reef spreads widely and is topped with small sea fans and plumes. Juvenile wrasse and chromis hover around the reef top and there are always angelfish and butterflyfish swimming around in pairs. Yellowhead jawfish (*Opistognathus aurifrons*) are comical to watch as they hover above the sand and retreat tail-first into their burrows.

32 Xaac Deep
★★★★

Location: due east from Xaac to the outer edge of the spur and groove reef.
Access: by boat only.
Conditions: moderate current on the outer edges, but always sheltered in the huge gullies and canyons of this convoluted reef.
Minimum depth: 20 m (66 ft)
Maximum depth: 28 m (90 ft)
Average visibility: more than 20 m (66 ft)

Large sections of the outer spur and groove reef have formed a mini-wall where it is a pleasure to drift slowly along in the slight current. The swimthroughs and gullies are a riot of colour from many different species of sponges, among them the erect rope sponge (*Amphimedon compressa*), which is a brilliant red colour. Large grouper are always seen and there is a fair chance in May and June of seeing turtles as they search out their traditional nesting sites along the Yucatán's Caribbean coast.

33 Xaac Xico
★★★★★★

Location: closer into the shore opposite Xaac.
Access: by boat only, although the inner edges can be accessed from the shore.
Conditions: shallow and sheltered, ideal for macro-photography.
Minimum depth: 5 m (17 ft)
Maximum depth: 12 m (40 ft)
Average visibility: more than 20 m (66 ft)

This is a smaller and shallower version of the outer reef and also very similar in formation to Aquario (Site 25). There are lots of fish species all over the reef to interest the diver and the photographer. There are more species of algae in these shallower waters, including some interesting ones, such as the mermaid's wine glass (*Acetabularia calyculus*); and numerous anemones, of which the most common is the giant anemone (*Condylactis gigantea*). Tiny featherworms dot the coral heads. They are light- and pressure-sensitive, so it is often difficult to get close enough to photograph them.

> ### Dive Flags
>
> The flag most commonly used by divers is the 'divers down' – a red flag with a white diagonal stripe running from top left to bottom right. The other flag used is the International Code 'A' flag. This consists of a white rectangular box on the inside and a blue box on the outside with an inverted 'V' shape cut out.
>
> It is an offence to show these flags if diving is not in progress; it is also an offence not to show the flag whenever diving is taking place.

34 Yal Ku Lagoon
★★★★★

Location: north of U-Nah-Kay.
Access: directly from the shore.
Conditions: reduced visibility.
Minimum depth: shoreline
Maximum depth: 5 m (17 ft)
Average visibility: about 6 m (20 ft)

This shallow dive in the Akumal area is popular with beginners and snorkellers. However, the sheltered bay is also a favourite with swimmers and other water sports enthusiasts, so underwater visibility is reduced. Take great care: there is always some boat traffic in the lagoon.

35 North Yal Ku
★★★★★

Location: west of Yal Ku Lagoon to the mid-section of the strip and patch reef.
Access: directly from the mooring at Akumal.
Conditions: shallow and sheltered, little or no current, reduced visibility.
Minimum depth: 9 m (30 ft)
Maximum depth: 15 m (50 ft)
Average visibility: about 12 m (40 ft)

This is an extensive reef system which covers the entrance to the lagoon, and is split by a wide sandy area before reforming into another reef. There is minimal current and lots of different fish species inhabit the reef. Although there is little good hard coral growth, there are numerous sea fans and other gorgonians. Snapper, grunts and parrotfish are everywhere on this stretch of reef. Christmas tree worms (*Spirobranchus giganteus*) can be found on most of the coral heads, and there are numerous anemones to be seen.

Opposite: *Erect rope sponges* (Amphimedon compressa) *make a vivid splash of red on the sea floor off the Yucatán's Caribbean coast.*

36 South Yal Ku
★★★

Location: south from North Yal Ku (Site 35) and along the fringing barrier reef for which this coast is famous.
Access: directly from the local dive shops at Akumal; the boat trip takes about 10 to 15 minutes.
Conditions: shallow and sheltered, ideal for macrophotography.
Minimum depth: 10 m (33 ft)
Maximum depth: 15 m (50 ft)
Average visibility: more than 15 m (50 ft)

This is similar to the northern dive (Site 35). Cushion sea stars (*Oreaster reticulatus*) can be seen on the coral rubble and brittle stars can be found under some of the larger dead coral blocks. (If you turn the blocks over to look for them, remember to turn them back afterwards for the protection of shade-loving animals.)

37 Yal Ku Deeps
★★★★

Location: east to the outer edge of the spur and groove reef.
Access: by dive boat from Akumal Bay or by live-aboard.
Conditions: there can be current.
Minimum depth: 20 m (66 ft)
Maximum depth: 27 m (90 ft)
Average visibility: 25 m (80 ft)

This reef is deep, and, as always, you should take care to monitor your time. There are no undertows, but fresh water enters these reefs from springs that start on the Yucatán mainland. There are some large coral build-ups with interesting canyons and swimthroughs, and the walls of these caverns are covered in small coral and sponge growths. Lobsters are evident in the recesses and octopus are common during night dives. Yal Ku is not favoured as a night dive but it is recommended for the variety of invertebrates that can be found there.

Manatees

The manatee or sea cow *(Trichechus manatus latirostrisis)* lives in coastal and inland waterways from Brazil to Virginia in the USA. They are common in the Crystal River area of Florida's west coast and around a number of Caribbean islands. In the western Caribbean they are most common around Guatemala and in the shallow rivers and cenotes around Chetumal, the state capital of Quintana Roo state in southern Yucatán.

MERMAIDS OF LEGEND

Sirenians – the manatee's family group – recalls the sirens, the mythical mermaids believed by the ancient Greeks to lure sailors to their deaths. Hundreds of years ago mariners believed that manatees and dugongs were indeed the mermaids of legend. Today this is hard to imagine.

The equable temperature of the waters of the western Caribbean, fed by Mexico's inland springs, and a constant 24°C (75°F), is ideal for these docile, fish-like underwater 'blimps' with their paddle-like tails. They are warm-blooded air-breathers and bear live young which suckle their mothers' milk. Their body fat insulates them from cold to some degree, but it is the warm water in which they swim that enables them to maintain a body temperature of 31°C (97.5°F) – very close to our 37°C (98.6°F).

The manatee is the largest vegetarian creature in the sea. It is often said to be a cross between a seal and a whale, but in fact it is a relative of the elephant. It can weigh more than 1,361 kg (3,000 lb) and will grow as long as 2.7 m to 4 m (9–13 ft). Manatees have no hind limbs, just a large, flattened, paddle-like tail, and their two forelimbs have evolved into flippers, with five bones on each, which look like finger nails and indicate that they were originally used for something else. Manatees have been around for millions of years; fossil evidence indicates that there were once more than a dozen species of sea cow.

CALVING

The centre of the inland springs, called 'the main boil', is where the cows give birth around the end of November each year. The newborn calf weighs about 37 kg (80 lb) and is approximately 1 m (3 ft) long at birth.

Males reach sexual maturity at six or seven years and mate with several females. They take no part in the rearing of the young. The females become sexually receptive at seven, and also mate with several males. Pregnancy lasts 13 months; twins are not uncommon.

From birth the calves are strong swimmers. Using their tail and flippers they stay close to the water surface, to which they rise every 20 seconds to breathe. As a calf grows older the intervals in this regular breathing rhythm slow to over four minutes. The rhythm is a reflex action; even when sleeping the young mammal rises automatically to take a breath at intervals of 12 to 20 minutes.

Unlike most land mammals, the newborn manatee can see, swim, hear and make noises.

A manatee grazing on sea grasses and weed in the coastal shallows.

Manatees

For two years the calf accompanies its mother as she migrates along the coast in the shallow lagoons which border the Caribbean and back again with the changing seasons, growing fat on her rich milk. This annual migration is vital to the survival of these gentle mammals. The coastal shallows provide a constant source of the manatee's diet – the incredibly fast-growing grass and weed found in freshwater springs. They are also a haven where they can breed in relative safety.

PROTECTING THE MANATEE

Manatees have been on the official endangered species list since 1973 and, being nomadic, they are a difficult creature to protect. There are no restrictions on their movements and many will travel for several kilometres or miles to reach their favoured coastal location.

Mexican federal law forbids the chasing or touching of manatees, but what can you do when a manatee comes up and touches you? These animals are normally very shy, but in areas where they are used to interacting with humans they can be so friendly and inquisitive it is impossible not to be moved – physically and emotionally – by these gentle giants. Elsewhere, you will have to be very lucky, patient and persevering to get a chance to snorkel near manatees.

More legislation is needed to protect these animals, which are not only friendly and approachable but so harmless that they will protect neither themselves nor even their babies when danger threatens. A Manatee Reserve has now been set up in the northern stretches of Bahía de Ascensión and Bahía de Chetumal. Manatees are very rare in Mexico. All we can do to ensure their survival is pray that schemes like this, and the continuing lobbying of conservationists, will protect them for future generations to enjoy.

The manatee is a threatened species and is now a very rare sight along the Yucatán coast.

38 La Langosta
★★★★

Location: directly opposite U-Nah-Kay and north of Half Moon Bay.
Access: by day boat only and primarily from Akumal, although the boats from Puerto Aventuras often venture this far south.
Conditions: shallow and sheltered.
Minimum depth: 10 m (33 ft)
Maximum depth: 12 m (40 ft)
Average visibility: 15 m (50 ft)
Massive elkhorn columns predominate on this reef, with its many coral caves and swimthroughs. More rays are evident over the sand patches and the yellow stingray (*Urolophus jamaicensis*) is commonly seen foraging in the soft sand for molluscs. There are southern stingrays (*Dasyatis americana*) around this site and they are always accompanied by the bar jack (*Caranx ruber*) which darts in and feeds on the marine life that has been disturbed by the ray.

39 Grouper Canyons
★★★★★

Location: east of La Langosta (Site 38).
Access: by boat only.
Conditions: there is a possibility of current.
Minimum depth: 19 m (62 ft)
Maximum depth: 42 m (140 ft)
Average visibility: about 25 m (80 ft)
This mini-wall drops in three sections: the first at 18 m (60 ft); the next at 33 m (110 ft); and the last step starts at 42 m (140 ft). It is a wonderful dive if you have the time and experience to go deeper than normal down through the narrow canyons which cut the various steps of the reef. It has a fairly classic spur and groove formation and you will find it rewarding to spend some of your time exploring the gullies – fish can be seen here that are rarely found elsewhere, such as the spotted drum (*Equetus punctatus*) and the harlequin pipefish (*Micrognathus crinitus*).

40 Half Moon Bay
★★★★★★★

Location: shallow scuba and snorkel dive in Half Moon Bay.
Access: directly from the shore. The dive centres also offer snorkelling trips from their premises into this bay.
Conditions: shallow and sheltered.
Minimum depth: 3 m (1 0ft)
Maximum depth: 5 m (17 ft)
Average visibility: 9 m (30 ft)
This dive location, very similar to Akumal Bay (Site 46), is a wide, sandy bay interspersed with large coral blocks. It is perfect for snorkelling among the large stands of staghorn coral. A boat channel cuts through the site and divers should be careful to avoid accidents in that area. About 20 cannon can be seen; they are of English and Spanish origin and date from 1741. Numerous lobster and octopus are seen at night.

41 Sixty Two Feet Reef
★★★★

Location: south of Grouper Canyons (Site 39), along the same spur and groove inner reef system.
Access: by boat only.
Conditions: the surface can be choppy during the cooler season; there is a slight-to-moderate current, but it is sheltered among the coral heads.
Minimum depth: 10 m (33 ft)
Maximum depth: 19 m (62 ft)
Average visibility: 15 m (50 ft)
The coral canyons are much tighter in this area than in Half Moon Bay (Site 40) and the site is similar to Morganis (Site 44) and Dick's Reef (Site 42). There are numerous rays in this area, and blue tang, and tilefish are found in the coral rubble inside and outside the reef. The area surrounding the coral heads is predominantly sand with some coral rubble. Conch are common.

42 Dick's Reef
★★★★

Location: southeast of the Villas Flamingo and northeast of Las Casitas hotel.
Access: by boat only.
Conditions: no current in the canyons.
Minimum depth: 9 m (30 ft)
Maximum depth: 16 m (52 ft)
Average visibility: about 15 m (50 ft)
Dick's Reef is a popular shallow dive amid some interesting coral canyons festooned with sea fans and plumes. Divers can swim through a very nice tunnel through the reef, which is composed predominantly of pillar coral (*Dendrogyra cylindrus*) and boulder star coral (*Monastrea annularis*). This whole reef section is well known for large varieties of coral, but not for its other marine life. However, there are large numbers of sea urchins in this area and divers should remember to keep a lookout for them (see page 172).

43 Doña Leticia
★★★★

Location: due east of Las Casitas, to the inner patch and strip reef barrier reef.
Access: by boat only.
Conditions: can be affected by the ocean surge.
Minimum depth: 10 m (33 ft)
Maximum depth: 17 m (55 ft)
Average visibility: 15 m (50 ft)

The corals in this area are good quality, but the fish life is somewhat poor. There are low encrusting sponges, small barrel sponges, vase sponges and some broken coral. The hurricane which passed through here in 1995 did some damage, but the reef is recovering nicely.

44 Morganis
★★★★

Location: east of Doña Leticia (Site 43).
Access: by boat only.
Conditions: shallow, sheltered, ideal for divers of all levels.
Minimum depth: 15 m (50 ft)
Maximum depth: 19 m (62 ft)
Average visibility: 15 m (50 ft)

Very similar to Sixty Two Feet Reef (Site 41), but with the canyons fairly tightly packed together. There are numerous sea fans and plumes, and lobster can be seen in almost all the crevices and caves. There are blue chromis and creole wrasse on the reef top, and the occasional whitespotted filefish (*Cantherhines macroceros*) may be glimpsed. Nurse sharks have been seen and the reef has a few blackcap basslet (*Gramma melacara*), which are instantly recognized by their almost fluorescent magenta and indigo coloration.

45 Cien Pies
★★★★

Location: south along same spur and groove reef as Morganis (Site 44).
Access: by boat only.
Conditions: there can be current along the outer wall.
Minimum depth: 15 m (50 ft)
Maximum depth: 19 m (62 ft)
Average visibility: 20 m (66 ft)

The coral canyons of this spur and groove mid-reef are much more tightly packed than those in Grouper Canyons (Site 39), resulting in some interesting swimthroughs and caves to explore on the outer edge of the reef. Purplemouth morays (*Gymnothorax vicinus*) and the chain moray (*Echidna catenata*) are common. Balloonfish (*Diodon holocanthus*) can also be seen in the recesses during the day. They should not be handled, as this can remove the protective mucus on the skin, which leaves the fish open to infection and possible death.

46 Akumal Bay
★★★★★★★★

Location: south along sheltered Akumal Bay.
Access: directly from anywhere along the shore and occasionally by boat.
Conditions: shallow and rather murky from a mix of sea water and fresh spring water flowing from the mainland.
Minimum depth: 3 m (10 ft)
Maximum depth: 5 m (17 ft)
Average visibility: below 9 m (30 ft)

Akumal Bay is similar to Half Moon Bay (Site 40), in that it is wide, sandy-bottomed and interspersed with some large, interesting coral blocks. But it is deeper overall, so more rays can be seen foraging among the eel grass and algae. There are lobster and octopus, and many varieties of small mollusc on the sand.

47 La Tortuga
★★★★

Location: south along same spur and groove reef as Cien Pies (Site 45).
Access: by boat only.
Conditions: there can be current along the outer wall.
Minimum depth: 15 m (50 ft)
Maximum depth: 25 m (80 ft)
Average visibility: 20 m (66 ft)

This site, with its gullies and canyons now splitting up into single, huge coral blocks, is known for sightings of the green turtle (*Chelonia mydas*). In fact, *akumal* is a Mayan word meaning 'place of the turtle'. The outer edges of these large, interesting coral blocks are a favourite with many divers. Concentration is difficult because you want to look at the marine life on the reef, yet you also want to spend your time scanning the ocean blue for signs of these majestic animals.

48 Gonzalo's
★★★★

Location: south from and similar to La Tortuga (Site 47), distinguished by the size of the separate reef coral heads.
Access: by boat only.
Conditions: there can be current along the outer wall.

Minimum depth: 15 m (50 ft)
Maximum depth: 25 m (80 ft)
Average visibility: 20 m (66 ft)

There are coral blocks of massive proportions here, cut by narrow gullies and canyons, which are much tighter than those at Site 47. The rare blue angelfish (*Holacanthus bermudensis*) is found in this area amid part of the wreckage of the fibreglass wheelhouse of a ship which has been submerged since 1980. French angelfish are also common and, during April and May, dolphins commonly accompany your dive boat. Whale sharks have also been noted in October and November.

49 Escula
★★★★★★★

Location: to the south of Akumal Bay along the fringing barrier reef which protects the bay from the worst of the oceanic swell.
Access: by boat only. Occasionally there is snorkelling from the dive boats in this vicinity.
Conditions: reduced visibility and surge conditions amid the large stands of staghorn coral.
Minimum depth: 6 m (20 ft)
Maximum depth: 9 m (30 ft)
Average visibility: about 9m (30 ft) from November to April but it improves dramatically during May and June Because of the shallow depth, snorkelling trips are often made to this section of reef. There are nice build-ups of staghorn and elkhorn coral. As you travel south there are more sponges among the corals and there is now more competition for space.

SAFETY TIPS FOR NIGHT-DIVING

Night-diving need not be dangerous if you learn these rules and always follow them:
1. Attend an instruction course in night-diving before embarking on a trip
2. Always dive with someone who is acquainted not only with the dive site but also with night conditions.
3. Begin by diving at dusk and acclimatize yourself to the dark gradually.
4. Carry a spare torch or two.
5. When entering the water take a compass bearing to the shore or a mooring buoy.
6. Before setting out, inform someone at your hotel or dive shop of your dive plan and your estimated time of exit from the water.
7. Have warm, dry clothing ready to change into after the dive.
8. Wear a protective suit of some kind to avoid being stung by planktonic sea stingers, which abound during the twilight hours and are generally too small to see.

DIVERS DOWN LIGHTS

These are used when divers are diving at night. They consist of a series of three lights – red over white over red – displayed vertically, with a 360° visibility at a maximum of 180 m (600 ft). It is an offence to show 'divers down' lights if diving is not in progress – and, conversely not to show them when diving is taking place.

---

50 Las Redes
★★★

Location: directly opposite the Akumal Dive Centre.
Access: by boat only, but only a five-minute trip.
Conditions: there is plenty of everything here, including surge and choppy conditions between November and April particularly.
Minimum depth: 9 m (30 ft)
Maximum depth: 15 m (50 ft)
Average visibility: 9 m (30 ft)

Las Redes is a nice, easy, popular dive directly opposite the dive shop, and it is a favourite with the shop for night-diving. The reef is in average condition, but this is never noticeable when your dive lights are continuing to pick out brightly coloured fish, crustaceans and molluscs. Small reef squid and juvenile queen triggerfish are often seen among the sea fans. Hermit crabs and cowrie shells are also common.

51 Tzim-Há
★★★★

Location: south along same spur and groove reef and a continuation of Gonzalo's (Site 48).
Access: by boat only.
Conditions: there is often some current along the outer wall.
Minimum depth: 15 m (50 ft)
Maximum depth: 25 m (80 ft)
Average visibility: 20 m (66 ft)

Much tighter gullies and canyons are found here than in Grouper Canyons (Site 39), and the remains of the wreckage of the small fishing boat at Site 48 can be seen in this section of reef. The reef here is beautiful and especially interesting since it is frequented by many different species of marine creatures. Garden eels are common and they are fun to watch as they retreat into their holes when you swim close to them.

Above: *File clams* (Lima scabra) *are sensitive to light and inhabit the recesses of undersea caves.*
Below: *Channel-clinging crabs* (Mithrax spinosissimus) *are aggressive predators on the reef at night.*

Spiny lobsters (Panulirus argus) *are common at night on almost all reefs along the Yucatán coast.*

52 Cuevas de Tiburones
★★★★★★★

Location: south from Escula (Site 49).
Access: by boat only.
Conditions: there can be current along the outer wall, but it is sheltered among the coral heads.
Minimum depth: 7 m (23 ft)
Maximum depth: 12 m (40 ft)
Average visibility: 15 m (50 ft)
There are large numbers of Spanish hogfish (*Bodianus rufus*) all over this reef. The juveniles act as cleaners for the large numbers of schooling jacks which come in to be cleaned of parasites. There are large stands of elkhorn and staghorn coral with their allied snapper and grunt sheltering under the overhangs.

SLIPPER LOBSTERS

These lobsters, members of the Paniluridae family, resemble the more common spiny lobster, but do not have its extended antennae or claws. The slipper lobster's shell, or carapace, has a rough, knobbly texture and is mottled in colour. Slipper lobsters can swim backward quickly by rapidly flicking their tail. They are rather timid creatures and are most commonly seen by divers at night.

53 Lobster Condominiums
★★★★

Location: south along same reef as Las Redes (Site 50).
Access: by boat only.
Conditions: varied, including surge and choppy conditions between April and October.
Minimum depth: 6 m (20 ft)
Maximum depth: 16 m (52 ft)
Average visibility: 20 m (66 ft)
Everything on this reef is larger and more abundant than at the sites described above. The numerous large coral heads are home to hundreds of spiny lobster (*Panulirus argus*). The spotted lobster (*Panulirus guttatus*) and the much rarer slipper lobster (*Parribacus antarcticus*) can also be seen, and hermit crabs are common. Beaugregory damselfish (*Stegastes leucosticus*) are aggressive when protecting their eggs, which they lay in coral crevices.

54 Trigger Fish Reef
★★★★

Location: due east of Hotel Akumal Cancún to the outer edge of the spur and groove reef.
Access: by boat only.
Conditions: varied, including surge and choppy conditions between November and April.

Minimum depth: 25 m (80 ft)
Maximum depth: 27 m (90 ft)
Average visibility: 20 m (66 ft)

This very flat, sandy sea bed has some huge single coral blocks covered in sponges, sea plumes and gorgonian sea fans. There are rays, garden eels, queen triggerfish (*Balistes vetula*) and sargassum triggerfish (*Xanthichthys ringens*), which are relatively unafraid and will come quite close to divers. The queen triggerfish has been known to attack divers if they approach too close to the nesting site, which is a shallow depression in sand and coral rubble.

55 South Akumal
★★★★

Location: southeast from the Hotel Akumal Cancún to the inner fringing barrier reef.
Access: by boat only.
Conditions: similar to Escula (Site 49). Can be choppy, with surge conditions between November and April. Take care when entering and exiting the water.
Minimum depth: 8 m (25 ft)
Maximum depth: 12 m (40 ft)
Average visibility: 20 m (66 ft)

Underneath the extensive coral build-ups and spurs there are numerous small caves and recesses where sharks have been found apparently sleeping at night. There is evidence of fresh water coming out from under the reef and it is thought that this has a slightly narcotic effect on the sharks. It is also thought to clean them of parasites. There are large fish populations all over this reef.

56 Tortuga Canyons
★★★★★

Location: south along same spur and groove strip reef as South Akumal (Site 55).
Access: by boat only.
Conditions: very similar to Site 57.
Minimum depth: 9 m (30 ft)
Maximum depth: 13 m (42 ft)
Average visibility: 20 m (66 ft)

Large, distinct and separated coral heads are the feature for which this reef is known and although the associated species are similar, each outcrop is of particular interest. Tilefish and jawfish can be found amid the coral rubble. There are many anemones all over each coral head.

57 Ak 100 Feet
★★★★★

Location: south along the outer edge of the reef to where the sand slope bottoms out.
Access: by boat only.
Conditions: current is to be expected in open water. Only experienced divers should try this type of deep dive, as it is important not to waste time in getting to the bottom.
Minimum depth: 25 m (80 ft)
Maximum depth: 30 m (100 ft)
Average visibility: 20 m (66 ft)

Red reef hermit crabs (Paguristes cadenati) *live inside their hard shell covered in purple algae.*

> **STINGING CELLS**
>
> Anemones, corals and jellyfish are armed with a battery of stinging cells called nematocysts. Each cell consists of a tiny barbed harpoon tipped with a paralyzing poison, which the creature will fire into any prey that happens to brush against it. These microscopic cells are particularly effective in the Portuguese man-of-war, whose tentacles may trail beneath it to a depth of more than 10 m (33 ft). In May and June large clusters of thimble jellyfish *(Linuche unguiculata)* can be found in the waters. A sting from one of these can cause irritation to soft human skin. There are local remedies for stings from all these sea creatures (see page 173).

A lovely deep dive, but limiting for the time spent at that depth. The coral heads are now widely spaced, with deep sand chutes. Each section is like a mini-wall with all the associated species of corals and sponges. There is a greater chance of seeing rays and other pelagic fish along the outer reef.

58 Las Esponjas
★★★★

Location: south from Tortuga Canyons (Site 56).
Access: by boat only.
Conditions: choppy and exposed between November and April. There can be current along the outer mini-wall.
Minimum depth: 15m (50ft)
Maximum depth: 19m (62ft)
Average visibility: 20m (66ft)

A mid-section spur and groove reef which is well developed with numerous swimthroughs and overhangs. There are some good, large specimens of brain coral (*Colpophyllia natans*) and lettuce coral (*Leptoseris cucullata*). Fish species include porkfish (*Anistotremus virginicus*) and yellow damselfish (*Microspathodon chrysurus*). There are also numerous parrotfish, wrasse and small grouper.

59 Grouper Gulch
★★★★

Location: east from Akumal to continue south from Ak 100 Feet (Site 57).
Access: by boat only.
Conditions: there can be current along the outer wall.
Minimum depth: 22m (71ft)
Maximum depth: 27m (90ft)
Average visibility: 20m (66ft)

An open, sandy area with large clumps of coral boulders. This area is a huge sand plain which can be seen clearly from the air. Below Akumal the reef starts once more and evolves into the spur and groove reef that is typical of the western Caribbean. This is a very interesting dive spent at depth. Although the coral heads rise above 22 m (71 ft), you tend to spend most of your time on or near the sea bed, only swimming up the reef on the way to the surface. It is a good area for rays, conch, cushion starfish and sand dollars (*Clypeaster subdepressus*).

The three-spot damselfish (Stegastes planifrons) *readily attacks divers to defend its nesting site.*

The porkfish (Anistotremus virginicus), *one of the larger grunts, is solitary by nature.*

60 Sailfish Reef
★★★★★

Location: south to the next delineated area of reef from Grouper Gulch (Site 59).
Access: by boat only.
Conditions: there can be current along the outer wall. Visibility can be very variable.
Minimum depth: 19 m (62 ft)
Maximum depth: 28 m (92 ft)
Average visibility: surprisingly low at 20 m (66 ft)
Another of those reefs that were named by someone who once saw a 'sailfish'. However, there is a good chance of seeing large pelagic fish along this section of reef. The coral formations are weird and wonderful, encrusted with brightly coloured sponges and gorgonian sea fans. Large grouper are often seen lurking in the shadows. The tight gullies and canyons are formed by fresh water seeping out through the reef formations, causing erosion.

61 Las Jolesias
★★★★

Location: south along to the next section of the same spur and groove reef as Site 60.
Access: by boat only.
Conditions: there is often some current along the outer wall.
Minimum depth: 22m (71ft)
Maximum depth: 30m (100ft)
Average visibility: 20m (66ft)
The reef sections on this site are tightly packed together, with too many caves and gullies to explore. The corkscrew anemone (*Bartholomea annulata*) and the hydroid (*Cnidoscyphus marginatus*), which tends to grow over colonial sponges, are common. There are lots of fish, including angelfish, butterflyfish, snapper and grunt.

62 Bad Head
★★★

Location: south along same spur and groove reef as Site 61.
Access: by boat only.
Conditions: there can be current along the outer wall, but no more than 0.9 km (29 knots).
Minimum depth: 6 m (20 ft)
Maximum depth: 12 m (40 ft)
Average visibility: 20 m (66 ft)
This is the closest good dive site to the dive shop and it is where you are taken if the dive masters are suffering from a 'bad head'. It is a long thin strip reef along the inner site. You can have a lovely dive watching marine life of every variety. There is good sponge growth and this dive is better known for its delicate corals than for the larger species. The author found the painted elysia nudibranch (*Elysia picta*) on some dead coral and the lettuce sea slug (*Tridachia crispata*) is also common seasonally.

63 Narcosis Ridge
★★★★

Location: south along same outer spur and groove reef as Site 61.
Access: by boat only.
Conditions: there can be current along the outer wall.
Minimum depth: 15 m (50 ft)
Maximum depth: beyond 45 m (150 ft)
Average visibility: 20 m (66 ft)

This huge, long spur is well named. It extends far out into the blue and drops to 37 m (120 ft) on the top before rolling over beyond 45 m (150 ft). This dive is not for the faint-hearted, but there is a very good chance of seeing sharks, turtle and rays. The coral forms at this depth are low and encrusting and the predominant growths are sponges.

64 Matanceros
★★★★★★★★★★

Location: south along the coast between Aventuras Akumal and Chemuyil.
Access: by boat and from the shore.
Conditions: there can be surge conditions between April and October.
Minimum depth: 3 m (10 ft)
Maximum depth: 10 m (33 ft)
Average visibility: 9 m (30 ft)

This site is the wreck of a Spanish galleon found in the shallows here (see opposite). She was a Spanish trading ship built in 1741 (she was carrying English cannons, so was first thought to have been an English ship; she has only recently been recorded as Spanish after the recovery from the sea bed of other trade goods). The ship was travelling on her own and the mate and captain were killed when she ran aground. The wreck's cargo was recently excavated by CEDAM Divers and many artefacts and trinkets were discovered, such as crucifixes, musket balls, cannon balls, doubloons, and packages of needles and pins. These were black market goods commonly carried by traders running to the Mexican port of Veracruz. Some are on display in the Maritime Museum in Puerto Aventuras. This is a site for snorkelling, as well as diving.

65 Roman's Reef
★★★★

Location: south along same spur and groove reef and a continuation of Narcosis Ridge (Site 63).
Access: by boat only.
Conditions: there can be current along the outer wall.
Minimum depth: 15 m (50 ft)
Maximum depth: beyond 34 m (130 ft)
Average visibility: 20 m (66 ft)

An excellent classic spur and groove formation with much tighter gullies and canyons than are found in the preceding section of reef. Huge growths of sheet coral (*Agaricia grahamae*) roll into the depths, creating interesting underhangs and crevices. Cactus coral (*Mycetophyllia lamarckiana*) appears almost luminous. The hanging vine algae (*Halimeda goreaui*) is also present in the shady areas. Blue chromis and creole wrasse abound on the reef top, and almost every section of hard coral has many species of gobies and blennies.

---

*The southern stingray (*Dasyatis americana*) burrows into the sand by flapping its wings in a search for molluscs and worms.*

El Matancero Wreck

On February 22, 1741, a ship now known as *El Matancero* struck a reef and ran aground in the coastal waters off the southern Yucatán Peninsula. Researchers exploring the massive archives in Spain tell us that the ship was officially named *Nuestra Señora de los Milagros (Our Lady of Miracles)* and that she plied the waters of the western Caribbean as a merchant ship. She was originally built in Cuba in the West Indies at a place called Matanzas, which accounts for her second name, the one now more commonly used.

The vessel's hull measured 23 m (73 ft) and was registered at 270 tons burthen. *El Matancero* was recorded as either a ship or a frigate, which term, when applied to a merchant ship, describes the characteristics of the hull. She was square-rigged, with three masts, and like all contemporary merchant ships carried 16 small iron cannon and 4 swivel guns, primarily as protection against pirates.

Breaking the Embargo

El Matancero was owned by Francisco Sánchez, Marqués de Casa Madrid, an influential merchant from the Spanish port of Cádiz, who was licensed to carry 1,000 tons of trade goods to the Spanish colonies in the Americas. At that time, however, the English Navy, commanded by Admiral Edward Vernon, was applying a stranglehold on Spanish shipping. Because of this there were no planned shipments of gold or silver bullion and trade between Spain and her New World colonies was virtually at a standstill. The ship's owner decided, nevertheless, that he could make a great profit by breaking this embargo and shipping trade goods to the Mexican port of Veracruz.

Rich Cargo

The cargo manifest tells us that El Matancero carried 50 tons/tonnes of household goods, including knives, spoons, scissors, needles, buttons, buckles, writing quills, paper and glassware. In addition, the ship carried 100 tons of pig iron, 25 tons of tempered steel, and 750 barrels, 400 casks, 204 cases and 21,200 bottles of brandy and wine. Among other items that have been discovered were military stores, including 240 sword blades. This unofficial cargo (which violated the stringent regulations imposed by Spain's Casa de Contratación or Board of Trade) would never have been discovered but for one fateful night when the ship was dashed to pieces on the jagged reefs along the southeast coast of the Yucatán Peninsula.

Scuba divers and marine archaeologists have recovered a large number of artefacts from the sea floor which were not on the original manifest, including crucifixes, religious medallions, costume jewellery set with green and white lead glass stones, and glass beads.

Expedition

In 1959, the newly formed organization called CEDAM (Club de Exploraciones y Deportes Acuáticos de Mexico), in cooperation with divers from the USA, mounted an expedition to recover and preserve more artefacts from *El Matancero*. At the time, the salvage was regarded as the most important of its kind by the USA's Smithsonian Institute, because of the value of the articles recovered. Their value was not monetary but historical: they provided priceless information and insight into Spanish colonial life during the 18th century. In essence, the ship was regarded as a time capsule. The articles recovered from the wreck now form the major part of the collection of the Maritime Museum in Puerto Aventuras, near the CEDAM Dive Centre.

Scuba divers and snorkellers can now swim around the wreck of *El Matancero* to see what is left of the galleon. It is of great historical interest – since Hurricane Roxanme in October 1995, marine archaeologists have unearthed objects including, buttons, buckles, pottery and glass shards, musket balls and gun flints. Anything found at the site must not be kept as a souvenir but should be handed in to the Maritime Museum at Puerto Aventuras.

66 Mike's Maze
★★★★★

Location: south to the next section of spur and groove reef opposite Chemuyil.
Access: by boat only.
Conditions: there can be current along the outer wall.
Minimum depth: 18 m (60 ft)
Maximum depth: 40 m (130 ft)
Average visibility: 20 m (66 ft)

The reef has now devolved into huge separate coral heads, like large islands, many metres or yards high and separated by sand chutes. You can swim in and out of these canyons with ease – all are filled with sea fans, plumes and many colourful sponges. Scores of angelfish, parrotfish, wrasse and snapper are everywhere. There are many more fish here than on Cozumel.

67 Two Cocos
★★★★★

Location: south of Chemuyil to the outer edge of the spur and groove reef.
Access: by boat only.
Conditions: there can be current along the outer wall.
Minimum depth: 18 m (60 ft)
Maximum depth: 40 m (130 ft)
Average visibility: 20 m (66 ft)

Two large and widely separated coral blocks loom up on the edge of the mini-wall, where the sandy sea bed appears to fold over into the depths. These coral heads are like islands of marine life, with all manner of coral, sponge and algae, topped with thousands of small fish. Chemuyil is said to be the best beach along the Tourist Corridor between Akumal and Tulum.

68 Xcacel
★★★★

Location: opposite Xcacel to the outer edge of the spur and groove reef.
Access: by boat only.
Conditions: there can be current along the outer wall.
Minimum depth: 18 m (60 ft)
Maximum depth: 40 m (130 ft)
Average visibility: 20 m (66 ft)

Here, widely spaced, wide sand chutes dissect to the outer barrier reef and you are less aware of the spur and groove formation, except when swimming well above the reef. There is a good chance of seeing rays and turtles cruising by. Large black grouper (*Mycteroperca bonaci*) and smooth trunkfish (*Lactophrys triqueter*) are common.

69 Xel-Há
★★★★

Location: inside the sheltered lagoon of Xel-Há.
Access: directly from the shore using TUBS (Tom's Underwater Breathing System).
Conditions: lots of fresh water flow through the lagoon reducing visibility.
Minimum depth: 2 m (6 ft)
Maximum depth: 4 m (13 ft)
Average visibility: under 5 m (16 ft)

This fun dive consists of some large old coral limestone blocks close to shore, and it is a great chance for anyone who has never been scuba-diving. An air cylinder is placed in a float and you are attached by means of a life jacket and a 3-m (10-ft) hose. Correctly weighted, you are able to dive and swim along the sea bed and around the coral reef pulling the air cylinder along behind you on the surface. The reef is fairly poor because it is bathed in the freshwater outflow from a cenote, in which coral cannot live. This also affects the clarity and visibility of the water. There are numerous wrasse, parrotfish and sergeant majors around.

Fitting TUBS (Tom's Underwater Breathing System) – an adapted aqualung with the air bottle carried in a float above the diver.

70 Punta Solyman
★★★★★

Location: south of Xel-Há to the next headland and bay.
Access: from the shore road or by boat.
Conditions: there can be surge between November and April making entry and exit difficult.
Minimum depth: 3 m (10 ft)
Maximum depth: 6 m (20 ft)
Average visibility: 6 m (20 ft)

This is a nice easy dive, but because the site is so shallow it is entirely dependent on the weather. There is often quite a lot of surge and you should take care around the shore. The old coral limestone shore or 'ironshore' has numerous small caverns and blowholes. Silverside minnows can often be found sheltering in these between May and August. There is not much coral but there are peacock flounders and rays in the shallows.

71 Punta Cadenas
★★★★★

Location: south of Punta Solyman along the coast road to the next sheltered lagoon.
Access: from the shore.
Conditions: a sheltered lagoon, but there can be surge and choppy seas between November and April.
Minimum depth: shoreline
Maximum depth: 6m (20ft)
Average visibility: 6m (20ft)

This is a beautiful location for snorkelling and diving. You can spend a long time at the maximum depth of only 6 m (20 ft) and examine the marine life at your leisure. If you are snorkelling you should take great care to protect yourself from the sun. Always wear a T-shirt or other clothing and apply a high-factor sunscreen to the backs of your legs and neck.

72 Tulum
★★★

Location: directly from the beach at Tulum.
Access: from the shore.
Conditions: sandy beach with light coral growth around the rocky headlands.
Minimum depth: shoreline
Maximum depth: 6 m (20 ft)
Average visibility: 6 m (20 ft)

This site is a lovely white sand beach sandwiched between some of the most impressive Maya ruins on this section of coast – it is in the ancient walled Maya port of Tulum. The bay is quite sheltered and makes a pleasant interlude from the heat of the day when you are sightseeing.

Corals on a reeftop in shallow waters can be viewed by snorkellers as well as divers.

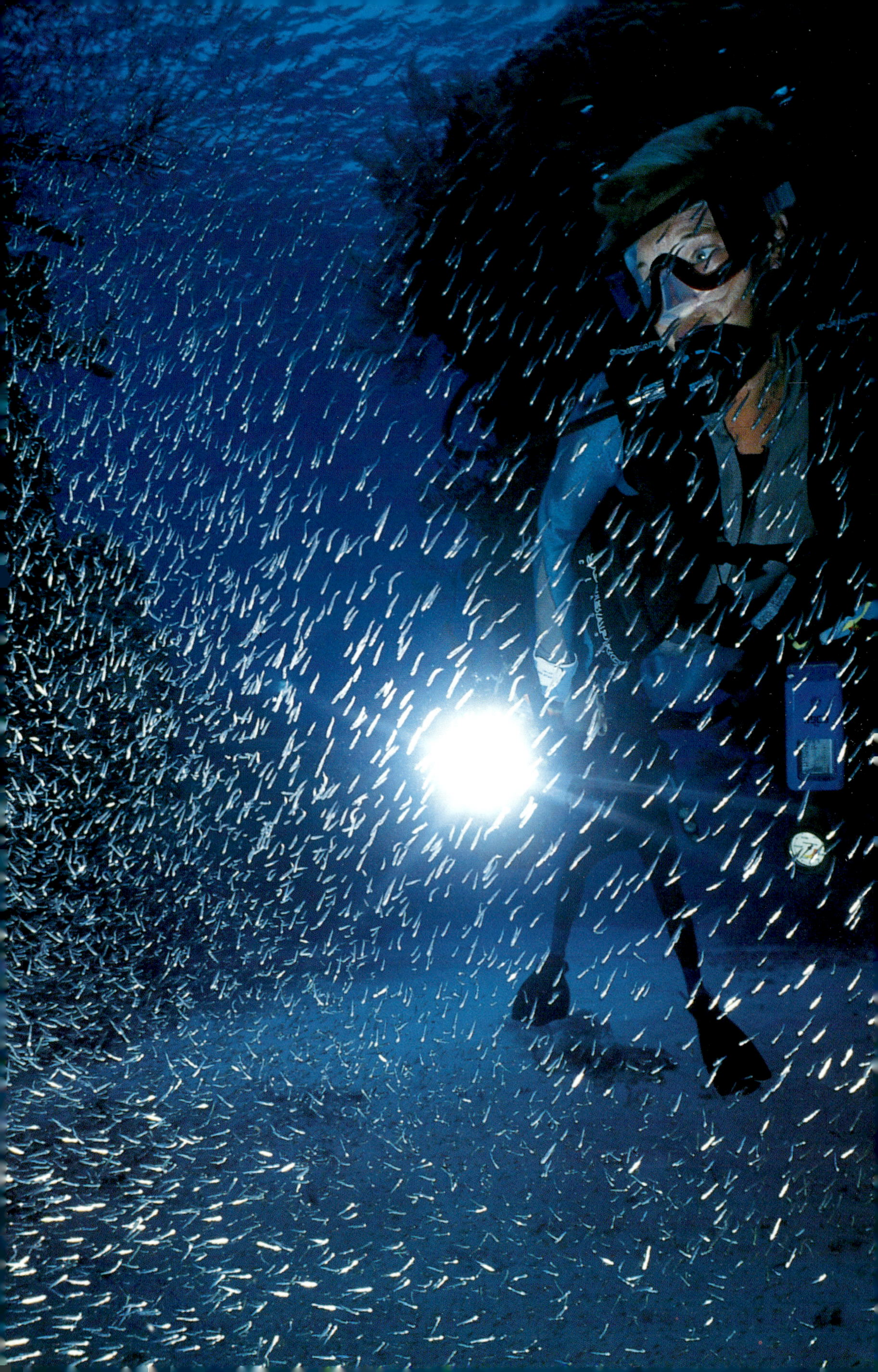

The Mayan Riviera

How to Get There

By air: there are major international airports at the state capital, Chetumal, and outside Cancún (see page 53).
Chetumal International Airport Avda Revolución, Chetumal, 277049, Quintana Roo, Mexico; tel (983) 23525/20465/ fax (983) 23898.
By bus: There is a first-class coach service between Cancún and Chetumal, operated by Autotransportes Caribe; and a second-class service between Playa del Carmen and Chetumal, operated along the same route by Autotransportes del Oriente. The services are very cheap and reliable, but the second-class buses run more frequently and make more stops on the way. Check with the local tourist office for details.
By car: Highway Mex 307 runs along the Quintana Roo coast from Cancún to Chetumal in the south (see page 25).

Where to Stay

As well as the many hotels, apartments and condominiums all along the Mayan Riviera, there are four timeshare resorts. There are several coastal campsites and trailer parks for visitors in camper vans, with tents, or who are backpacking. Some sites are in areas of outstanding scenery.

The Cancún Hotel Association's star-rating system extends along the Mayan Riviera. Only a representative number of the many hotels in the region is listed on this page. A full list of Hotel Association members is available from their office in Cancún.

Asociación de Hoteles de Cancún, A.C, Avda Ignacio García de la Torre 6 S.M.1, Apdo Postal 1339, Cancún, Quintana Roo, Mexico 77500; tel (988) 42853/45895/fax (988) 47115.

Mexican Tourism Promotion Office, Avda Ignacio García de la Torre 6 1 S.M, Apdo Postal 1339, Cancún, Quintana Roo, Mexico 77500; tel (988) 42853/fax (988) 47115.

Hotels
This list covers hotels south from Cancún toward Chetumal. The hotels are chosen for price and location but are not necessarily recommended. Phone well ahead to book.

Akumal Cancún, km 104, Akumal, Tulum Corridor, Quintana Roo, Mexico 77710; tel (987) 22453. Beachfront, a pool and a restaurant, full water sports and cenote dive centre nearby.

Opposite: *Millions of silversides glitter in a diver's splotight.*

Blue Parrot Inn, Playa del Carmen, Tulum Corridor, Quintana Roo, Mexico 77780; tel (987) 30083/fax (987) 30002. An exclusive beach-front club with pools, restaurants, tennis courts, and a dive centre; 41 rooms.

Cabañas Tulum, km 127 Tulum, Tulum Corridor, Quintana Roo, Mexico 77780. Small cabins on the beach, few facilities; popular with backpackers.

Caribbean Reef Club at Villa Marina, Puerto Morelos, Tulum Corridor, Quintana Roo, Mexico 77750; tel (987) 10191. Beachfront, but next to ferry port, with 21 rooms, a pool and a restaurant.

Costa de Cocos, Xcalak, Tulum Corridor, Quintana Roo, Mexico 77780; tel (303) 674 9615; www.costadecocos.com. Fourteen small beach cabins, a restaurant and a dive centre. Book well ahead.

Hotel Acuario, km 127, Tulum, Tulum Corridor, Quintana Roo, Mexico 77780; tel (987) 12195/fax (987) 12194; www.hotelacuario.com. Small cabins on the beach; few facilities but good food.

Hotel Club Akumal Caribe, km 104, Akumal, Tulum Corridor, Quintana Roo, Mexico 77710; tel (987) 59012; www.hotelakumalcaribe.com. A beach-front hotel with, 48 rooms, a pool, a restaurant and a cenote dive centre.

Hotel Continental Plaza, south of where the ferry docks, Playa del Carmen, Tulum Corridor, Quintana Roo, Mexico 77780; tel (987) 30100/fax (987) 30105. Huge beach-front resort; allwatersports, a pool and a restaurant.

Hotel Mayan Paradise, Avda 10 and Calle 12, Playa del Carmen, Tulum Corridor, Quintana Roo, Mexico 77780; tel (987) 30933/fax (987) 32015. Forty rooms arranged around a pool and gardens.

Las Casitas Akumal, Akumal, Tulum Corridor, Quintana Roo, Mexico 77710; tel (987) 22554/fax (987) 42371. Eighteen beachfront units with water sports facilities and cenote dive centre nearby.

Los Cocos, Avda de los Héroes, Chetumal, Tulum Corridor, Quintana Roo, Mexico 77710; tel/fax (983) 20544. A good-value hotel in town, with restaurant.

Maranatha Hotel, Avda Juárez s/n, Playa del Carmen, Tulum Corridor, Quintana Roo, Mexico 77780; tel (987) 30143. A small, medium-priced hotel with a small pool, ten minutes' walk from beach.

Maroma Hotel, Lucero Street, Puerto Morelos, Tulum Corridor, Quintana Roo, Mexico 77750; tel (987) 844729. Small, intimate with a pool and a restaurant.

Omni Club de Playa, km 98, Puerto Aventuras, Tulum Corridor, Quintana Roo, Mexico 77750; tel (987) 35101/fax (987) 35051. Exclusive club with pools and restaurants; all watersports catered for; set back from the beach.

Omni Puerto Aventuras, km 98, Puerto Aventuras, Tulum Corridor, Quintana Roo, Mexico 77750; tel (987) 35101/ fax (987) 35102; www.omnihotels.com. A modern hotel with 30 rooms near the marina. It has three connecting pools and three restaurants.

Posado del Capitán Lafitte, Punta Bete, Tulum Corridor, Quintana Roo, Mexico 77780; tel (987) 30212; email lafitte@qroo1.telmex.net.mx. Beachfront; 62 comfortable rooms with pools and a restaurant.

San Carlos Hotel, km 98, Puerto Aventuras, Tulum Corridor, Quintana Roo, Mexico 77750. A typical Mexican hotel, comfortable and reasonably priced with a cenote dive centre nearby.

Shangrila/Las Palapas, km 69.5 Playa del Carmen, Tulum Corridor, Quintana Roo, Mexico 77780; tel/fax (987) 22888. A beachside hotel with cabin-style rooms, pools, restaurants and an integrated dive centre.

Villas Aventuras Akumal, km 104, Akumal, Tulum Corridor, Quintana Roo, Mexico 77710; tel/fax (987) 22804. Villas style set back from beach, some with views, cenote dive centre.

Villas Flamingo, Half Moon Bay, Akumal, Tulum Corridor, Quintana Roo, Mexico 77710; tel (800) 343 1440. Beach cabins, a pool, a restaurant; cenote dive centre nearby.

Trailer Parks
Acamaya Reef Trailer Park, km 29 Tulum Corridor, Quintana Roo, Mexico 77710; tel (987) 10132. A beach site. Facilities include showers, a bar and a small restaurant.

Chemuyil Trailer Park, Playa Chemuyil, Tulum Corridor, Quintana Roo, Mexico 77710. A beach site. Facilities include showers, a bar and a small restaurant.

Paamul Trailer Park, km 85 Paamul, Tulum Corridor, Quintana Roo, Mexico 77710; tel (987) 259422. A beach site. Facilities

The Mayan Riviera

include showers, a bar and a small restaurant.

Trailer Park Playa Xcalacoco, km 296 Chetumal, Tulum Corridor, Quintana Roo, Mexico 77710. A beach site. Facilities include showers, a bar and a small restaurant.

Where to Eat

Eating out in the Mayan Riviera is good value in the international hotels – including the hotels listed opposite under 'Where to Stay' –.and in local restaurants.

All the international hotels offer good-value, buffet-style evening dinners. Most of the local restaurants are typically Tex-Mex in style, specializing in excellent local seafood and traditional Mexican dishes. 'Turf and Surf' establishments are numerous and very popular with divers, although they are often rather impersonal and noisy. Some bars and the palapas also offer good-value food.

The restaurants listed on this page are a small sample of the many that can be found all the way along the riviera. They have been selected in the main towns and resorts – the selection is not necessarily a recommendation. It is not usually necessary to book.

Playa del Carmen
Lobster Pub, Playa del Carmen, Tulum Corridor, Quintana Roo, Mexico 77780. Traditional Mexican and seafood.
Calipso House, Playa del Carmen, Tulum Corridor, Quintana Roo, Mexico 77780; tel (987) 30119. Caribbean and Tex-Mex.
Chicago, Playa del Carmen, Tulum Corridor, Quintana Roo, Mexico 77780; tel (987) 30208. Steaks, burgers and Tex-Mex.
El Tacolote, Playa del Carmen, Tulum Corridor, Quintana Roo, Mexico 77710; tel (987) 30066. Mexican and seafood.

Puerto Aventuras
Papay Republic, Puerto Aventuras Resort, Tulum Corridor, Quintana Roo, Mexico 77750; tel/fax (987) 35170. Gourmet, traditional Mexican and international.
Carlos 'n' Charlies, km 98, Puerto Aventuras, Tulum Corridor, Quintana Roo, Mexico 77750; tel (987) 35131. Tex-Mex, buckets of beer and rock music.
Mama Mía, km 98, Puerto Aventuras, Tulum Corridor, Quintana Roo, Mexico 77750; tel (987) 35130. Italian-style and traditional Mexican.

Puerto Morelos
Maroma, Puerto Morelos, Tulum Corridor, Quintana Roo, Mexico 77580; tel/fax (987) 844729. International, Mexican and seafood specialities.
Ciao, Puerto Morelos, Tulum Corridor, Quintana Roo, Mexico 77500; tel/fax (987) 841216. Italian and Mexican.

Tulum
Osha Oasis, Tulum, Tulum Corridor, Quintana Roo, Mexico 77780; tel (987) 42772/fax (987) 30230. Vegetarian and seafood.

Xcaret
La Cocina, Xcaret, Tulum Corridor, Quintana Roo, Mexico 77500; tel/fax (988) 30654/30743/fax (988) 33709. Traditional Mexican.

Xel-Há
Subway, Xel-Há National Park, Tulum Corridor, Quintana Roo, Mexico 77710; tel (988) 33277/fax (988) 33281. Light easy French bread and Mexican food.

Dive Facilities

There are a small number of seasonal dive shops which operate as subsidiaries of larger operations during the summer months. These are almost always closed during the winter from late November until April. If trying to dive 'on spec', it is best to use one of the more professional organisations, all of which usually have accomodation on the premises or nearby.

It is always recommended to contact the diving operations prior to your trip to check out the facilities and whether they are still prepared to take divers out when there are reduced numbers or whether they only travel with a full boat and perhaps with no room or facilities for rinsing camera equipment. The specialized cave diving operators always handle small numbers and even if you are travelling on your own, they will be more than happy to help you dive accompanied into these vast underground caverns.

General
Scuba Mex, Paamul, Tulum Corridor, Quintana Roo, Mexico 77710; tel (987) 41729.
Aqua Adventures, Puerto Morelos, Tulum Corridor, Quintana Roo, Mexico 77710; tel (987) 20761/30204.

Playa del Carmen south to Puerto Aventuras
Cenotemania, Lote 1 Mza 147 Esq, Calle 40N and Av 15, Playa del Carmen, Quintana Roo, Mexico 77710; tel/fax (987) 31756; email cenotemania@playadelcarmen.com.mx.
Dressel Divers Club, Hotel Iberostar Quetzal/Tucan, Playa del Carmen, Quintana Roo, Mexico 77000; tel (987) 30424/fax (987) 32921; email clubbuceo@playadelcarmen.com
Mayatech, PO Box 397, Playa del Carmen, Quintana Roo, Mexico 77710; tel (987) 62506; email info@mayatechdiving.com.

Phocea Caribe, 5a Ave Norte, between 12 and 14, Playa del Carmen, Quintana Roo, Mexico 77710; tel (987) 31210/fax (987) 31024; email phocea@playadelcarmen.com.
Scuba Mex, PO Box 80, Playa del Carmen, Quintana Roo, Mexico 77710; tel/fax (987) 51079; email scubamex@playadelcarmen.com.
Seafari Divers, Avda 5 between 2 Norte and Juárez, Playa del Carmen, Quintana Roo, Mexico 77600; tel (987) 51447/fax (987) 52179; email seafari@spin.com.mx.
Studio Blue, Hotel Molcas Local 5, Playa del Carmen, Quintana Roo, Mexico 77710; tel (987) 31088/fax (987) 24330; email seafari@spin.com.mx.
Tank-Ha Dive Centre, Avda 5 between 8 and 10, Playa del Carmen, Quintana Roo, Mexico 77710; tel (987) 30302; email tankha@playadelcarmen.com.
Viva Diving Maya-Azteca, Club Viva Maya, Playacar, Playa del Carmen, Quintana Roo, Mexico 77710; tel (987) 34600 ext. 8851; www.vivaresorts.com.

Puerto Aventuras south to Akumal
Aquanauts Dive Rite Tek Center, Local 2a Marina Puerto Aventuras km 269.5, Puerto Aventuras, Quintana Roo, Mexico 77750; tel/fax (987) 35280; email info@aquanauts-online.com.
CEDAM Dive Centres, PO Box 1, Puerto Aventuras, Quintana Roo, Mexico 77750; tel (987) 35147/fax (987) 35129; www.cedamdive.com.
DIR Mexico, Apt 62, Puerto Aventuras, Quintana Roo, Mexico 77750; tel (987) 456556; email danny@dir-mexico.com.
Servi Scuba, Centro Comercial Marine, Loc.5A and 5B, Puerta Aventuras, Quintana Roo, Mexico 77750; tel (987) 35151/fax (987) 30901.
Xcaret Dive Centre, Xcaret Ecological Park, km 55, Quintana Roo, Mexico 77780; tel (987) 14000/fax (987) 14005; email xcacuati@playa.com.mx.
Yucatech University of Diving, Omni Carr Chetumal, km 269.5, Quintana Roo, Mexico 77750; tel (987) 35031/fax (987) 35129; email diveadventuresi@ptoadventures.com.

Akumal south to Chetumal
Akumal Dive Centre, PO Box 714, Carretera Tulum km 104, Akumal, Quintana Roo, Mexico 77500; tel/fax (987) 59025; email dive@akumaldivecentre.com.
Akumal Dive Shop, PO Box 1, Akumal, Quintana Roo, Mexico 77710; tel (987) 41259/fax (988) 73164; www.akumal.com.
Bahia Divers, Marina de Buceo y Deportes Acuaticos, Akumal, Quintana Roo, Mexico 77500; tel (987) 55041; www.bahiadivers.com.
Dive Aventuras, PO Box 25, Aventuras Akumal 35, Tulum, Quintana Roo, Mexico 77780; tel/fax (987) 41271; email info@

The Mayan Riviera

diveaventuras.com.mex.
Dos Ojos Hidden Worlds Cenotes, km 111, Tulum Corridor, Quintana Roo, Mexico 77710; tel (987) 44081; email info@hiddenworlds.com.mx.
Yax-Há Dive Centre, Yax-Há, Tulum Corridor, Quintana Roo, Mexico 77710; tel (987) 22888.
Xhel-Há TUBS, Xel-Há, km 122, Mayan Corridor, Tulum, Quintana Roo, Mexico 77710; tel (987) 54070/fax (987) 54075; email briones@mail.xel-ha.com.mx.
Xcalak Costa de Cocos, Apdo 44 Xcalak, Chetumal, Quintana Roo, Mexico 77000; tel/fax (983) 10110; email ccocos@astro.net.mx.
Xcalak Dive Centre, Apdo 62, Chetumal, Quintana Roo, Mexico 77000; tel (510) 490 5597/fax (510) 490 8374.
Xcalak to Chinchorro Dive Resort, PO Box 21, North Road, Xcalak, Quintana Roo, Mexico 77710; tel/fax (987) 65331; www.xcalak.com.mx.

EMERGENCY SERVICES

Recompression (Hyperbaric) chambers:
It is planned that a new recompression chamber will soon be installed in Playa del Carmen on the mainland coast of Quintana Roo. Meanwhile all the diving operations along the coast use the services of the recompression chamber on Cozumel Island. The hyperbaric chamber is privately owned by Sub-Aquatic Safety Services, who installed it in 1987. The facility has a 135-cm (54-in) diameter hyperbaric chamber with a double lock. The recompression chamber operates on a 24-hour service in tandem with a fully equipped medical clinic where any diving-related incident will be treated by highly trained medical staff. The medical facilities in the chamber include the use of IV fluids, EKG machines, ventilators, other emergency equipment, two rooms for patients, a surgery room, an emergency room, X-ray machines and a closed-circuit television link.

The hyperbaric chamber staff administer a US$1 charge per diver, which goes toward the upkeep of the recompression chamber and toward the treatment costs of anyone using the chamber who does not have private medical insurance or the means to pay.

Cozumel Recompression Chamber; tel (987) 20140/22387/21430.

Life Flight (Houston Texas) for delivery to recompression chamber in the USA; tel (800) 392-4357 (713) 797-4357.

Air-Evac (San Diego, California) for delivery to recompression chamber in the USA; tel (800) 854-2567 (619) 278-3822.

Divers' Alert Network; tel (919) 648-8111.

General medical emergencies
Hospitals air service: Belize Link, San Pedro Airstrip; tel (026) 2851, 2073. (DAN)

General Hospital, Avda Andrés, Chetumal, Tulum Corridor, Quintana Roo, Mexico 77710; tel (983) 21932.

Centro de Salúd, Avda Juárez at Avda 15a, Playa del Carmen, Tulum Corridor, Quintana Roo, Mexico 77780; tel (987) 21230.

Dr. Victor Macias Orozco; tel (987) 30493.

Chemists
There are small pharmacies on almost every street in each town. As long as you know what medication you need you are unlikely to need a prescription:

Farmacia Social Mechaca, Avda Independencia 134c, Chetumal, Tulum Corridor, Quintana Roo, Mexico 77780; tel (983) 20044.

LOCAL HIGHLIGHTS

Croco-Cun km 30 Tulum Corridor, Quintana Roo, Mexico 77500; tel/fax (988) 41709. This is a crocodile farm and a miniature zoo situated 29 km (18 miles) south of Cancún.

Xcaret Ecoarchaeological Park km 55 Tulum Corridor, Quintana Roo, Mexico 77780; tel (988) 30654, (988) 30743/fax (988) 33709. For detailed information on this national park, see pages 112–113.

Xel-Há Tourism Lagoon and natural aquarium, km122 Tulum Corridor, Quintana Roo, Mexico 77780; tel (988) 33277/fax (988) 33281.

Sian Ka'an Biosphere Reserve, UNESCO Biosphere Reserve, Tulum Corridor, Quintana Roo, Mexico 77780. This UNESCO reserve is described on pages 14–15.

VEHICLE HIRE

Four-wheel-drive Volkswagens and jeeps are the vehicles most easily available for hire. There are very few petrol stations along Highway Mex 307 and you should always keep your tank full in case of emergencies. The main coastal highway may be the only major road you will need to drive along – it is the route you take for excursions into the coastal towns, to the dive centres and to the various cenotes. You must show a full driving licence and proof of identity.

Mopeds and scooters are a simple way of getting from hotel to town. Traffic can be quite heavy on the main road and there may be frequent road blocks manned by the military police, at which papers are checked and, if necessary, searches made for imported illegal drugs and arms. When you are stopped, just be patient. Avis, Hertz and the other major car rental companies have offices in Cancún. There are also local car-hire companies, but very few. Most people use taxis for short journeys.

Budget, Playacar Hotel, Playa del Carmen, Tulum Corridor, Quintana Roo, Mexico 77710; tel (987) 23554. Km104, Akumal, Tulum Corridor, Quintana Roo, Mexico 77710; tel (987) 22453.

Continental Car Rental, Avda. Norte 10A, Playa del Carmen, Tulum Corridor, Quintana Roo, Mexico 77710; tel (987) 30580.

Holiday Car Hire, Playa del Carmen, Tulum Corridor, Quintana Roo, Mexico 77710; tel (987) 30959.

Nautical Car Hire, Hotel Mollas, Playa del Carmen, Tulum Corridor, Quintana Roo, Mexico 77710; tel (987) 30360.

Petrol Stations
There are petrol stations in Puerto Morelos, Playa del Carmen, Tulum, Felipe Carillo Puerto, and Chetumal. Always fill up as you travel, bearing in mind that you may have to keep going further than planned if you have not booked accommodation.

FILM PROCESSING

Kodak Film Lab, 1a Sur c/z FM, Playa del Carmen, Tulum Corridor, Quintana Roo, Mexico 77710.

Photo Omega, Avdas 10 and Juárez, Playa del Carmen, Tulum Corridor, Quintana Roo, Mexico 77710; tel (987) 30031.

USEFUL TIPS

This region is in the tropics and at sea level, so it is very hot. June, September and October are the wettest months, so be prepared, not only for the rain but also the massive jump in humidity – which can be debilitating if you are not used to it. Always carry a swimsuit and insect repellent on any excursions. Also carry your tourist card with you all the time as there are border checks around each of the main crossroads.

The World Ocean

It never ceases to be astonishing that the same species of marine life are found in more than one location around the world, despite the fact that these areas are separated by landmasses or by strong tidal streams of different salinity, temperature and strength.

Christmas tree worms *(Spirobranchus giganteus)* are common throughout the Caribbean – and they also give great pleasure to marine photographers in the Red Sea. The anemone *Alicia mirabilis* and the scrawled filefish *(Aluterus scriptus)* are found in all tropical seas; and the jellyfish *Aurelia aurita* in every ocean. banded coral shrimps *(Stenopus hispidus)* have been recorded from Cozumel to Sodwana Bay in South Africa and all the way to the major coral reefs of Malaysia and Australia. The sargassum anglerfish *(Histrio histrio)* is found wherever there is sargassum weed – from Bermuda to Cozumel to Borneo – and the balloonfish *(Diodon holocanthus)* has been recorded in the Caribbean, the Red Sea, Indonesia and the Philippines.

THE PREHISTORIC OCEAN

All these and many other examples have given rise to the notion that the world's oceans were linked at one time, millions of years ago. As tectonic movements have shifted the Earth's crust, many species have moved with the land, and have evolved, yet have maintained fundamental similarities, given that the water temperature and salinity of their habitats remained almost the same.

Although it may be difficult to believe that the distribution of many animals and plants can be so wide, it must be recognized that species that look merely similar may, on close examination, turn out to be identical. For example, the sergeant major, *Abudefduf saxatilis,* is found in the Caribbean and the Atlantic Ocean as far to the southeast as Africa; and *A. vaigiensis* is known to be widespread in the Indo-Pacific ocean. The two species are very similar and may in fact be sub-species.

Larger pelagic species of fish such as the manta ray *(Manta birostris)*, the great barracuda *(Sphyraena barracuda)* and many members of the shark family are well known for their wide species distribution. This may sometimes be a natural phenomenon. When marine species reproduce, they spend a short time in the plankton, the life blood of the oceans. During this time, many animals are

The slow-moving, photogenic scrawled filefish (Aluterus scriptus) *is uncommon in the Mexican Caribbean.*

The World Ocean

Christmas tree worms (Spirobranchus giganteus) *have been found as far as Sodwana Bay in South Africa, the Red Sea, Malaysia, and the South Pacific.*

distributed perhaps thousands of miles, to wash up on some distant shore. So long as the conditions at their destination are similar to those of its native habitat, an alien species may occasionally establish itself in a new place – perhaps upsetting a stable community.

Human Intervention

This is rare, however; the fact is that 'aliens' are usually introduced into a distant community by human activity. The 20th century has seen the opening of the Suez and Panama Canals creating a channel between oceans where none existed previously. Although the Panama Canal is controlled by a series of locks, species from the Caribbean Sea and the Pacific Ocean are forever mixing in this region and spreading to much more distant locations. The Suez Canal is open all the time, allowing a continuous intermingling of marine life between the Red Sea and the Mediterranean.

Couple these factors with the construction of huge ocean-going liners, tankers and container ships which often use sea water as ballast when they are travelling empty, means that large congregations of plankton and small fish can be transported to the other side of the world, where they may be released when the ship takes on its next cargo.

Exceptions to the Rule

There are curious anomalies, however. Why, for example, are there no true anemonefish or clownfish in the Caribbean, when near-identical species of every other family are represented there, from lizardfish to shrimps, and many species of corals?

Like every other part of the oceans, the Yucatán coastal waters have been affected by these phenomena: a curious mix of species is found there – and some of its native species now inhabit far-distant seas. When you dive there, your underwater exploration could become even more fascinating if you think about the creatures that especially interest you, and take time afterwards to read about them and find out whether they are native to the area or interlopers from another ocean.

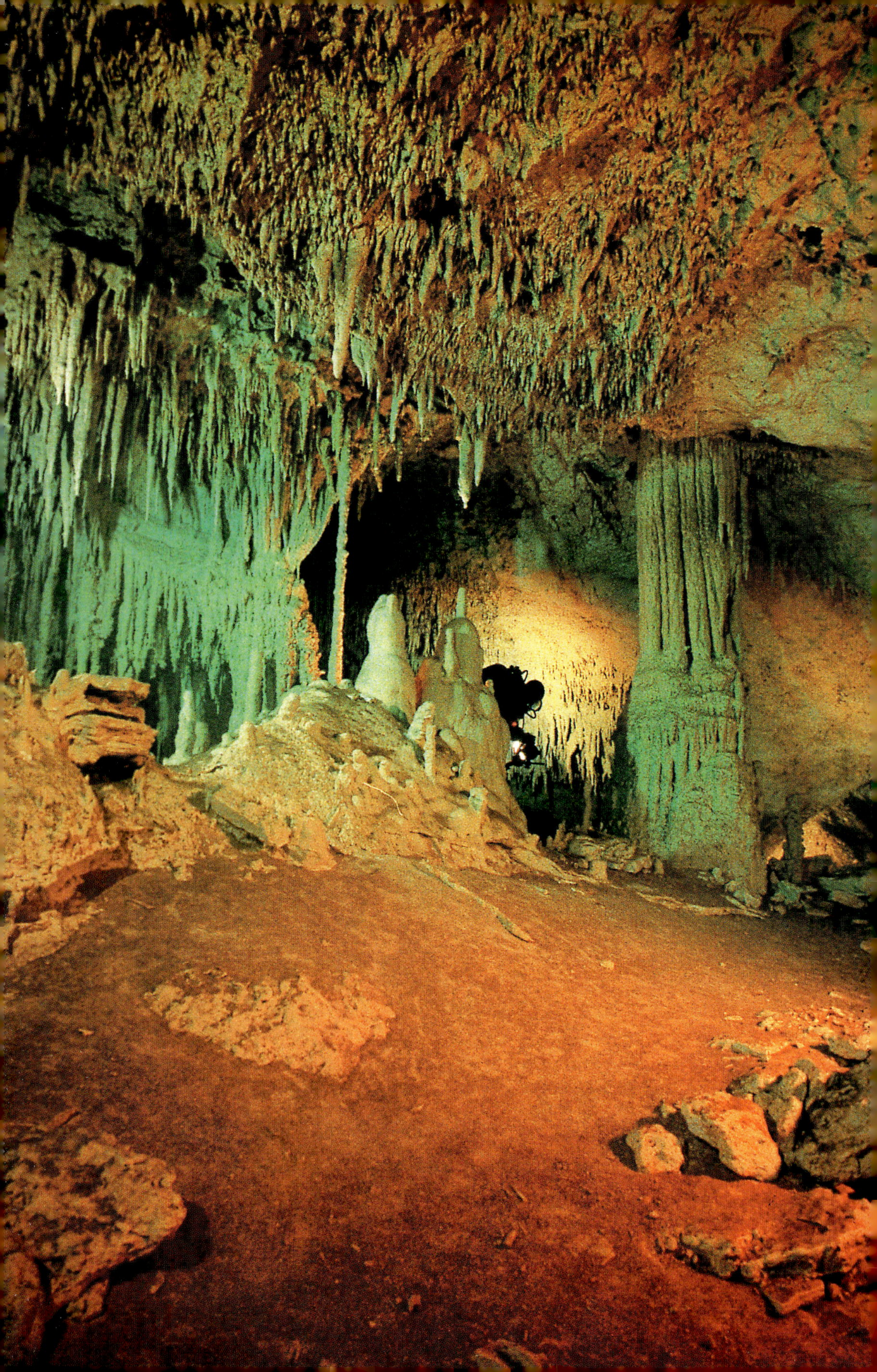

DIVING THE CENOTES

Cenote-diving is the new frontier of diving. It has evolved only since the 1980s, exclusively in the Yucatán and specifically along the Tourist Corridor, which has become a major dive destination for cave divers from around the world.

The name cenote comes from the Mayan word *tzonott*, which means 'well'. Cenotes are geological formations found all over Central America. Until recently in geological time, North and South America were two separate continents and Central America – the land bridge that unites them – was under water. During the last Ice Age, which lasted from about 1 million to 10,000 years ago, the sea level dropped, exposing this land bridge – a shallow, raised limestone plateau. Over centuries, rainwater seeped through the soft, porous limestone and eroded beneath its surface caves and tunnels, filling them with water. In some places the water eroded caverns so huge that in time their roofs collapsed, leaving mysterious pools – some of them the size of a lake, and some immeasurably deep. These are cenotes.

SACRED WELLS OF THE ANCIENTS
The cenotes were the primary source of fresh water for the peoples who lived around them, and they were revered as sacred. Great Mesoamerican cities were built around certain cenotes. One example is Chichen Itzá, whose focus is the great Cenote Sagrado, where the Maya prayed and offered sacrifices to Chac Mool, their rain god. Local people always believed that this Sacred Well was bottomless, but archaeological explorations initiated by the US consul at the turn of the 20th century revealed its maximum depth to be 20 m (66 ft). Human bones were found in it, indicating that the victims were mainly children (or, since the ancient Maya were a very small people, there may be truth behind the myth that virgins were cast into this cenote). Treasures excavated from the well were taken to the Peabody Museum at the USA's Harvard University. As a site of great archaeological importance, the cenote at Chichen Itzá is permanently off-limits to divers.

Divers began to explore the cenotes for recreation only in the early 1980s. Some 80 to 90 have been located in the Yucatán. Some, such as the popular Cenote Carwash (Site 1), are easily accessible; but others, such as Dos Ojos (Site 2), can be reached only by a four-

---

Opposite: *A diver glimpses the colourful stalacmites and stalactites in Nohoch Na Chich.*
Above: *A packhorse is needed to carry cenote-diving equipment into the rainforest.*

DIVING THE CENOTES

wheel-drive vehicle along a forest track; and visiting Nohoch Nah Chich (Site 6) involves a trek through the rainforest to the west of Tulum with a packhorse to carry equipment.

Some cenotes are round or crescent-shaped pools, while others look more like muddy ponds. Nohoch Na Chich, more than 150 m (500 ft) across, has the largest surface area. Near Chetumal on Quintana Roo's southern border is Cenote Azul, the deepest cenote so far discovered, more than 100 m (330 ft) deep. From its clear surface, 185 m (607 ft) in diameter and fringed with mangroves, the water drops to many underhanging caves and caverns leading off the sinkhole. By contrast, some cenotes are shallow. Cenote Naharon south of the junction of the Tulum/Coba roads is a pond only a few metres deep; and the centre of El Grande Cenote (Site 4), was filled in by its collapsed cavern roof. It consists of a circular channel of water around the perimeter of the filled-in sinkhole, open to the sky.

However, even the shallowest cenotes have an underwater entry and exit point for the stream that keeps them filled with water. It is the tunnels along which these underground streams flow that divers explore. They average only 5–12 m (17–40 ft) in depth and at such depths divers can spend hours at a time submerged without incurring any time penalties or decompression stops. This accounts for the extent to which the underwater cave networks have already been explored.

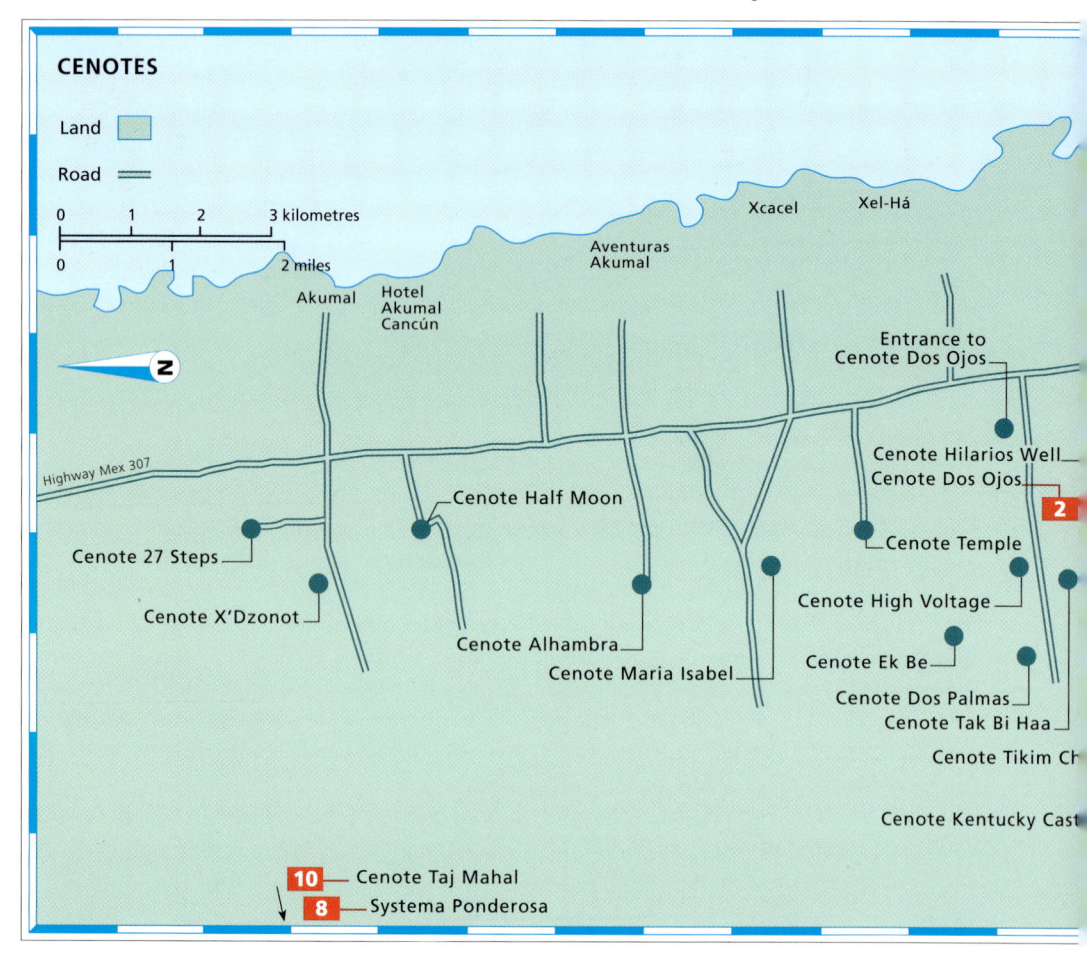

To facilitate access for divers, platforms have been built across the surface of Cenote Carwash, but to enter Mundo Escondido (Site 5) divers have to drop 6 m (20 ft) down a very narrow well shaft. A few cenotes have tiny entrances and divers have to squeeze between a cave wall and drop downward through 6 m (20 ft) of open cavern before they reach the water. The centre of Cenote Carwash is piled high with rubble from the collapsed cave roof and you can only reach the water by climbing a rustic step ladder.

All the cenote diving takes place on private land. There are crude changing huts around some cenotes. You will be required to pay at least US$5 per person per dive to the landowner, plus a small tip to the 'man at the gate'.

FAIRYTALE WORLD

The waters of Cenote Azul are, as its Spanish name implies, azure; but Cenote Sagrado at Chichen Itzá is an impenetrable green because the top few metres of its surface waters are dense with algae. Many cenotes are affected by algal bloom in the dry season. It cuts out light, so these cenotes are dived from November to April when the water is clear. However, the water in the cenotes is unpolluted and in most it is so clear that the light penetrates into the submerged caverns and tunnels that open out from them. Perhaps the main attraction of exploring this newly discovered underwater world is to see the spectacular limestone formations – stalactites, stalagmites, flowstone and other beautiful rock forms – that decorate the caverns and tunnels. Many are brilliantly coloured and patterned with minerals dissolved in the rainwater that seeped through the bedrock of the Yucatán plateau.

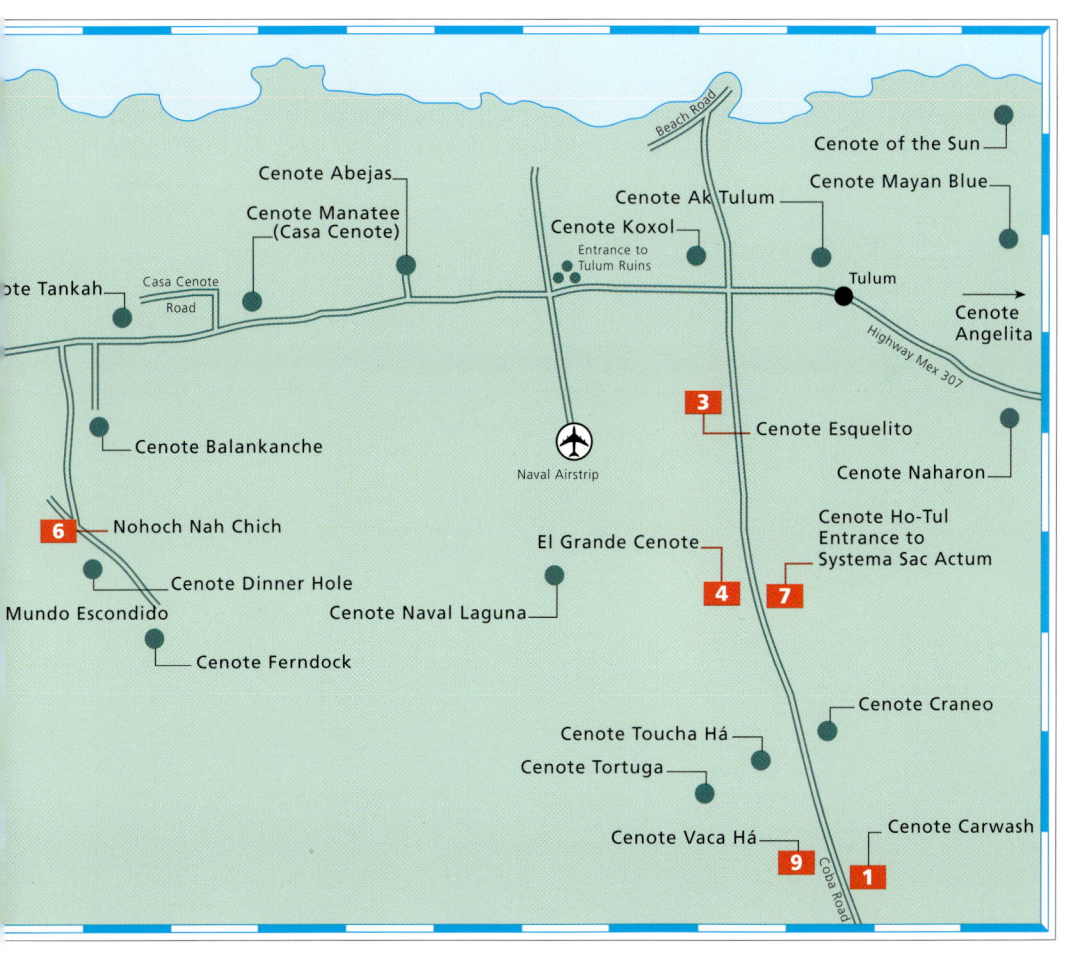

Pathways to the Sea

In 1987 Mike Madden, who operates CEDAM (Conservation, Education, Diving, Archaeology and Museums) Divers in Puerto Aventuras discovered what is now the most famous cenote, Nohoch Nah Chich (see pages 152–53). While exploring it with a team of divers, he made the astonishing discovery that Nohoch Nah Chich forms part of a vast, interconnecting system of water-filled caves and passageways that links many cenotes. Much of this vast subterranean network is still unexplored, but since the 1980s more than 160 km (100 miles) of underground waterways have been surveyed.

The magnitude of Mike Madden's discovery became evident only as the subterranean waterway network began to be mapped – for since 1992 Nohoch Nah Chich has been recorded in *The Guinness Book of Records* as the world's largest cave system. CEDAM Divers have now discovered more than 50 km (30 miles or 158,432 ft) of surveyed passageways. This network, they now know, is connected to the sea – there are both saltwater and freshwater passageways in a number of cenotes.

Subsequent explorations traced other cenote systems to the sea. Cenote Tankah, for instance, is a large, open pool of clear water fringed by rainforest. Its submerged passage drops slowly as you swim along it, eventually opening out into the sea at Tankah Beach. It is clear from these discoveries that a cenote is, in effect, a window in the rainforest looking down into the underground rivers that honeycomb the Yucatán Peninsula.

Diving Caves and Caverns

Exploring cave systems is dangerous and during explorations the divers carry an automatic dispenser reel from which they unwind a trace – a fine, lightweight nylon line – as they swim. Many of the underground caves and passageways have since been laid with a gold Kermalite line, which is recognized as the strongest water-resistant line to use for marking underwater passageways. Because parts of the system are now marked, cenote-diving is practicable for all experienced divers visiting the Yucatán.

The surface of the Cenote Sagrado (Sacred Cenote) at Chichen Itzá is covered in algae.

Diving the Cenotes

Cenote-diving is now divided into cavern dives, defined as staying in sight of the entrance to a cave or cavern, and considered safe for beginners and for snorkellers and scuba divers; and cave dives, defined as moving well away from sunlight into a cave system. Cave divers must have received instruction from a certified cave-diving operation. Even divers qualified in cave-diving should not explore the seaward caverns of systems such as Nohoch Na Chich unless accompanied and supervised by an expert on the system.

Mike Madden of CEDAM divers, Steve Gerrard of Aquatec in Aventuras Akumal, and Tony and Nancy DeRosa at Aquatec, now offer cavern and cave-diving instruction to the highest safety standards; and the region's oldest-established diving centre, The Akumal Dive Centre, run by Don Brewer, offers cave-diving as an alternative to tropical reef-diving. Other diving operators from Mexico, California, Florida and Texas run cave-diving excursions but all liaise with one of these three established specialist centres.

In the exploration of the caves all three centres have maintained a 100 per cent safety record. Divers have been lost, however – all at the hands of unscrupulous operators who are not qualified to dive in the Nohoch Nah Chich labyrinth of caves and passageways.

Top Ten Cenote Dives

There are about 50 cenotes along the Tourist Corridor and these are shown on the map on pages 145–146. However, although they are now well mapped, they are not yet all completely explored. For guidance the author, kindly assisted by Mike Madden of CEDAM Divers and Steve Gerrard of Aquatec, has compiled the following list of top ten cenote dive sites. Though a novice cave and cavern diver, the author can testify to the excellence of each one. They are listed not in order of their geographical location – like the dive sites in preceding chapters of this book – but in 'Top 10' order, based on their appeal to a wide range of divers, their spectacular underwater scenery and other interesting features.

1 Cenote Carwash (The Room of Tears and Beyond)
★★★★★★★

Cavern/cave dive only for properly qualified diivers.
Location: west along the Coba road – well signposted.
Access: 10 m (33 ft) from the small car park. The crescent-shaped lagoon of the cenote has two wooden platforms extending over the water, which make entry and exit very easy.
Conditions: excellent, extremely safe, and photogenic.
Average visibility: 60 m (200 ft).
Fee: US$5.

Parker Turner and Mike Madden found The Room of Tears in 1958. It is still regarded as a classic. The cave is now so well known that calls are being made for a permanent gold Kermalite guideline to be placed in it, not only to guide divers but to ensure that damage is kept to a minimum in the most distant passages.

Carwash is the most popular cenote with divers in this part of the Yucatán because of its accessibility through a huge cavern entrance and its very clear water. It is easy enough for scuba divers to see and explore the underwater environment, no matter what their level of skill or experience and even if they are not qualified to dive.

Two notes about safety: First, you must always wear a protective suit and hood when diving, as the freshwater fish in this cenote – such as tetra and mollies are voracious. They may be small but they have sharp teeth and can be a real menace to divers. And second, you will need to have reached a high level of ability before extending your range beyond the point where daylight penetrates the cenote. You should assess your own levels of skill and competence realistically before venturing this far and beyond.

2 Dos Ojos (Two Eyes)
★★★★★★★

Cavern/cave dive only for properly qualified divers.
Location: just off Highway Mex 307 south of Aventuras Akumal. The site is well signposted.
Access: via a sturdy track; four-wheel-drive vehicles are recommended.
Conditions: tremendous.
Average visibility: excessive.
Fee: US$5.

This is the world's second largest underground cave system and even as you read this, an underground river connection may already have been made to Nohoch Nah

Chich. Dos Ojos was first dived by Jim Coke and Johanna DeGroot back in 1986. The maximum depth is only 11 m (36 ft) and the average depth is only 5 m (16 ft). The main traverse is more than 1,600 m (5,500 ft) long and spans four openings (or possible bail-out points). The dive is upstream because of the strength of the water drainage flowing downstream. Following the continuous guideline, after 45 minutes you will reach Cenote Dos Palmas, then after another 35 minutes you will reach Cenote High Voltage or 'Tic-Te-Há'. Each section can be traversed within the safe one-third air rule. The dive concludes by passing through Cenote Tapir's End to Cenote Monolith. This dive will take approximately 110 minutes, which should allow you a safety margin on twin 80 cu ft tanks. Each section of the dive is worth exploring separately and divers should not rush on to the next traverse simply to say that they have done it all. This is cave-diving to dream about.

3 Cenote Esquelito (The Skeleton or Cenote Temple of Doom)
★★★★★
Cave dive only for properly qualified divers.
Location: just after the turning of the Coba road from Highway 307, on the west side.
Access: down a narrow opening which bells out inside.
Conditions: superb.
Average visibility: staggering.
Fee: US$5.
This cenote was discovered by Mike Madden and his former brother-in-law, Denny Atkinson, after a tip-off by a local taxi driver. Since their first explorations in July 1986, passageways covering distances of more than 3,800 m (13,000 ft) have already been mapped.

This cenote is a beautiful place to visit. The walls and floor are snow white, contrasting with the cobalt blue salt water. You can swim along the Kermalite guideline 180 m (600 ft) to a T-junction. If you turn right you enter the Coliseum Room, which leads in a short circuit back to the cenote; if you turn left and travel another 75 m (250 ft) you will enter a cavern the size of a football field called The Fang. From this point at the next offshoot divers are now exploring the continuing passageway.

4 El Grande Cenote (The Big Well)
★★★★★★★★
Cavern/cave dive only for properly qualified divers.
Location: off the Coba/Tulum road to the north.
Access: 6 m (20 ft) down a rickety wooden ladder and along the platform to the left.
Conditions: spectacular.
Average visibility: more than 60 m (200 ft).
Fee: US$5.
Gauging visibility is always difficult, but when you are more than 60 m (200 ft) into a cavern and you can see someone snorkelling at the entrance, you know it is high. This cenote is a huge circular hole – a collapsed cavern with the centre completely filled in – and you dive round the perimeter, from where the cavern system extends well beyond natural daylight to connect eventually with other cenotes. There are stalactites, stalagmites, flowstone and other formations that only an expert could identify. Divers seen from a distance can look when they are not breathing as if they are suspended in mid-air among cathedral-sized columns.

5 Mundo Escondido (Hidden World)
★★★★★
Cave dive only for properly qualified divers.
Location: between the two largest cave systems – Nohoch Nah Chich and Dos Ojos.
Access: by four-wheel-drive vehicle to site, then a 6-m (20-ft) drop down a well shaft (large enough for only one diver at a time).
Conditions: awesome.
Average visibility: excessive.
Fee: US$5.
This cenote was first explored by two pioneering divers of the Yucatán cave system, Buddy Quattlebaum and Gary Walton, in March 1994. The site presents a logistical challenge, not only to get to it but also to lower all your equipment down the 6-m (20-ft) well shaft. It may be easy on the way in, but it can be a nightmare on the way out. However, the effort is well worth it. The water is so clear that swimming is more like flying – and it makes the limestone formations so clear that the details appear slightly magnified. You find yourself forgetting to let out your breath as you swim through the narrow passages.

6 Nohoch Nah Chich (The Giant Birdhouse)
★★★★★★★★★★
Cavern/cave dive only for properly qualified divers.
Location: off Highway Mex 307, south of Akumal and Dos Ojos. Divers must obtain permission from the owner of the land where the cenote is located before entering this cave system.
Access: difficulty depends on which point you use to enter and exit the site.
Conditions: varied in this massive system, with snorkel sections, shallow dives and deep dives. Many cenotes are traversed during the diving.
Average visibility: well over 60 m (200 ft). Divers must be accompanied by staff from CEDAM Divers.
Fee: US$5.
This, the world's longest underground cave system (see pages 152–53), was first discovered by Mike Madden of CEDAM Divers in November 1987. The caves consist of gigantic hallways – to call them 'huge' is an understatement – from which the name of the site is derived. Most of the passageways are no deeper than 7 m

Above: *A diver exploring the Cenote Carwash has crystal-clear visibility.*
Below: *A cavern in the labyrinthine Nohoch Na Chich system, which has been traced to the sea.*

(23 ft), however, and the cenote pool is more than 150 m (500 ft) across, so snorkellers are able to explore an area well underground safely.

One diver could not explore this cave system in a lifetime. Most settle for following the route of the underground river, and it is impossible to say which part is the best. The easiest to see are the Disneyland and Heaven's Gate caverns, but the further upstream you start your dive the better it will be. This involves a 50-minute hike into the rainforest utilizing packhorses to carry equipment; this can be expensive.

7 Systema Sac Actun (The White Cave)
★★★★★

Cave dive only for properly qualified divers.
Location: the other side of the road from El Grande Cenote (Site 4) and in through a section called Cuzah Nah in Cenote Ho-Tul.
Access: a difficult hike into the rainforest, but it is well rewarded.
Conditions: probably the favourite of all cenote dives.
Average visibility: excessive.
Fee: US$5.

This cenote was discovered by pioneering explorers Steve DeCarlo and Jim Coke in November 1988 (about the same time that the Nohoch Na Chich system was discovered by Mike Madden). Its maximum depth is only 14 m (45ft) and the water maintains a constant temperature of 24°C (74°F). The site is so decorative it is never disappointing. It is a photographer's dream, with thousands of limestone columns of every size, from straws to chandeliers. More than 5,000 m (17,000 ft) of passageways have been explored.

8 Systema Ponderosa
★★★★★★★★★★

Cave/cavern dive, only for properly qualified divers.
Location: 12 km (7 1/2 miles) north and west of Aventuras Akumal.
Access: a difficult 4-m (13-ft) drop to the water.
Conditions: absolutely fantastic.
Average visibility: awesome, but where the longer caves connect with the sea, divers can experience hydrology (halocline) – a mix of fresh water toward the surface and salt water below – the composition depending on the strength of swell in the Caribbean Sea, which is over 4 km (2.5 miles) away.
Fee: US$5.

When first shown this cenote in June 1990, Tony and Nancy DeRosa of Aventuras Akumal first jumped in with only single tanks and immediately saw another cenote 90 m (300 ft) away. This was a typical circular cave-roof collapse, the forest floor surrounding the cenote packed tightly with palm trees and mangroves, forming a sunken forest below the rainforest. Within the cenote there is a huge cavern called The Pool Hall, which is more than 90 m (300 ft) long, topped by a huge air space called The Chapel. A gold Kermalite divers' guideline has now been led to it from the cenote, creating a dive that takes approximately 42 to 45 minutes. More than 10 km (6 m) of passages have now been mapped, connecting Systema Ponderosa to at least 19 other cenotes. This amazing system will keep the most ardent cave diver very happy indeed.

9 Cenote Vaca Ha (The Cow Well)
★★★★★

Cave dive only for properly qualified divers.
Location: along the Coba road, on the north side opposite Cenote Carwash (Site 1).
Access: a difficult, tight entrance and a tight squeeze from the hallway.
Conditions: for experienced cave divers only.
Average visibility: well over 60 m (200 ft).
Fee: US$5.

This is one of the most beautiful caves to be found along the Quintana Roo coast. It was first dived by Steve Gerrard and Tony DeRosa at Aquatec in Aventuras Akumal and to date only about 1,100 m (4,000 ft) of passages have been surveyed. The first 175 m (60 ft) of fresh water are filled with columns and multiple decorative features; from there the cenote develops into a fault-line passage just above the salt water and is like a subway tunnel. Although Vaca Ha is very close to Carwash (Site 1) no connection between the two has yet been made. This is a rewarding and stimulating dive.

10 Cenote Taj Mahal (The Palace of Ornaments)
★★★★★

Cave dive only for properly qualified divers.
Location: 8 km (5 miles) north of Aventuras Akumal.
Access: by rough bulldozed track directly to the entrance.
Conditions: absolutely fantastic.
Average visibility: like being in clear air.
Fee: US$5.

This cave system was known for over four years before it was first dived in 1994 by Nancy DeRosa and her brother Wayne Nefzger. Its maximum depth is only 12 m (40 ft), Pushing on for a distance of 700 m (2,400 ft) to a new cenote called Shah Jahan, reached through a passageway more than 240 m (787 ft) long and of extraordinary size, they discovered a cavern loaded with the fossilized remains of shells, sea urchins and corals. This massive conduit clearly displays its geological past. There are boulders the size of houses and massive slabs of limestone. A superb dive not to be missed.

Diving the Cenotes

How to get There

Many of the most spectacular cenotes are located along the Tourist Corridor off Highway Mex 307 and along the Coba road to the west of the highway. Most are easily reached from local hotels. The most accessible are well signposted from the main highways.

A hired car is usually the best means of transporting dive equipment. Unless you have a qualification in cave-diving, you must be accompanied on a cenote dive by a qualified cave-diving expert who knows the cenotes you intend to dive.

In addition to the hotels, restaurants and other facilities and services listed on this page, many of those listed in the regional directory for The Mayan Riviera (see pages 137–139) may be relevant to anyone intending to dive in the cenotes.

Where to Stay

Akumal Cancún, km 104, Akumal, Tulum Corridor, Quintana Roo, Mexico 77710; tel (987) 22453. A beachfront hotel with a pool and a restaurant, full water sports facilities, and a cenote dive centre nearby.

Hotel Club Akumal Caribe, km104, Akumal, Tulum Corridor, Quintana Roo, Mexico 77710; tel (987) 59012; www.hotelakumalcaribe.com. A beachfront hotel with, 48 rooms, a pool, a restaurant and a cenote dive centre.

Las Casitas Akumal, Akumal, Tulum Corridor, Quintana Roo, Mexico 77710; tel (987) 22554/fax (987) 42371. Consists of 18 beachfront units. Water sports facilities and a cenote dive centre nearby.

Omni Club de Playa, km 98, Puerto Aventuras, Tulum Corridor, Quintana Roo, Mexico 77750; tel (987) 35101/fax (987) 35051. Exclusive club with pools and restaurants; all watersports catered for; set back from the beach.

Omni Puerto Aventuras, km 98, Puerto Aventuras, Tulum Corridor, Quintana Roo, Mexico 77750; tel (987) 35101/ fax (987) 35102; www.omnihotels.com. A modern hotel with 30 rooms near the marina. It has three connecting pools and three restaurants.

Villas Aventuras Akumal, km 104, Akumal, Tulum Corridor, Quintana Roo, Mexico 77710; tel/fax (987) 22804. A villa-style hotel with a cenote dive centre.

Villas Flamingo, Half Moon Bay, Akumal, Tulum Corridor, Quintana Roo, Mexico 77710; tel (800) 343 1440. Cabin-style hotel on the beach with pool and restaurant. Cenote dive centre nearby.

Where to Eat

Most cenotes are rather remote from the tourist resorts and you have to make an expedition to them, taking food and water. Local stores may not have the variety of the larger supermarkets in Cancún, but fruit and vegetables are generally fresh. The small local supermarkets are much cheaper than those in the tourist centres. Otherwise you will usually eat in the resort where you are staying. Most hotels offer a full package deal with meals included – and there is plenty of self-catering accommodation in the Akumal area.

Dive Facilities

Akumal Dive Centre, PO Box 714, Carretera Tulum km 104, Quintana Roo, Mexico 77750; tel/fax (987) 59025; email dive@akumaldivecentre.com.

Akumal Dive Shop, PO Box 1, Akumal, Playa del Carmen, Quintana Roo, Mexico 77710; tel (987) 41259/fax (988) 73164; www.akumal.com. One of the three leading cenote-diving centres along the Quintana Roo coast.

Aquanauts Dive Rite Tek Center, Local 2a Marina Puerto Aventuras km 269.5, Puerto Aventuras, Quintana Roo, Mexico 77750; tel/fax (987) 35280; email info@aquanauts-online.com.

CEDAM Dive Centres, PO Box 1, Puerto Aventuras, Quintana Roo, Mexico 77750; tel (987) 35147/fax (987) 35129; www.cedamdive.com. The leading specialist cenote-diving centre.

Dive Aventuras, PO Box 25, Aventuras Akumal 35, Tulum, Quintana Roo, Mexico 77780; tel/fax (987) 41271; email info@diveaventuras.com.mex.

Dos Ojos Hidden Worlds Cenotes, km 111, Tulum Corridor, Quintana Roo, Mexico 77710; tel (987) 44081; email info@hiddenworlds.com.mx. Specialists in cenote-diving.

Servi Scuba, Centro Comercial Marine, Loc.5A and 5B, Puerta Aventuras, Quintana Roo, Mexico 77750; tel (987) 35151/fax (987) 30901.

Tank-Ha Dive Centre, Avda 5 between 8 and 10, Playa del Carmen, Quintana Roo, Mexico 77710; tel (987) 30302; email tankha@playadelcarmen.com.

Yax-Há Dive Centre, Yax-Há, Tulum Corridor, Quintana Roo, Mexico 77710; tel (987) 22888.

Medical Services

Many of the cenotes are some distance from medical help, so you must consider your safety at all times. NEVER dive alone in the cenotes – you should always be accompanied by a dive guide from one of the specialist cenote-diving centres who knows the cenote. It is advisable to attend a cave-diving course first.

Recompression Chamber: tel (987) 20140/22387/21430.

Radio:
La Costera (Coastguard), Channel 16 (canal número dieciseis), **Belize Link**, San Pedro Airstrip; tel 026 2851, 2073.

DAN (Divers' Alert Network) tel (919) 648 -8111.

Life Flight, Houston, Texas, USA (for delivery to recompression chamber in the USA); tel (800) 392-4357/(713) 797-4357.

Air-Evac, San Diego, California, USA (for delivery to recompression chamber in the USA); tel (800) 854-2567/(619) 278-3822.

Doctor:
Dr Victor Macias Orozco, Calle 35 & Calle 2 Norte, Playa del Carmen, Tulum Corridor, Quintana Roo, Mexico 77780; tel (987) 30493.

Film Processing

Carmen, Tulum Corridor, Quintana Roo, Mexico 77810.
Photo Omega, Avenida 10 and Avenida Juárez, Playa del Carmen, Tulum Corridor, Quintana Roo, Mexico 77710; tel (987) 30031.

Cenote Diving Courses

The very specialized courses in cave and cavern-diving run by Mike Madden's **CEDAM Dive Centres**, Aquatech, and **The Akumal Dive Shop** consist of over 12 hours of lectures and a minimum of 14 cave dives using double tanks. Students develop a safe working knowledge of the cave environment and are briefed in: dive planning; air management and the use of oxygen; guidelines and reels; guideline techniques and protocol; equipment configuration; decompression theory and procedures; accident analysis; emergency procedures; stress management and other psychological aspects of diving; landowner relations; and team management. The courses cost about US$600.

The Discovery of Nohoch Nah Chich

There remain only a few areas of the earth to explore, but investigating the ocean depths remains as great a challenge to ingenuity and the desire to go where no one has been before as does the exploration of outer space. Beneath the apparently solid limestone floor of the Yucatán Peninsula lies a huge network of caves that have been submerged probably for thousands of years. Advanced diving techniques and equipment have made the penetration of these caves a possibility and have opened a new frontier for exploration.

Nohoch Nah Chich

One of the most exciting moments in the history of cave-diving and exploration came in late 1987, when a cave system was discovered in a cenote – an ancient well – 100 km (62 miles) south of Cancún near the ancient walled city of Tulum, about 2 km (1 1/4 miles) into the rainforest from the main highway.

On the recommendation of a local Maya friend, Mike Madden of CEDAM divers hiked into the rainforest to see a cenote someone had named 'The Big One'. Adjacent to a Maya ranch Mike found a depression, 240 m (800 ft) in diameter and 6 m (20 ft) deep, with huge cave entrances at its northern and southern ends. He carried only snorkelling equipment and a small diving light, but was able to swim into the cavern in clear water.

The following day Mike organized the first cave-diving expedition into the cave system now called Nohoch Nah Chich. Translated from Mayan, *nohoch* means 'huge', 'large' or 'giant' and *nah chich* means 'the birdhouse'. But words scarcely convey the vast scale of the gigantic, water-filled labyrinth that was waiting to be discovered. With the help of the rancher and an overburdened packhorse, Mike and his three colleagues next moved the tons of equipment they needed to explore the cave system into the rainforest so that they could begin their explorations.

On their first dive, they reeled out nearly 1 km (1.6 m) of line through exquisite, water-filled galleries of natural rock sculptures. They explored further than anyone had ventured in a single day. Day two was even better: their powerful diving lights illuminated endless passageways. These two days marked the beginning of an obsession that was to consume the team for years.

Underwater Wonders

The Nohoch cave system has been recorded since 1992 in *The Guinness Book of Records* as the world's longest underwater cave system, with more than 50 km (30 miles or 158,432 ft) of surveyed passageways. Nohoch Nah Chich is unique not only because of its size but also for the majestic rock formations that adorn the walls. Huge stalagmites, stalactites, flowstone and other speleological wonders rival even the best of the terrestrial air caves, such as the Carlsbad Caverns in New Mexico, USA and Postojnska Jama in former Yugoslavia. Cave-diving in Nohoch is like scuba-diving through kilometres of azure passages bejewelled with sparkling columns. Every so often you find another cenote – a window into the terrestrial world above.

Teamwork

The exploration has been carried out exclusively by the CEDAM cave diving team led by Mike Madden. Its divers, scientists and cartographers make an annual expedition to the caves to continue exploration and research. In 1995 they made a breakthrough of massive importance by connecting the cave system to the Caribbean Sea at Cenote del Manatee (Casa Cenote). They added a further 7 km (4 miles) to the known length of the system during their month-long exploration. Plans are now being made to explore the network further to discover how it connects with other cenotes in the region, which are dived regularly.

Each member of the CEDAM Team represents the best of what the word 'explorer' means. Each contributes expertise that helps to push the limits of discovery and to further document the dimension and understanding of this vast new frontier.

The Discovery of Nohoch Nah Chich

Above: *Lawson Wood and Mike Madden with a map of the Nohoch Nah Chich cave system.*
Below: *A diver exploring the fantastic underwater caverns of the Nohoch Nah Chich system.*

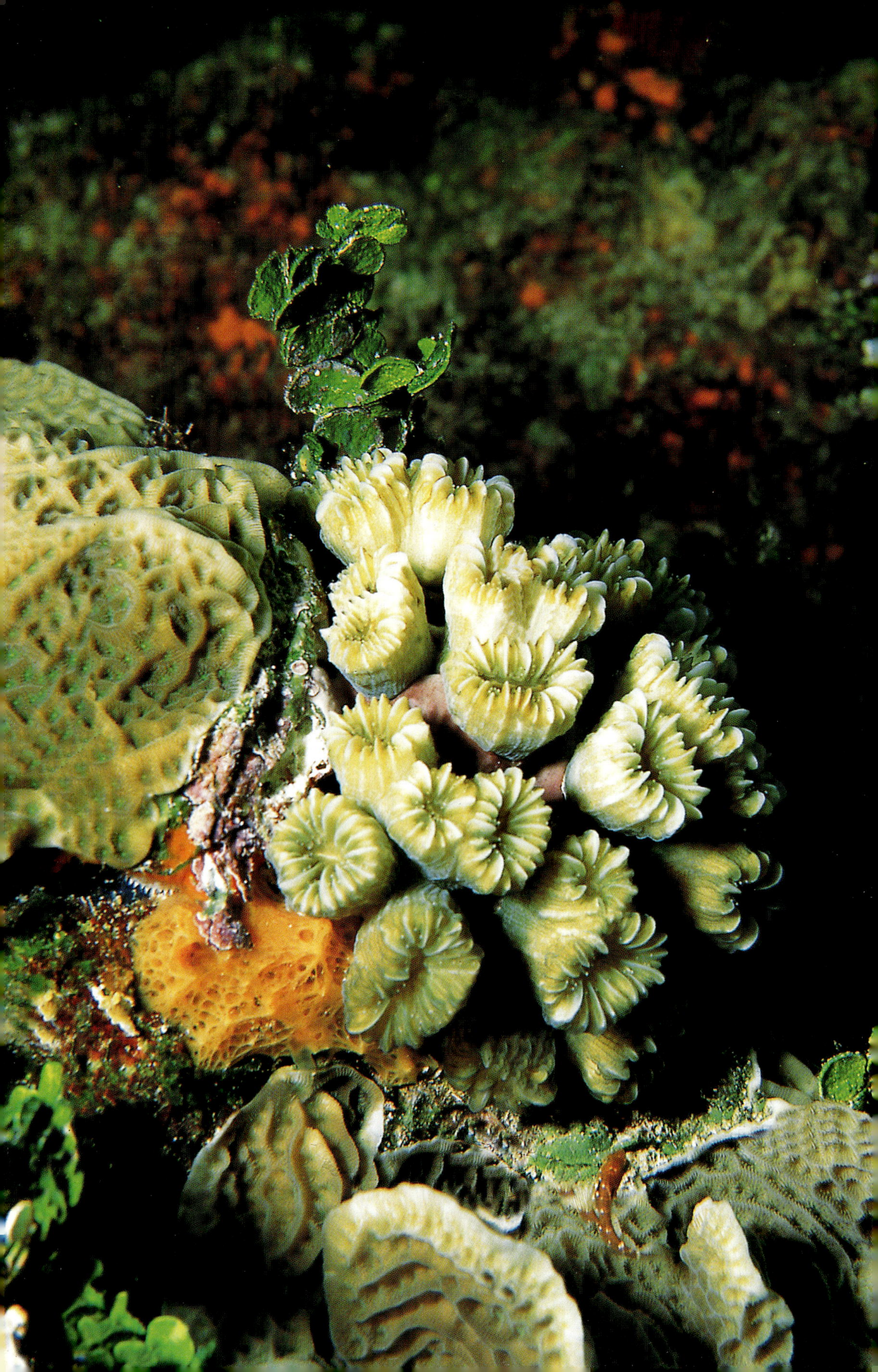

The Marine Environment

The coast of the Yucatán Peninsula is a vast limestone platform, riddled with cenotes (natural wells or sinkholes) leading to huge underground caverns and labyrinthine cave systems. The only rivers are those formed underground by rainwater runoff, which percolates down through the porous limestone into the cave systems and makes its way along them to the sea. Consequently, the coast and the offshore islands are surrounded by clear, clean water.

Much of the peninsula's long eastern coast is protected by shallow fringing reefs, but beyond them, about 32 km (20 miles) from shore, is the Great Maya Barrier Reef. Extending from Honduras in the south all along the coasts of Belize and of Quintana Roo state as far as Cancún in the north, it is the largest barrier reef in the northern hemisphere and the second largest in the world. The sheltered lagoon between the two reef systems is a major breeding area for many species of fish and invertebrates.

TYPES OF REEF
A **fringing reef** is the type of reef that occurs closest to the shoreline. It is usually fairly flat and sandy on top due to the constant battering it has received over the centuries from waves and exposure to the air – and, along the western Caribbean coast, by stormy weather and sometimes people. In this habitat you find an occasional knob of hard coral or a sea fan (fan-shaped coral). Turtle grass usually grows in the open, sandy areas in the reef.

These sandy areas often drop to an outer fringing reef on the other side of a lagoon, but they may also give way to a **barrier reef**, which is much larger. Barrier reefs are formed by corals such as elkhorn and staghorn. These reefs usually grow parallel to the coast.

Beyond where the sandy areas make a shallow drop there occurs a steeply inclined sand stage interspersed with large clumps of hard coral and sea fans. This formation is sometimes called a bommie, but it is more generally called a **patch reef**. The patch reef is where you usually find the highest proportion of marine life and most night-diving takes place in this environment.

These coral formations gradually take on the characteristics of a **spur and groove reef**. The spur is a finger of coral growth; the groove is a sand chute – a sand-filled channel formed by erosion caused by surge – in which hard corals have been unable to grow. Sand chutes start in the shallows and run into deep water. Both spur and chute may lead over the edge of the reef – called the wall or drop-off.

Spur and groove reefs are characteristic of this particular, exposed, region of the Caribbean Sea. They are formed by the action of waves, particularly during adverse weather conditions. They always run perpendicular to the shore, so if you are exploring this type of reef you will find it easy to make your way back into shallow water.

In the shallows, the reef systems merge into one and the wall may start very close to the shore. In deep water the spur and groove reef merges into the start of the reef wall or drop-off. Large coral heads or pinnacles form the top of the wall and mark where the reef plunges into the depths. The outer reef drop-offs are interspersed with canyons, gullies, tunnels, caves, chimneys, and sand chutes.

CORALS
Most of the reef is a thin crust of living organisms called polyps, which form corals. Coral polyps live within their rigid limestone skeletons; successive generations form new skeletons on top of those of their predecessors. The part of a reef you can see is, in fact, only its outer, most recent, layers. The reef has grown as the coral polyps have built new skeletons over the ancient skeletons of past organisms. The reef changes in shape and structure as the environment around it changes.

Corals come in many different shapes and sizes. The hard or stony corals are the major reef builders, and the largest of these is the great star coral *(Montastrea cavernosa)*. The boulder star coral *(Montastrea annularis)* has a more knobbly appearance. A colony can grow up to 3 m (10 ft). Brain corals, such as *Colpophyllia natans*, can grow up to 2 m (7 ft). Perhaps the species of brain coral that most closely resembles the convolutions of the human brain is *Diploria labyrinthiformis*. Sheet coral *(Agaricia grahamae)* is found on the outer edges of the wall, while lettuce coral *(Agaricia tenuifolia)* is more often found on the reef top.

Sea fans and sea plumes, a type of coral called a gorgonian, which is shaped rather like ostrich feathers – are also much in evidence in this region. There are many different species. Always take care when approaching these corals because they are very delicate and they bend and sway in the current, making it very easy for a diver to misjudge distance under water and perhaps bump into and damage them. Fan corals are home to a vast number of invertebrates (see page 161).

Opposite: *Flower coral* (Eusmilia fastigiata) *on a reef off the eastern Yucatán coast.*

A GUIDE TO THE COMMON FISH OF THE WESTERN CARIBBEAN

The waters along the Quintana Roo coast are among the clearest and least polluted in the world. Since the Yucatán Peninsula has no major terrestrial rivers and because, in this region, scarcely any sewage is pumped into the sea to pollute the waters and damage the reefs and the marine environment, there is relatively little sedimentation.

Cozumel and Cancún are famed for two species of toadfish represented in their waters: the brightly coloured splendid toadfish (*Sanopus splendidus*) and the large eye toadfish (*Batrachoides gilberti*); (see page 100) and for its angelfish, especially the queen angelfish (see pages 56–57), which, unusually, schools in small numbers in Bahía de Mujeres.

Other flamboyant and colourful inhabitants of the region's reefs are described on these pages. Several are poisonous, or may sting, bite or exhibit some other means of defence, so always take care and observe safety and buoyancy rules when you are diving on the reefs.

Blennies (family Clinidae, Blenniidae, Tripterygiidae)
Blennies live on coral heads in association with gobies. Most are bottom-dwellers living in cracks or holes which they defend vigorously. The sailfin blenny (*Emblemaria pandionis*), a comical-looking fish with a large, sail-like dorsal fin, lives in small burrows. The blackedge triplefin (*Enneanectes atrorus*) commonly lives on sponges. The diamond-backed blenny (*Malacoctenus boehlkei*) associates with the giant anemone (*Condylactis gigantea*).

Diamond-backed blenny *Malacoctenus boehlkei*

Butterflyfish (family Chaetodontidae)
Among the prettiest of the six species of brilliantly coloured butterflyfish in the waters off the Yucatán coast is the spotfin butterflyfish (*Chaetodon ocellatus*). It has a white body with a yellow trim and a black vertical band through the face and eye. The foureye butterflyfish (*Chaetodon capistratus*) is marked with dark thin lines and a darker bar through the eye, and a large pair of eyes 'painted' near the tail as a defensive device.

Foureye butterflyfish *Chaetodon capistratus*

Damselfish (family Pomacentridae)
The sergeant major (*Abudefduf saxatilis*, one of the most common species of damselfish, lives in upper water areas. It has five vertical black body bars and grows up to 17 cm (7 in) long. The yellowtail damselfish (*Microspathodon chrysurus*) is a small, oval fish with a dark body, iridescent blue spots along its back, and a yellow tail. Longfin damselfish (*Stegastes diencaeus*) go through amazing colour changes from juvenile to adulthood.

Longfin damselfish *Stegastes diencaeus*

Gobies (family Gobiidae)
Gobies are often found with blennies, but they colonize a wider variety of substrate, from corals to muddy bottoms. The pallid goby (*Coryphopterus eidolon*) inhabits sand and coral rubble, while the peppermint goby (*Coryphopterus lipernes*) usually perches on stony corals. Cleaning gobies (*Gobiosoma genie*) wait at 'cleaning stations' (see page 109) for fish to clean of parasites. The neon goby (*Gobiosoma oceanops*) is a similar species.

Neon goby *Gobiosoma oceanops*

THE MARINE ENVIRONMENT

Grouper (family Serranidae)
There are some 16 species in this family. The tiger grouper *(Mycteroperca tigris)* is one of the most common of those found off the Yucatán coast. It can grow up to 1 m (3 ft), but the jewfish, the largest of the family, grows up to 2 m (7 ft) long. It is now rare due to predation by humans over the centuries. A common small grouper is the coney *(Cephalopholis fulvus)*, which comes in colour variations from a dark reddish brown to a bright yellow.

Coney (golden phase) *Cephalopholis fulvus*

Grunts (family Haemulidae)
Grunts are commonly seen with their close relatives, the snappers, but they are much smaller and lack the snapper's sharp canine teeth. They emit an unusual grunting sound when the grinding noise made by their teeth deep within their throats is amplified by the air bladder. The white grunt *(Haemulon plumieri)* has blue stripes on its head. It stacks up on the outer edges of the reef with the white margate *(Haemulon album)*.

White grunt *Haemulon plumieri*

Jacks (family Carangidae)
Bar jacks *(Caranx ruber)* are very common on the sand flats among the compact coral heads. They are often in mating pairs, and, while one stays silvery blue the mate turns almost completely black and looks and acts like the other's shadow. They are seen feeding beside southern stingrays. Several species of jack, including the bar jack, will dart into schools of silverside minnows and pick off fish at random, apparently working together as a pack.

Bar jack *Caranx ruber*

Moray eels (Muraenidae)
Green morays *(Gymnothorax funebris)* are the largest eels in the western Caribbean, growing up to 2 m (7 ft). Spotted morays *(Gymnothorax moringa)*, only 60 cm (2 ft) long, are among the most common and are active predators by night. The goldentail moray *(Gymnothorax miliaris)* at under 60 cm (2 ft) in length, is the smallest moray in the region. Its head often protrudes from the reef. Morays open and close their mouths to aid respiration, which makes them look threatening.

Goldentail moray eel *Gymnothorax miliaris*

Parrotfish (family Scaridae)
The princess parrotfish *(Scarus taeniopterus)* supermale (which begins life as a female and later changes sex) grows only to 32 cm (13 in) and females and juveniles, which have distinctive dark stripes, to 10–18 cm (4–7 in). The stoplight parrotfish *(Sparisoma viride)* is larger – it undergoes several colour phases before reaching the supermale size of 60 cm (2 ft). Adult redband parrotfish *(Sparisoma aurofrenatum)* have a striking red ring round the eye and a red band from the eye to the gills.

Redband parrotfish *Sparisoma aurofrenatum*

Rays (order Rajiforms)
The electric or torpedo ray *(Torpedo nobiliana)*, up to 1.5 m (5 ft) long, and the much smaller, rare *Narcine brasiliensis* are the region's most dangerous rays. Two electrical organs in their rounded bodies deliver a 14–37 volt charge to stun prey. Yellow stingrays *(Urolophus jamaicensis)*, up to 50 cm (15 in) long, are common in the coastal shallows. Like southern stingrays *(Dasyatis americana)* they have a strong tail with a venomous spine near the end.

Yellow stingray *Urolophus jamaicensis*

Snappers (family Lutjanidae)
Snappers such as the schoolmaster *(Lutjanus apodus)* are often seen around the outcrops of elkhorn coral in the eastern Yucatán's coastal waters. The yellowtail snapper *(Ocyurus chrysurus)* is perhaps the most common member of the snapper family. These inquisitive fish often congregate in fairly large schools and are forever following divers about looking for tasty morsels, tending to get in the way of underwater photographers.

Yellowtail snapper *Ocyurus chrysurus*

Squirrelfish (family Holocentridae)
Squirrelfish are fairly common around the reef; several individuals congregate with blackbar soldierfish *(Myripristis jacobus)* in caves and recesses. Common squirrelfish *(Holocentrus ascensionis)* have white triangular markings on the tips of their dorsal spines and are reddish in colour with light silvery stripes running horizontally along the body. Bigeyes *(Priacanthus arenatus)*, close relatives, are usually a uniform dark red. They drift in small groups and are most commonly seen at night.

Common squirrelfish *Holocentrus ascensionis*

Surgeonfish (family Acanthuridae)
These fish tend to swim over all areas of the reef in loose congregations. They have a uniform body colour. There are several species in this family, and common to all is a sharp, scalpel-like appendage near the base of the body before the tail, which they use to great effect when defending their nesting areas by sweeping in fast and slicing with their tail. Surgeonfish feed on algae and are often seen in a head-down position.

Ocean surgeonfish *Acanthurus bahianus*

Wrasse (family Labridae)
One of the largest Caribbean species in the wrasse family is probably the pudding wife *(Halichoeres radiatus)*. It has greenish blue scrolls on its head and is blue to green overall, occasionally with a mid-white body bar. It grows up to 50 cm (18 in). Smaller species include the yellowhead wrasse *(Halichoeres garnoti)* and the bluehead wrasse *(Thalassoma bifasciatum)*. Both species undergo several colour changes before maturity.

Pudding wife *Halichoeres radiatus*

OTHER FISH TO LOOK OUT FOR

Barracuda
The great barracuda *(Sphyraena barracuda)* is the largest of the silvery predators on the reef. It can grow up to 1.8 m (6 ft) and, with its streamlined body and and sinister-looking jaws, it seems aggressive. However, these fish, though predators, rarely attack divers. They usually swim alone and may be found close to mooring buoys, lying in wait for prey in the shadow of a tied-up dive boat.

Blackcap basslet
The blackcap basslet *(Gramma melacara)* is only 7.5 cm (3 in) long, but its magenta and indigo colouring make it a real eye-catcher. These fish flit about around small recesses and near the mouths of smaller caves.

Creole fish
The creole fish *(Paranthias furcifer)* is black-faced with a blue body and a yellowish underside and tail. It is found on the deeper slopes off the wall. Creole fish inhabit large vase sponges and often drift in small shoals. They are found on parts of the reef where there are strong currents.

Eels
In addition to the moray eels (see page 157), two species of snake and conger eels are common in the region. Snake eels, which have a fin along the back, live under the sand by day and forage at night. Two species recorded in Caribbean waters – both very rare – are the sharptail eel *(Myrichthys breviceps)* and the goldspotted eel *(Myrichthys ocellatus)*. They have poor eyesight, so can be approached easily. The garden eel *(Heteroconger halis)* lives in vertical burrows in soft sand. Large numbers are seen picking off plankton drifting past, swaying in the current. They withdraw into their burrows long before you reach them.

Manta rays and eagle rays
The rays belong to several families. The manta ray *(Manta birostris)* is the largest of the five species of ray found in western Caribbean waters, with a wingspan up to 6 m (20 ft). It is often seen in the channel between Cozumel and the mainland. The spotted eagle ray *(Aetobatus narinari)*, with a wingspan up to 2.5 m (7 ft), is common further to the south. It digs in the sand with its pig-like snout for crustaceans and molluscs.

Goatfish
Long, whisker-like barbels give the goatfish its name. Using their barbels, groups of up to six yellow goatfish *(Mulloidichthys martinicus)* forage in the sand for worms and small crustaceans or molluscs. When they are not feeding they swim slowly over the reefs in large, colourful shoals.

Hamlets
These members of the sea bass family have several striking representatives in western Caribbean waters. The barred hamlet *(Hypoplectrus puella)*, the most common, is found as far away as Bermuda. The golden hamlet *(Hypoplectrus gummingatta)*, perhaps the brightest, has a golden body and curious blue and black cheek markings.

Hawkfish
Hawkfish perch on top of the corals and sea fans waiting for small animals to swim by. When approached they dart off a short distance and resume their stance. They are rather timid but if you can get close enough they make an excellent photographic subject. The redspotted hawkfish *(Amblycirrhites pinos)* is the only Caribbean species.

Hogfish
Hogfish belong to the same family as wrasse. They are constantly swimming and often follow feeding stingrays. The common hogfish *(Lachnolaimus maximus)* and the Spanish hogfish *(Bodianus rufus)* are represented in the western Caribbean. Common hogfish, which grow up to 1 m (3 ft) long, forage among the sand flats of the mid-reef. The Spanish hogfish is smaller and the forebody has a purple upper band which merges into a yellow-gold belly and tail. Larger adults develop a snout and the first three spines of the dorsal fin are long.

Jawfish
A curious fish found amid coral rubble, the jawfish *(Opistognathus aurifrons)* has a yellowish head and a pale body, and can be seen hovering above its burrow. The male incubates the eggs in its mouth.

Lizardfish
Lizardfish *(Synodus sp.)* have lizard-like heads with protruding eyes and rounded jaws. They can swim, but have no swim bladder, so sink to the bottom where they remain motionless, perfectly camouflaged against the coral rubble, waiting for prey. They closely resemble species found in the Pacific.

Peacock flounder
The peacock flounder *(Bothus lunatus)* is a flatfish, a sand-dweller related to the common flounder. It has dark blotches on the upper body and a large, plumelike adapted fin which it raises during its mating rituals. It is skittish, retreating into its burrows under coral rubble if a diver approaches.

Pufferfish
When threatened, a pufferfish inflates itself into a large sphere by sucking water into its abdomen, so that a predator cannot swallow it. Sharpnose puffers *(Canthigaster rostrata)* are seen on night

dives resting in sponges or on sea fans. Bandtail puffers *(Sphoeroides spengleri)* rest in shallow depressions in the sand. Their relatives, the porcupinefish and the boxfish, are quite common. The balloonfish *(Diodon holocanthus)* and the smooth trunkfish *(Lactophrys triqueter)* are comical-looking reef dwellers and are commonly seen. If these species are handled their skin may become diseased – and many are highly poisonous.

Sand tilefish
Sand tilefish *(Malacanthus plumieri)* are elongated white fish with a yellow, crescent-shaped tail. They are common on coral rubble areas of the inner reef and on eel grass beds. They build burrows and are often seen hovering over them in mid-water.

Saucereye porgy and Bermuda chub
The saucereye porgy *(Calamus calamus)* and the Bermuda chub *(Kyphosus sectatrix)* are both silvery fish. The porgy has a steeply sloping head with a blue crescent under the eye and yellow markings on the scales on its back. Bermuda chub are oval-shaped with dark fins and tail. The two species are not related, but they are both commonly seen together in fairly large schools travelling through or over the reef. They seem unafraid of divers.

Scorpionfish
Excellent camouflage ensures that these warty-looking fish are rarely seen. They change colour to match their background; but at night divers' torches pick up their brightly coloured pectoral fins as they swim off if disturbed. The plumed scorpionfish *(Scorpaena grandicornis)* is found in turtle grass and algae in sand flats. Scorpionfish unleash up to 12 venomous spines if touched.

Sharks
Sharks are uncommon in the western Caribbean. The most frequently seen is the nurse shark *(Ginglymostoma cirratum)*, distinguishable by its small mouth and the two barbels on the top of its lip. It is fairly docile unless disturbed. The Sleeping Shark Caves off Isla Mujeres (see page 62) is a well-known site where nurse sharks and bull sharks *(Carcharhinus leucas)* have been seen apparently sleeping.

Silversides
The smallest of the silvery fish most likely to attract a diver's attention are the silversides. These grow no larger than 8 cm (3 in). The common name describes several species, including anchovies (Atherinidae family), herring (Clupeidae family) and scad (Engraulidae family) and jacks (Carangidae family). Silversides are at their most vulnerable at the juvenile stage, when they form huge shoals among the gullies and caves of patch reefs.

Suckerfish
Look closely at any manta ray that swims past you in the channel between Cozumel and the mainland. It may have a couple of remora or suckerfish attached to its flanks by a vacuum suction pad on top of its head. The remora *(Echeneis naucrates)* hitches a ride on manta rays, sharks and turtles, and eats any scraps left behind by its host.

Trumpetfish and cornetfish
Trumpetfish *(Aulostomus maculatus)*, with their distinctive, trumpet-shaped mouth, and their close relatives, the cornetfish *(Fistularia tabacaria)*, are a fairly common sight around the reefs of this region. Trumpetfish can grow up to 1 m (3 ft) long. They exhibit many different colour variations, from yellow to a bright reds. The cornetfish grows up to 1.8 m (6 ft) and has a long tail filament and blue dashes or spots on the body.

A GUIDE TO THE COMMON INVERTEBRATES OF THE WESTERN CARIBBEAN

A very large proportion of the living creatures in the sea are invertebrates. The western Caribbean Sea is influenced by the Gulf Stream, which sweeps up the coast of the Yucatán and between the island of Cozumel and the mainland. As a result it has a very high proportion of all the invertebrate species found around the Americas. There are sponges, jellyfish, hydroids, anemones, corals, tube worms, flat worms, segmented worms, crustaceans, molluscs, echinoderms, bryozoans and tunicates. Their lives make up the stuff on which virtually everything else is dependent.

Invertebrates are so diverse, they have perhaps the most interest for the inquisitive diver and underwater photographer. Many are brightly coloured and some seem very comical in appearance, movements and activities. Altogether they are a delight to study.

Anemones (class Anthozoa)

The giant anemone *(Condylactis gigantea)*, with quite long tentacles tipped with a purple knob, is most common on the inner reefs of Cancún Bay. The corkscrew anemone *(Bartholomea annulata)* is usually found in shallower water among coral rubble, often in association with the red snapping shrimp.

Giant anemone *Condylactis gigantea*

Crabs (crustaceans)

The red reef hermit crab *(Paguristes cadenati)* is rather wary and retreats into its shell when divers appear. It grows only 2–3 cm (1 inch) long; the white speckled hermit crab *(Paguristes punticeps)* is much larger and can grow up to 12 cm (5 in). The arrow crab *(Stenorhynchus seticornis)* is common but most likely to be seen at night. Stareye hermit crabs *(Dardanus venosus)* are covered in minute bristles and some have lavender-coloured claws.

Stareye hermit crab *Dardanus venosus*

Nudibranchs (gastropods)

These molluscs, also called sea slugs, are brightly coloured and very attractive. They feed on a number of different animals and algae. The lettuce sea slug *(Tridachia crispata)* is difficult to find because it is usually camouflaged by surrounding algae. The painted elysia *(Elysia picta)* is common on algae growing over dead coralline limestone.

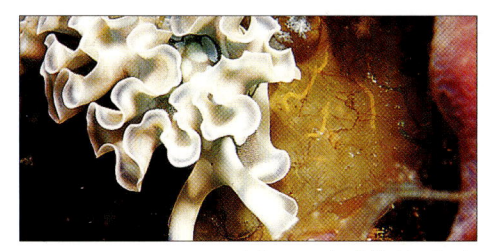

Lettuce sea slug *Tridachia crispata*

Snails (molluscs)

Snails form an extensive group within the large and diverse mollusc phylum. The group includes cowries, such as the Atlantic deer cowrie *(Cypraea cervus)*, which browses on algae at night; and the Atlantic grey cowrie *(Cypraea cinerea)*, which inhabits the undersides of ledges and overhangs; and the conches, of which the queen conch *(Strombus gigas)* is harvested by local populations (see pages 66–67).

Atlantic grey cowrie *Cypraea cinerea*

Sponges (phylum Porifera)
Several species of sponges are found in the western Caribbean, including the yellow tube sponge *(Aplysina fistularis)* and the pink vase sponge *(Niphates digitalis)*, and, on the deeper reefs off the wall, the rope sponges *(Aplysina cauliformis* and *Aplysina fulva)*. Perhaps the most dramatic is the giant barrel sponge *(Xestospongia muta)*, which grows up to 2 m (7 ft) high.

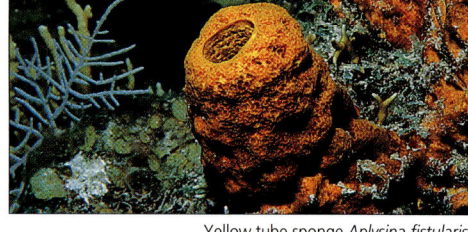

Yellow tube sponge *Aplysina fistularis*

Tube worms (family Serpulidae and Sabellidae)
The most colourful of the segmented or tube worms found in the western Caribbean are the social featherduster worm *(Bispira brunnea)* and the magnificent featherduster worm *(Sabellastarte magnifica)*. Both are abundant off Cancún, but *Sabellastarte* has been seen only once off Cozumel. The Christmas tree worm *(Spirobranchus giganteus)*, only 3 cm (1.5 in) high, comes in a multitude of different colours.

Social featherduster worm *Bispira brunnea*

OTHER INVERTEBRATES TO LOOK OUT FOR

Bearded fireworm
The exotic-looking bearded fireworm *(Hermodice carunculata)* can grow up to 15 cm (6 in). The fine hairs or bristles along its body can easily penetrate the skin and cause a painful skin irritation.

Jellyfish and hydroids
These are closely related to each other and to the anemones. The jellyfish is essentially a free-swimming stage of the hydroid. All species are armed with stinging cells with which they paralyze their prey. The moon jellyfish *(Aurelia aurita)* is found in every ocean of the world. The Portuguese man-of-war *(Physalia physalis)* has long tentacles which can trail over 10 m (33 ft). The featherlike plumes of the stinging hydroid *(Aglaophenia latecarinata)* can inflict a rather nasty sting.

Octopus, squid, sea stars and sea urchins
Many of these prowl the reefs at night – squid in particular seem to be fascinated by divers' lights and the food they attract. Crinoids or featherstars crawl on to the coral at nightfall and brittle stars curl round sea fans and whips. Basket stars extend their multi-jointed arms into the current and sea urchins vie for space amid sponges and corals.

Shells
Olives and ceriths are molluscs belonging to the snail group, which are found on all types of reef substrate, from sandy floors to corals. Perhaps one of the more brightly coloured of the Caribbean shells is the flamingo tongue *(Cyphoma gibbosum)*, which feeds on sea fans. It can be found in shallow reefs, particularly off Chankanaab Marine National Park in Cozumel. Its speckled mantle folds up round the body of the shell.

Shrimps
The banded coral shrimp *(Stenopus hispidus)* lives in all tropical oceans. It is small and colourful with long pincers. Divers are often attracted by its waving antennae. The peppermint shrimp *(Lysmata wurdemanni)* can be seen at night in and around a number of sponge species. The red night shrimp *(Rhynchocinetes rigens)* is usually glimpsed at night. It hides in the coral recesses, but its bright green reflective eyes are clearly visible.

Tunicates
These are sea squirts and they are fairly common. You are sure to see the tiny lightbulb tunicate *(Clavelina picta)*, which is found in clumps from a few to several hundred individuals, usually attached to gorgonian fan corals and black coral.

REEF DAMAGE AND CONSERVATION

The Island of Cozumel is an ancient coral reef situated on top of an extinct submarine volcano. Isla Mujeres and Isla Contoy are coral islands formed by the deposition of corals and sand over centuries– they began as submerged reefs. Coral reefs everywhere in the world are fragile, living communities made up of many thousands of individuals,. They are just one link in one of the earth's most complex ecosystems: the underwater environment. More than 1,000 species of animals and plants can be found in the near-shore waters of the Yucatán's east coast. Nearly all the animals are interdependent and so they survive only because of the very fragile balance that exists between them.

A FRAGILE ECOSYSTEM

The major inhabitants of a reef are corals and algae. These are in constant competition with each other. Marine algae are among the fastest-growing living things. By contrast, the average yearly growth of coral is incredibly small: brain coral grows about 1 cm (0.5 in) a year and elkhorn, the fastest-growing coral, grows up to 10 cm (4 in) in a year. If a coral is accidentally damaged, therefore, algae takes a very fast grip on the damaged area and can soon smother and kill the coral.

All corals are animals – they are a relative of the common anemone. Some varieties of coral, such as staghorn, are particularly fragile and you can easily break a piece off with a misplaced fin. The living tissue in all corals is found on and just below the surface. To destroy this outer layer, by accident or design, may kill the entire colony. Even putting your hand on the coral can remove its protective mucus and expose it to stress and damage.

Sea fans, sea plumes and sea whips look like plants but they are also animals. So are sponges, which look more robust than delicate corals, but are also fragile and easily harmed. Barrel sponges are a target for divers. Some of the larger species grow bigger than 2 m (7 ft), and divers sometimes climb inside them for fun. These organisms are very fragile and to climb inside one may kill it.

Most reef fish have slow growth rates, so if an area of coral, which is the marine habitat for fish and invertebrates, is damaged, the effect on the rest of the reef's population can be catastrophic. A small reduction in the coral community not only makes a reef look less inviting or pretty to the visiting diver but it also reduces the numbers of fish and other creatures, such as shrimp, lobster and octopus, living on it.

PROTECTING MARINE LIFE

All the marine life that inhabits the reef environment must be treated with sensitivity and empathy. In order not to cause damage, divers must always approach reefs carefully. And divers should always bear in mind that the reefs around Cozumel Island are a protected conservation zone. To be able to exercise control and avoid harming marine creatures it is imperative that divers know how to manage their buoyancy (see page 118).

Turtles are fascinating and graceful creatures. During the summer months they can be seen in large numbers along the lower coast between Tulum and Chetumal, where they are approaching their traditional nesting grounds. You must never try to hold on to them. If you find one sleeping at night, stay well clear, because to grab hold of it could give the creature such a shock that it may blunder into a cave and be drowned or seriously damage itself and the corals around it.

Pufferfish (see page 160) should also be left untouched. They have a natural defence mechanism, which involves sucking in water very rapidly until they become spherical, with their defensive spines jutting out. They look comical when inflated and they cannot swim properly, but that is no reason to try to touch them. Continual handling of these fish will remove the protective mucus membrane covering their skin. As a result, infection can set in and the fish will die.

Long-spined black sea urchins must also be treated cautiously. Some divers, keen to get good photographs, cut them up to feed other animals (see page 80). Apart from the danger of losing control and getting the spines embedded in soft parts of your flesh, it is illegal to do it. The urchins are important in controlling algae and they are only just beginning to recover after being almost wiped out by disease in the Caribbean in 1983.

UNDERWATER PHOTOGRAPHY

For those who want to record their dives more accurately than is possible in a logbook or a diary, underwater photography is the answer. During my early days of diving I could never completely remember every single detail of a dive or describe the intricacies of the colour markings on a species of fish in order to try to identify it properly. There were very few identification books available at the time. In the past 30 years however, all that has changed dramatically. The first amphibious camera for the mass market was designed in 1949 by Jean de Wouters d'Oplinter, a Belgian, and developed by a Frenchman, Jacques Yves Cousteau. The industry since has since developed specialized lenses, flashes and waterproof housings for the most advanced camera systems.

On my introduction to underwater photography I quickly discovered that not only did I have a recording tool but that I was able to bring the wonders of the underwater world to the attention of a much wider audience. My interest in underwater photography has never been the same since.

EQUIPMENT

For the beginner, perhaps the best way to start is with one of the instant disposable cameras. They are inexpensive and you will be able to get instant results. Most of these cameras are only good for about 2 m (6 ft) of depth, and others are useful to about 8 m (30 ft), but you can rent a waterproof box that allows you to use the camera down to 30 m (100 ft). In Cancún, disposable underwater cameras are sold from auto-dispensers on many beaches.

To take photographs under water you must think beyond using just the camera of your choice. You must be certain that as your ability progresses, your camera can evolve into an operational system, compatible with as wide a variety of equipment as possible. This will include the camera, a choice of lenses, a flash, and a device to connect it to the camera. If you are unsure of which system to buy, perhaps you should hire an outfit from one of the two main photo retailers in Cozumel or Cancún, and perhaps attend an instruction course to acquaint yourself with the intricacies and pitfalls of each type of camera system.

When choosing equipment, submersible waterproof housings are always an option for your land camera, bearing in mind that you already know how your camera works. They can be bulky but they are strong and reliable and work out cheaper than the Nikonos RS-AF. Lighting is always with a waterproof flash of some type and most are compatible with a very wide range of cameras and housings. Again, a specialist photographic shop will supply the necessary advice.

No matter which type of system you plan to choose – the amphibious type, such as the Nikonos or Sea & Sea system, or a housed land SLR camera in a waterproof box – you must always treat it with the greatest respect and care. Before any trip, you must ensure that all the connections are clean and that all 'O' rings are free of dust and are given a fresh light coat of silicone grease. Also check for any nicks or cuts in the seals. Ensure that the flash fires correctly with the camera shutter and that you have sufficient power to operate it. If you have a rechargeable flash, make certain that the recharger works and that it is compatible with the electrical supply in the area.

Film stock used is generally slide or transparency variety, with film speeds of between 50 and 100 ISO. This allows for better quality of sharpness and colour reproduction. For the more instant type of camera, print film is more usually used to produce those instant 'happy snappies' of your holidays and this film speed is around 200–400 ISO.

35MM FORMAT

This is by far the most popular type of photography for perspective photographs of the deeper canyons and gullies off Palancar and Santa Rosa on Cozumel. To see a diver surrounded by huge sponges against a deep blue background gives you a feel for the vista you are shooting. Wide-angle photographs are the type most often published by magazines; and, if you were to ask any number of professional underwater photographers what their preferred lens would be if they could have only one, they would chose a wide-angle lens.

Macro photography is a specialized form of underwater photography in which the camera lens is positioned very close to a subject to record a relatively large image on the film and produce an image

---

WIDE-ANGLE LENS SHOTS

This format is most suitable for:
- cliff and reef drop-off panoramas
- exteriors of shipwrecks
- interiors of shipwrecks and caves
- divers in action
- divers and fish/animal interaction
- wide-angle flash and flash-fill techniques
- large fish
- close focus attention
- available light and silhouettes.

Macro Photography

The benefits of this format are:
- a different perspective
- high magnification
- maximum colour saturation
- sharp focus
- ease of learning and execution
- can be done anywhere, under almost any conditions
- easiest form of photography to use on night dives
- greatest return for the least investment.

of high magnification of the subject. I personally recommend that you start underwater photography with a macro system because it is undoubtedly the easiest form of underwater photography. Frustrations common to many other types of photography are minimized and very soon you will be amazed by the sharp images and vibrant colours that only macro photography produces.

The different perspective macro photography gives opens up a whole new world of tiny animals and plants not normally seen during average diving conditions. Your eyes get trained very quickly to find creatures small enough to fit into the format you are using. What once seemed boring dives on gravel beds or sandy bottoms or under jetties now suddenly reveal a wealth of life.

You can seem to become an expert overnight, but the pursuit of underwater images is a life-long experience. You can achieve very good pictures very quickly and steadily improve your techniques as you learn about composition.

Before embarking on this new underwater adventure with a camera, it is recommended that you attend an underwater photography workshop. Several centres specialize in this type of instruction. Classes are scheduled through the year. Even non-photographer 'buddies' will benefit from them because modelling, composition and buoyancy are very important.

Three Useful Tips

1. Buy all the film you think you will need before you leave. If you have to buy it locally, go to a hotel or a store where it will have been stored in cool conditions. Keep it refrigerated and give it time to defrost (about two hours) before using it.
2. Do not leave your underwater camera exposed to direct sun light as the lens or inside of the housing's port will mist up when you take the camera into the water, which will be cooler.
3. If you assemble or store your underwater camera in an air-conditioned room, condensation will make it mist up when you take it into the hot outdoor environment. You will have to wait for ten minutes or more before the condensation will dissipate and you can take clear photographs again.

The Beginner's Guide To Taking Successful Underwater Photographs

1. Approach one photographic technique or problem at a time. Do not try to do everything at once.
2. Record the technical details of each photograph as you take it to find out which settings (aperture, speed, distance, etc.) get the best results.
3. Keep your flash or strobe well away from the camera (unless you are working in a macro situation). Position it to the top left of the camera so that the light beam makes an angle of 45° along the camera-to-subject axis.
4. Pre-aim your flash out of the water at first to obtain the correct counter for the effects of light refraction.
5. Find the aperture that produces the most consistent results for you. Next time you take photographs at that setting, take an extra photograph, one either side of that aperture (one stop lower and one stop higher). This is called 'bracketing'; it will take care of subjects reflecting different degrees of brightness.
6. Get as close as you can to your subject. Close-ups have the most impact and better colour saturation.
7. Note the position of the sun when you enter the water. Use the sun to create back-lit shots to add depth and interest.
8. Never take a picture below you; always shoot horizontally or upward.
9. Pre-set your focus and allow the subject and you to approach each other gently and sympathetically.
10. Take photographs in clear water and bright sunlight if you can.
11. Never use the flash when the camera-to-subject distance is greater than one-fifth of the underwater visibility. If the visibility is 5 m (17 ft), focus and use the flash at only 1 m (3 ft). This will cut down the reflection or back-scatter of particles in suspension in the water.
12. Set your camera to the fastest aperture that the flash will synchronize to (unless you are using an automatic housed system).
13. Attend an underwater photography instruction course.
14. Be ruthless. Really, the only way you learn is by self-criticism: put as much film through the camera as possible and learn from your mistakes.

UNDERWATER VIDEO

Choosing the correct video system is always a problem because it is extremely difficult to keep up with progress in the technology of underwater video. Almost all the videos on the market were originally designed for the terrestrial holiday market and some have had waterproof housings of various degrees of sophistication developed around them. Housings come in a variety of styles and sizes. All will have waterproof controls to allow you to use all your camera's functions, but some are rather awkward to handle, especially with lights attached. It is best to choose a system for which the manufacturer offers a good-quality housing, such as Sony. Very many housing manufacturers have built their business around videos made by Sony, Panasonic and other well-known manufacturers. These are readily available by mail order from most diving-related magazines.

CAMERA

While video cameras have decreased in size, the quality of the image has improved by leaps and bounds. Cameras are becoming smaller and lighter with no loss of quality whatsoever. The image produced is now of broadcast quality and there is an even chance that if you were in the right place at the right time to record some spectacular underwater event, it could be used in that evening's television news. Modern systems are so lightweight that this can cause a problem: with hand-held shots, you may get camera shake. Whenever possible, for close-up work or a study of marine life, use a tripod, even underwater.

A great advantage of video is that there is no waste. You can reuse the tape at any time. The greatest problem you are likely to encounter is with the use of the rechargeable power packs. Always change each pack before you dive and always be certain that you have enough power to catch that magic moment.

LIGHTING

Lighting systems have also undergone a revolution over the last few years. Many of the lights fixed on the video housing weigh very little and the bulky and heavy battery pack is extended to a clamp which attaches it to your diving air tank. On a number of housings the battery pack is held in a sling under the housing and this helps to stabilize the system.

SHOOTING SEQUENCES

Try to plan shooting sequences before entering the water and stick to that plan as best you can. Of course, there is always the chance that something totally unexpected can happen and you have to be ready for all eventualities. Avoid diving with inexperienced divers or trainees, as they will inevitably get in the way. Train your buddy to help you.

Try not to prolong the sequence you are filming; too long a sequence is boring and more difficult to edit. Keep the direction of movement of divers constant and whenever possible have the divers and fish swimming toward the camera. It is a good idea for your diving buddy or model to swim to the other side of the reef and then swim toward you. As he or she approaches, the fish in front of the person will automatically find themselves also swimming toward you, making a more interesting shot. Take cut-away shots. These are small vignettes of diver portraits, fish behaviour, close-ups of anemone tentacles, and so on.

EDITING

Editing a video is fun, but it is also incredibly frustrating, as you have to be ruthless with your choice of clips. The difficulty is not what to leave in, but rather what to take out. Your audience will soon get bored if the video is too long and the subject matter does not change. Look at wildlife films on television and try to emulate them. Studying these films is as good a way as any for learning technique. Your video will also be greatly enhanced by the addition of sound and a commentary. Again, try not to get too technical or boring and perhaps use someone else's voice instead of your own – you could ask an amateur actor to do a voice-over to add a touch of professionalism.

THE MOVING IMAGE

Stills photography is all very well in recording a moment in the life of a marine subject. But when you are faced with swimming through a hole in the wall surrounded by millions of silversides, video is what you need. People are transfixed by the moving image and nothing tells this story of the Earth's marine wonders better than video. Several of the dive stores have underwater video equipment for hire and you will soon be able to see for yourself exactly which system you prefer. The only drawback if you decide to buy one is that the format is changing constantly and your state-of-the-art video and housing may soon be obsolete.

Health and Safety for Divers

The information on first aid and safety in this part of the book is intended as a guide only. It is based on currently accepted health and safety guidelines, but it is merely a summary and is no substitute for a comprehensive manual on the subject – or, even better, for first aid training. We strongly advise you to buy a recognized manual on diving safety and medicine before setting off on a diving trip, to read it through during the journey, and to carry it with you to refer to during the trip. It would also be sensible to take a short course in first aid.

We urge anyone who reads these pages for advice on emergency treatment to see a doctor as soon as possible.

WHAT TO DO IN AN EMERGENCY

- Divers who have suffered any injury or symptom of an injury, no matter how minor, related to diving, should consult a doctor, preferably a specialist in diving medicine, as soon as possible after the symptom or injury occurs.
- No matter how confident you are in making a diagnosis, remember that you are an amateur diver and an unqualified medical practitioner.
- If you are the victim of a diving injury do not let fear of ridicule prevent you from revealing your symptoms. Apparently minor symptoms can mask or even develop into a life-threatening illness. It is better to be honest with yourself and live to dive another day.
- Always err on the conservative side when treating an illness or an injury, if you find that the condition is only minor you – and the doctor – will both be relieved.

FIRST AID
The basic principles of first aid are to:
- do no harm
- sustain life
- prevent deterioration
- promote recovery.

If you have to treat an ill or injured person:
- First try to secure the safety of yourself and the ill or injured person by getting the two of you out of the threatening environment: the water.
- Think before you act: do not do anything that will further endanger either of you.
- Then follow a simple sequence of patient assessment and management:
  1. Assess whether you are dealing with a life-threatening condition.
  2. If so try to define which one.
  3. Then try to manage the condition.

Assessing the ABCs:
Learn the basic checks – the ABCs:
A: for AIRWAY (with care of the neck)
B: for BREATHING
C: for CIRCULATION
D: for DECREASED level of consciousness
E: for EXPOSURE (a patient must be exposed enough for a proper examination to be made).

- **Airway (with attention to the neck):** check whether the patient has a neck injury. Are the mouth and nose free from obstruction? Noisy breathing is a sign of airway obstruction.

- **Breathing:** look at the chest to see if it is rising and falling. Listen for air movement at the nose and mouth. Feel for the movement of air against your cheek.

- **Circulation:** feel for a pulse (the carotid artery) next to the windpipe.

- **Decreased level of consciousness:** does the patient respond in any of the following ways?
  A - Awake, Aware, Spontaneous speech.
  V - Verbal Stimuli: does he or she answer to 'Wake up?'
  P - Painful Stimuli: does he or she respond to a pinch?
  U - Unresponsive.

- **Exposure:** preserve the dignity of the patient as much as you can, but remove clothes as necessary to carry out your treatment.

Now, send for help
If, after your assessment, you think the condition of the patient is serious, you must send or call for help from the nearest emergency services (ambulance, paramedics). Tell whoever you send for help to come back and let you know whether help is on the way.

Recovery position
If the patient is unconscious but breathing normally there is a risk that he or she may vomit and choke on the vomit. It is therefore critical that the patient be turned on one side with arms outstretched in front of the body. This is called the recovery position and it is illustrated in all first aid manuals.

If you suspect injury to the spine or neck, immobilize the patient in a straight line before you turn him or her on one side.

If the patient is unconscious, does not seem to be breathing, and you cannot feel a pulse, do not try to turn him or her into the recovery position.

If you cannot feel a pulse
If your patient has no pulse you will have to carry out CPR (CardioPulmonary Resuscitation). This consists of techniques to:

- ventilate the patient's lungs (expired air resuscitation).
- pump the patient's heart (external cardiac compression).

CPR (Cardiopulmonary Resuscitation)

Airway
Open the patient's airway by gently extending the head (head tilt) and lifting the chin with two fingers (chin lift). This lifts the patient's tongue away from the back of the throat and opens the airway. If the patient is unconscious and you think something may be blocking the airway, sweep your finger across the back of the tongue from one side to the other. If you find anything, remove it. Do not try this if the patient is conscious or semi-conscious because he or she may bite your finger or vomit.

Breathing:EAR (Expired Air Resuscitation)
If the patient is not breathing you need to give the 'kiss off life', or expired air resuscitation (EAR) – you breathe into his or her lungs. The 16 per cent of oxygen in the air you expire is enough to keep your patient alive:
1. Pinch the patient's nose to close the nostrils.
2. Place your open mouth fully over the patient's mouth, making as good a seal as possible.
3. Exhale into the patient's mouth hard enough to make the chest rise and fall. Give two long slow breaths.
4. If the patient's chest fails to rise, try adjusting the position of the airway.
5. Check the patient's pulse. If you cannot feel one, follow the instructions under 'Circulation' below. If you can, continue breathing for the patient once every five seconds, checking the pulse after every ten breaths.
- If the patient begins breathing, turn him or her into the recovery position (see page 167).

Circulation
If, after giving expired air resuscitation you cannot feel a pulse, you should try external cardiac compression:
1. Kneel next to the patient's chest.
2. Measure two finger breadths above the notch where the ribs meet the lower end of the breast bone.
3. Place the heel of your left hand just above your two fingers in the centre of the breast bone.
4. Place the heel of your right hand on your left hand.
5. Straighten your elbows.
6. Place your shoulders perpendicularly above the patient's breast bone.
7. Compress the breast bone 4–5 cm (1½–2 in) to a rhythm of 'one, two, three ...'
8. Carry out 15 compressions.

Continue giving cycles of 2 breaths and 15 compressions checking for a pulse after every 5 cycles. The aim of CPR is to keep the patient alive until paramedics or a doctor arrive with the necessary equipment.

Check before you dive that you and your buddy are both trained in CPR. If not, get some training – it could mean the difference between life and death for either of you or for someone else.

DIVING DISEASES AND ILLNESSES

Acute decompression illness
Acute decompression illness is any illness arising from the decompression of a diver – in other words, by the diver moving from an area of high ambient pressure to an area of low pressure. There are two types of acute decompression illness:
- decompression sickness (the 'bends')
- barotrauma with arterial gas embolism.

It is not important for the diver or first aider to be able to differentiate between the two conditions because both are serious, life-threatening illnesses, and both require the same emergency treatment. The important thing is to be able to recognize acute decompression illness and to initiate emergency treatment. The box below outlines the signs and symptoms to look out for.

ROUGH AND READY NONSPECIALIST TESTS FOR THE BENDS

If you suspect a diver may be suffering from the bends, carry out these tests. If the results of your checks do not seem normal, the diver may be suffering from the bends and you must take emergency action (see page 169). Take the appropriate action outlined on page 169 even if you are not sure of your assessment – the bends is a life-threatening illness

1. Does the diver know:
   who he/she is?
   where he/she is?
   what the time is?
2. Can the diver see and count the number of fingers you hold up? Hold your hand 50 cm (20 in) in front of the diver's face and ask him/her to follow your hand with his/her eyes as you move it from side to side and up and down. Be sure that both eyes follow in each direction, and look out for any rapid oscillation or jerky movements of the eyeballs.
3. Ask the diver to smile, and check that both sides of the face have the same expression. Run the back of a finger across each side of the diver's forehead, cheeks and chin, and ask whether he/she can feel it.
4. Check that the diver can hear you whisper when his/her eyes are closed.
5. Ask the diver to shrug his/her shoulders. Both should move equally.
6. Ask the diver to swallow. Check that the adam's apple moves up and down.
7. Ask the diver to stick out his/her tongue at the centre of the mouth – deviation to either side indicates a problem.
8. Check the diver has equal muscle strength on both sides of the body. You do this by pulling/pushing each of the diver's arms and legs away from and back toward the body, asking him/her to resist you.
9. Run your finger lightly across the diver's shoulders, down the back, across the chest and abdomen, and along the arms and legs, feeling upper and underside surfaces. Check that the diver can feel your finger moving along each surface.
10. On firm ground (not on a boat) check that the diver can walk in a straight line and, with eyes closed, stand upright with feet together and arms outstretched.

The bends (decompression sickness)

Decompression sickness or 'the bends' occurs when a diver has not been adequately decompressed. Exposure to higher ambient pressure under water causes nitrogen to dissolve in increasing amounts in the body tissues. If this pressure is released gradually during correct and adequate decompression procedures, the nitrogen escapes naturally into the blood and is exhaled through the lungs. If the release of pressure is too rapid, the nitrogen cannot escape quickly enough and bubbles of nitrogen gas form in the tissues. The symptoms and signs of the disease are related to the tissues in which the bubbles form and it is described by the tissues affected – joint bend, for example.

Symptoms and signs include:
- nausea and vomiting
- dizziness
- malaise
- weakness
- pains in the joints
- paralysis
- numbness
- itching of skin
- incontinence.

Barotrauma with arterial gas embolism

Barotrauma is the damage that occurs when the tissue surrounding a gaseous space is injured followed a change in the volume of air in that space. An arterial gas embolism is a gas bubble that moves in a blood vessel; this usually leads to the obstruction of that blood vessel or a vessel further downstream.

Barotrauma can occur in any tissue surrounding a gas-filled space. Common sites and types of barotrauma are:
- the ears (middle ear squeeze) • burst/ear drum
- the sinuses (sinus squeeze) • sinus pain • nose bleeds
- the lungs (lung squeeze) • burst lung
- the face (mask squeeze) • swollen, bloodshot eyes
- the teeth (tooth squeeze) • toothache

Burst lung is the most serious of these since it can result in arterial gas embolism. It occurs following a rapid ascent during which the diver does not exhale adequately. The rising pressure of expanding air in the lungs bursts the delicate alveoli – air sacs in the lungs – and forces air into the blood vessels that carry blood back to the heart and, ultimately, the brain. In the brain these air bubbles block blood vessels and obstruct the supply of blood and oxygen to the brain. This causes brain damage.

The symptoms and signs of lung barotrauma and arterial gas embolism include:
- shortness of breath
- chest pain
- unconsciousness.

Treatment of acute decompression Illness:
- ABCs and CPR (see pages 167–68) as necessary
- position the patient in the recovery position (see page 167) with no tilt or raising of the legs
- give 100 per cent oxygen by mask or demand valve
- keep the patient warm
- remove to the nearest hospital as soon a possible. The hospital or emergency services will arrange for recompression treatment.

Carbon dioxide or monoxide poisoning

Carbon dioxide poisoning can occur as a result of skip breathing (diver holds breath on SCUBA); heavy exercise on SCUBA or malfunctioning rebreather systems. Carbon monoxide poisoning occurs as a result of: exhaust gases being pumped into cylinders; hookah systems; air intake too close to exhaust fumes.

Symptoms and signs of carbon monoxide poisoning:
- blue colour of the skin
- shortness of breath
- loss of consciousness.

Treatment of carbon monoxide poisoning:
- get the patient to a safe environment
- ABCs and CPR (see pages 167–68) as necessary
- 100 per cent oxygen through a mask or demand valve
- get the patient to hospital.

Head injury

Any head injury should be treated as serious.

Treatment of a head injury:
- the diver must surface and do no more diving until a doctor has been consulted
- disinfect the wound
- if the diver is unconscious, contact the emergency services
- if breathing and/or pulse has stopped, administer CPR (see page 168)
- if the diver is breathing and has a pulse, check for bleeding and other injuries, and treat for shock
- if the wounds permit, put the injured person into the recovery position and, if possible, give 100 per cent oxygen
- keep the patient warm and comfortable and monitor pulse and respiration constantly.

DO NOT give fluids to unconscious or semi-conscious divers.

Hyperthermia (raised body temperature)

A rise in body temperature results form a combination of overheating, normally due to exercise, and inadequate fluid intake. A person with hyperthermia will progress through heat exhaustion to heat stroke with will eventually collapse. Heat stroke is an emergency: if the diver is not cooled and rehydrated he or she will die.

Treatment of hyperthermia:
- move the diver as quickly as possible into a cooler place and remove all clothes
- call the emergency services

- sponge the diver's body with a damp cloth and fan him or her manually or with an electric fan.
- if the patient is unconscious, put him or her into the recovery position (see page 167) and monitor the ABCs (see pages 167–68) as necessary
- if the patient is conscious you can give him or her a cold drink

Hypothermia

Normal internal body temperature is just under 37°C (98.4°F). If for any reason it falls much below this – usually, in diving, because of inadequate protective clothing – progressively more serious symptoms may follow and the person will eventually die if the condition is not treated rapidly. A drop of 1°C (2°F) causes shivering and discomfort. A 2°C (3°F) drop induces the body's self-heating mechanisms to react: blood flow to the hands and feet is reduced and shivering becomes extreme. A 3°C (5°F) drop results in memory loss, confusion, disorientation, irregular heartbeat and breathing,.and eventually to death.

Treatment of hypothermia:
- move the diver as quickly as possible into a sheltered and warm place; or:
- prevent further heat loss: use an exposure bag; surround the diver with buddies' bodies; cover his or her head and neck with a woolly hat, warm towels or anything else suitable
- if you have managed to get the diver into sheltered warmth, remove wet clothing, dress your patient in warm, dry clothing and wrap him or her in an exposure bag or heat blanket. If you are still in the open, the diver is best left in existing garments
- if the diver is conscious and coherent administer a warm shower or bath and a warm, sweet drink
- if the diver is unconscious, check the ABCs (see page 167), call the emergency services, make the patient as warm as possible, and treat for shock (see below).

Near-drowning

Near-drowning is a medical condition in which a diver has inhaled some water – water in the lungs interferes with the normal transport of oxygen from the lungs into the bloodstream. A person in a near-drowning condition may be conscious or unconscious.

Near-drowning victims sometimes develop secondary drowning, a condition in which fluid oozes into the lungs causing the diver to drown in internal secretions, so all near-drowning patients must be monitored in a hospital.

Treatment of near-drowning:
- get the diver out of the water and check the ABCs (see page 167). Depending on your findings, begin EAR or CPR (see page 168) as appropriate
- if possible, administer oxygen by mask or demand valve
- call the emergency services and get the diver to a hospital for observation, even if he/she appears to have recovered from the experience.

Nitrogen narcosis

Air consists of about 80 per cent nitrogen. Breathing the standard diving mixture under compression can lead to symptoms very much like those of drunkenness (nitrogen narcosis is popularly known as 'rapture of the deep'). Some divers experience nitrogen narcosis at depths of 30–40 m (100–130 ft). Down to a depth of about 60 m (200 ft) – which is beyond the legal maximum depth for sport-diving in the UK and the USA – the symptoms are not always serious; but below about 80 m (260 ft) a diver is likely to lose consciousness. Symptoms can occur very suddenly. Nitrogen narcosis is not a serious condition, but a diver suffering from it may do something dangerous.

Treatment of nitrogen narcosis: the only treatment for this condition is to get the diver to ascend immediately to shallower waters.

Shock

Shock is a medical condition and not just the emotional trauma of a frightening experience. Medical shock results from poor blood and oxygen delivery to the tissues. As a result of oxygen and blood deprivation the tissues cannot carry out their functions. There are many causes; the most common is loss of blood.

Treatment for medical shock:
This is directed at restoring blood and oxygen delivery to the tissues:
- check the ABCs (see page 167)
- give 100 per cent oxygen
- control any external bleeding by pressing hard on the wound and/or pressure points (the location of the pressure points is illustrated in first-aid manuals). Raise the injured limb or other part of the body
- use a tourniquet only as a last resort and only on the arms and legs
- if the diver is conscious, lay him/her on the back with the legs raised and the head to one side; if unconscious, turn him or her on the left side in the recovery position (see page 167).

TRAVELLING MEDICINE

Many doctors decline to issue drugs, particularly antibiotics, to people who want them 'just in case'; but a diving holiday can be ruined by an ear or sinus infection, especially in a remote area or on a live-aboard boat, where the nearest doctor or pharmacy is a long and difficult journey away.

Many travelling divers therefore carry with them medical kits that could lead the uninitiated to think they are hypochondriacs. Nasal sprays, ear drops, antihistamine creams, anti-diarrhoea medicines, antibiotics, sea-sickness remedies ... Forearmed, such divers can take immediate action as soon as they realize something is wrong. At the very least, this may minimize their loss of diving time.

Always bear in mind that most decongestants and remedies for sea-sickness can make you drowsy and therefore should NEVER be taken before diving.

MARINE-RELATED AILMENTS

Sunburn, coral cuts, fire-coral stings, swimmers' ear, sea sickness and bites from various insects are perhaps the most common divers' complaints – but there are more serious, marine-related illnesses you should know about.

Cuts and abrasions

Divers should wear appropriate abrasive protection for the undersea environment. Hands, knees, elbows and feet are the areas most commonly affected. The danger with abrasions is that they become infected, so all wounds must be thoroughly washed and rinsed with water and an antiseptic as soon as possible after the injury. Infection may progress to a stage where antibiotics are necessary. If the site of an apparently minor injury becomes inflamed, and the inflammation spreads, consult a doctor immediately – you may need antibiotics to prevent the infection spreading to the bloodstream.

Swimmer's ear

Swimmer's ear is an infection of the external ear canal caused by constantly wet ears. The condition is often a combined fungal and bacterial infection. To prevent it, always dry your ears thoroughly after diving. If you know you are susceptible to the condition, insert alcohol drops after diving. If an infection occurs, the best treatment is to stop diving or swimming for a few days and apply ear drops such as:

- 5 per cent acetic acid in isopropyl alcohol; *or*
- aluminium acetate/acetic acid solution.

Sea or motion sickness

Motion sickness can be an annoying complication on a diving holiday involving boat dives. If you suffer from motion sickness, discuss the problem with a doctor before your holiday – or at least before boarding the boat. But bear in mind that many medicines formulated to prevent travel sickness contain antihistamines, which make you drowsy and will impair your ability to think quickly while you are diving.

Tropical diseases

Visit the doctor before your trip and make sure you have the appropriate vaccinations for Mexico and for any other countries you intend to visit on your trip.

Biting Insects

Some areas of the Mexico's eastern coasts are notorious for biting insects. Take a good insect repellent on your diving grips, and some antihistamine cream to relieve the effects of insect bites and stings.

Fish that bite
- **Barracudas**
  Barracudas very rarely bite divers, although they have been known to bite in turbid or murky, shallow water, where sunlight flashing on a knife blade, a camera lens or jewellery has confused the fish into thinking they are attacking their normal prey.

> **SUNBURN**
>
> Each year thousands of tourists visit Mexico intending to return home with a suntan. However, many get sunburned on their first day and spend a very sore and uncomfortable few days recovering, thus ruining their holiday. It is recommended that you gradually increase your exposure in the following way if you are not used to the strength of the sun's rays.
>
> - day 1: 10 minutes in direct sunlight
> - day 2: 15 minutes
> - day 3: 25 minutes
> - day 4: 35 minutes
> - day 5: 50 minutes
> - day 6: 75 minutes
>
> Keep yourself and your children well protected with a sun screen of factor 30 or higher, and pay particular attention to the top of the head (always wear a hat), the nose, the backs of the knees and the tops of the feet.

  Treatment: clean the wounds thoroughly and use antiseptic or antibiotic cream. Bad bites will also need antibiotic and anti-tetanus treatment.

- **Moray eels**
  Probably more divers are bitten by morays than by all other sea creatures added together – usually through putting their hands into holes to collect shells or lobsters, remove anchors, or hide baitfish. Once it bites, a moray often refuses to let go, so you may have to persuade it to by gripping it behind the head and exerting pressure with your finger and thumb until it opens its jaw. You can make the wound worse by tearing your flesh as you pull the fish off.

  Treatment: thorough cleaning and usually stitching. The bites always go septic, so have antibiotics and anti-tetanus available.

- **Sharks**
  Sharks rarely attack divers, but divers should always treat these fish with respect. Do not swim too close to them. Above, all, **never try to handle a shark.** Most of the bites from sharks that have been recorded in the Caribbean were inflicted by normally docile creatures that a diver had tried to touch or otherwise handle.

  One of the most common species in the western Caribbean is the nurse shark, which is often found apparently sleeping under a coral ledge.

  Other species divers might see in this region are the lemon shark and the Caribbean reef shark. None of these species is considered harmful to divers, unless provoked. If, however, you are ever confronted by a shark and feel frightened, do not panic. Calmly back up to the reef or your boat and get out of the water.

Treatment: a person who has been bitten by a shark usually has severe injuries and is suffering from shock (see page 170). If possible, stop any bleeding by applying pressure (see page 170). The patient will need to be stabilized with blood or plasma transfusions, so call an ambulance or get the diver to hospital. Even minor wounds are likely to become infected, so the diver will need antibiotic and antitetanus treatment.

- **Triggerfish** Large triggerfish – usually males guarding eggs in 'nests' – are particularly aggressive and will attack divers who get too close. Their teeth are very strong, and can go through rubber fins and draw blood through a 4-mm (⅙-in) wet suit.

  Treatment: clean the wound and treat it with antiseptic cream.

Venomous sea creatures
Many venomous sea creatures are bottom-dwellers – they hide among coral or rest on or burrow into sand. If you need to move along the sea bottom, shuffle along, so that you push such creatures out of the way and minimize the risk of stepping directly onto sharp venomous spines, many of which can pierce rubber fins. Antivenins require specialist medical supervision, do not work for all species, and need refrigerated storage, so they are rarely available when they are needed. Most of the venoms are proteins of high molecular weight that break down under heat.

Treatment: tie a broad bandage at a point between the limb and the body and tighten it. Remember to release it every 15 minutes. Immerse the limb in hot water (perhaps the cooling water from an outboard motor if no other supply is available) at 50°C (120°F) for two hours, until the pain stops. Several injections around the wound of local anaesthetic (such as procaine hydrochloride), if available, will ease the pain. Young or weak people may need CPR (see page 167). Remember that venoms may still be active in fish that have been dead for 48 hours.

- **Cone shells** Live cone shells should never be handled without gloves: the animal has a mobile, tubelike organ that shoots a poison dart. This causes numbness at first, followed by local muscular paralysis, which may extend to respiratory paralysis and heart failure.

  Treatment: tie a bandage between the wound and the body, tighten it, and release it every 15 minutes. CPR (see page 168) may be necessary.

- **Fire coral** Corals of the genus Millepora are not true corals but members of the class Hydrozoa – i.e., they are more closely related to the stinging hydroids. Many people react violently from the slightest brush with them – producing blisters sometimes as large as 15 cm (6 in) across, which can last for as long as several weeks.

  Treatment: as for stinging hydroids.

- **Fire worms** These attractive small worms with clumps of white hairs along their sides display bristles when they are touched. These bristles easily break off in the skin and cause a painful burning feeling and intense irritation.

  Treatment: bathe with a solution of hot water and vinegar.

- **Jellyfish** Most jellyfish sting, but few are dangerous. When seasonal changes are in their favour you can encounter the Portuguese man-of-war (*Physalia physalis*). These are highly toxic jellyfish and prolonged exposure to their stinging cells may require hospital treatment.

- **Scorpionfish** These are not considered dangerous in Caribbean waters, but divers should be careful not to brush against the spines on the top of the dorsal fin.

  Treatment: If you are stung, the pain can be eased by bathing the affected part of the body in very hot water.

- **Sea urchins** The spines of some sea urchins are poisonous and all sea urchin spines can puncture the skin, even through gloves, and break off, leaving painful wounds that often go septic.

  Treatment: for bad cases bathe the affected part of the body in very hot water. This softens the spines, which makes it easier for the body to reject them. Soothing creams or a magnesium sulphate compress will help reduce the pain, as will the application of the flesh of papaya fruit. Septic wounds need to be treated with antibiotics.

- **Sea wasps** (*Carybdea alata*) can be found in shallow warm water at night and are attracted to light. These creatures often swarm. Their stings can be severe, causing muscle cramps, nausea and breathing difficulties. Whenever conditions are favourable for thimble jellyfish (*Linuche unguiculata*), there is always the chance that sea wasps and much smaller and almost invisible microorganisms may be in the water column. You should wear protection, such as a wet suit or a Lycra skin suit. You can try local remedies for stings, but acetic acid or vinegar is adequate.

  Treatment: In cases of severe stinging, medical attention will be necessary.

- **Stinging hydroids** Stinging hydroids often go unnoticed on wrecks, old anchor ropes and chains until you put your hand on them, when their nematocysts are fired into your skin. The wounds are not serious but they are very painful, and large blisters can be raised on sensitive skin, which can last for some time.

  Treatment: bathe the affected part in methylated spirit or vinegar (acetic acid). Local anaesthetic may be required to ease the pain, though antihistamine cream is usually enough.

- **Stinging plankton** You cannot see stinging plankton, and so cannot take evasive measures. If there are reports of any in the area, keep as much of your body covered as you can.

  Treatment: as for stinging hydroids.

- **Electric rays** Electric (torpedo) rays can give a severe electric shock (200–2000 volts); the main problem here is that the victim may be knocked unconscious in the water and drown.

- **Stingrays** Stingrays vary considerably in size from a few centimetres to several metres across. The sting consists of one or more spines on top of the tail; although these point backward they can sting in any direction. The rays thrash out and sting when they are trodden on or caught. The wounds may be large and severely lacerated.

Treatment: clean the wound and remove any spines. Bathe or immerse in very hot water and apply a local anaesthetic if one is available; follow up with antibiotics and anti-tetanus.

- **Other stinging creatures**
  Venoms can also occur in soft corals, the anemones associated with clownfish and the nudibranchs that feed on stinging hydroids. If you have sensitive skin, do not touch any of them.

Cuts

Underwater cuts and scrapes, especially those caused by coral, barnacles and sharp metal, will usually, if they are not cleaned out and treated quickly, go septic; absorption of the resulting poisons into the body can cause more serious medical conditions

After every dive, clean and disinfect any wounds, no matter how small. Larger wounds will often refuse to heal unless you stay out of seawater for a couple of days. Surgeonfish have sharp fins on each side of the caudal peduncle; they use these when lashing out at other fish with a sweep of the tail, and they occasionally use them to defend their territory against a trespassing diver. Their 'scalpels' may be covered in toxic mucus, so wounds must be cleaned and treated with antibiotic cream.

As a preventive measure against cuts in general, the golden rule is: do not touch. Learn good buoyancy control so that you can avoid touching anything unnecessarily - never forget for an instant that every area of the coral you touch will inevitably be killed.

BIBLIOGRAPHY

Berg, Daniel & Denise *Tropical Shipwrecks* (1989), Aqua Explorers Inc., New York, USA

Cardenas, Luís Gómez *Dive Mexico* (1993), Editorial Fotográfica, Cancún, Mexico

Cummings, Susanne & Stuart *Watersports Guide to Cancún* (1993), Gulf Publishing Co., Texas, USA

Farley, Michael & Lauren *Diver's Guide to Underwater Mexico* (1986), Marcor Publishing, California, USA

Fielding's Mexico (1995) Fielding Worldwide Inc., Calfiornia, USA

Hartdegen, Tom *Dive Paradise Guide to Cozumel* (1995), Dive Paradise, Cozumel, Mexico

Humann, Paul 'Reef Identification' series: *Reef Coral Identification*; *Reef Fish Identification*; and *Reef Creature Identification* (1993) New World Publications, Florida, USA

Lewbel, G.S. & Martin, L.R. *Diving and Snorkelling Guide to Cozumel* (1991), Gulf Publishing Co., Texas, USA

The Mayas (1995), Monclem Ediciones, Mexico

Rosenberg, Steve *Diving Cozumel* (1992), Aquaquest Publications, New York, USA

Vine, Dr. Peter *Caribbean Divers' Guide* (1991), Immel Publishing, London, UK

Wood, Dr. Elizabeth *Corals of the World:* (1983), T.F.H. Publications, Neptune City, New Jersey, USA

Wood, Dr. Elizabeth & Wood, Lawson *Caribbean Reef Fishes, Corals and Invertebrates* (2001), New Holland Publishers (UK) Ltd

Wood, Lawson *Top Dive Sites of the Caribbean* (1999), New Holland Publishers (UK) Ltd

Index

A page reference in **bold type** indicates a major entry; a page reference in *italic type* indicates a photograph.

Air travel 23, 53, 101, 137
 charter aircraft 23, *23*
 Cozumel 101
 domestic flights 25
 international flights 23
 on the Mayan Riviera 137
 through Cancún 53
 through Cozumel 101
Airport departure tax 23, 27
Akumal 13, 25
Alacran Banks 46
Algae .46, 65, 87, 97, *108*, 121, 146, 160, 163
 hanging vine 87, 132
 pinecone algae 108
Aquaworld diving platform . .*36*, ...*37*, 52
Anemones 130, 140, 161
 giant anemone 161, *161*
Angelfish **56**, *57*, 56, 64, 84
 blue angelfish . . **56**, *59*, 126
 French angelfish **56**, *111*
 grey angelfish **56**
 queen angelfish *13*, **56**, *57*, 114
 rock beauty **56**, *56*
Atlantis submarine 48, 55

Bacalar, Laguna 107
Bahía de Mujeres 38, *42*, **46**, 48, 62, 100
Balloonfish 140, 160
Barracuda 159, 171
 great barracuda 140, 159
Barrier reefs 12

See also Great Maya Barrier Reef
Beaches 112
 access to dive sites from . .42
 Cancún 45, **46**
 Chemuyil 134
 Isla Mujeres 58, 60, **71**
 Playa Norte 60, 71
 Tulum 135
Bearded fireworm . .98, 99, **162**
Belize 9, 12
Bends, the (decompression
 sickness) 43, **168–69**
Bermuda chub **160**
Bigeyes 158
Biosphere reserves 42
 See also Sian Ka'an
Blackcap basslet 95, 159
Blennies **156**
 diamond-backed blenny .*156*
Blue chromis 83
Boat trips 36
 See also Atlantis submarine;
 Nautibus submarine.
Bommie (patch reef) . . .12, 155
Boxfish 160
BS-AC (British Sub-Aqua Club) 38, 40
Buddy system 38, 40, 43
buoyancy 43, **118**, 163
 vests 42, 79
Buses 25, 71, 105
Butterflyfish **156**
 spotfin butterflyfish 156
 foureye butterflyfish *156*

'C'-card 40
Campeche City 9, 18
Campeche state 9, 12

Campsites and trailer parks . .23, **137–38**
Cancún .8, 9, 12, 20, *21*, 23, 25, 26, 30, *30*, 35, *36*, **45–58**, 105, ... 107, 137
 Hotel Zone .*21*, *44*, 45, *54*, 55
 sports 31
 water visibility 34
Caribbean Sea . . . .9, 12, 34–35, 36, 75, 105, 140–41, 150, . . 152, 155
Cave- and cavern-diving .33, 35, 40, 85, 92, 94–5, 138
CEDAM Divers (Club de Exploraciones y Deportes Acuáticos de Mexico) . . .133, 138, 146, 151, 152, *153*
Cenote-diving 26, 30, 33, 36, 37, 107, 112 **114**, 139, **143–53**, 155
 Cenote Azul 144, 145
 Cenote Carwash . . .143, 144, 145, **147**
 Cenote del Manatee (Casa Cenote) 152
 Cenote Dos Ojos .143, **147–8**
 Cenote Naharon 144
 Cenote Nohoch Nah Chich *142*, 144, 146, 148–150, *149*, **150**, **152**, *153*
 Cenote Sagrado, Chichen Itzá 31, 143, 145, *146*
 Cenote Tankah 146
 El Grande Cenote . .144, **148**
 Mundo Escondido . .144, **148**
 water visibility in 35
Ceriths 162
Chac-Mool *30*, 143

INDEX

Chankanaab National Park . . **84,** 85, 103, 162
Chetumal . . .9, 14, 25, 26, 105, 107, 122, 137, 163
Chichen Itzá .16, *16, 17,* 29, **30,** 46
   Cenote Sagrado 31, 143, 145, *146*
Chinchorro atoll (Banco Chinchorro) . .14–15, 33, 38, 105, 107
Chinchorro Reef Resort 138
Christmas tree worm .140, 141, 162
Clams
   file clam *127*
Cleaning stations .92, **109,** 114, *115*
Climate 21, 139
Coba 29, **31,** 146
Conchs . . **66–67,** 78, 124, 161
   queen conch . . **66–67,** *66, 161*
Cone shells 172
Conservation .14, 15, 33–34, 38, 67, **68,** 79, 80, 91, 120, 121, **163**
Coral . .12, 46, 79, 89, *93,* 124, *135,* **155, 163**
   black **90**
   brain 155, 162
   elkhorn 163
   fire **111,** 172
   flower *154*
   gorgonian (sea fans) . .***88,*** *89,* 155, 162, 163
   lettuce 155
   sheet 155
   soft 173
   staghorn 163
   star 155
   stinging 130
Cornetfish 160
Costa Turquesa 46
Coral reef **155**
   atolls .14–15, 33, 38, 105, 107
   barrier 12, 155
   conservation of **163**
   fringing 73, 108, 155
   patch 12, 155
   types of 155
Cornetfish **160**
Cousteau, Jacques 62
Cousteau, Jean Michel 82
Cowries 161
   Atlantic deer cowrie 161
   Atlantic grey cowrie .161, *161*
Cozumel . .9, 20, 23, 25, 26, 28, 33, 35, 36, 37, **73–101,** 140, 146, 160, 162
   biodiversity of 76, 98
   diving and snorkelling in 74–6
   history 73–5
   Museum 77
   sports 31
   water visibility 34
Crabs **161**
   arrow crab 86

channel-clinging *127*
   red reef hermit *129*
   stareye hermit *161*
Creole fish 159
Croco-cun crocodile farm . . .139
Currency 25, 27–8
Current 36, 42
   Yucatán Current 33
Customs and Immigration 23, 24

Damselfish 156
   longfin damselfish *156*
   spotfin damselfish 156
   three-spot damselfish . . .130
Day of the Dead (Día de los Muertos) 18
Disabled divers 40
Dive boats . . .22, 25, *32,* 34, *37, 37,* 60
Dive Paradise, Cozumel *33*
Divers Down Lights 126
Dive shops 42, 54, 102 3, 138
Dive sites
   descriptions 6
   star-rating system 7
   symbols 7
Diving
   deep 96, 108–9
   equipment 43
   for families 40, 42
   night 34
   off Cancún 46
   off Mayan Riviera 105
   planning 34
   training . .38, 39, 40, 147
   water conditions for 34–5
Dolphins .71, 95, 112, *113,* 126
Drift dives 36, 46, 59, 75

Eels **159**
   garden eel 159
   goldspotted eel 159
   goldentail moray . . .157, *157*
   green moray 157
   moray 2, *115,* **157,** *157,* 171
   sharptail eel 159
   snake eel 159
   spotted moray 157
Electricity 25

Fairy basslet 154
Fiesta Americana Cozumel Reef Hotel *27,* 84
Filefish
   scrawled filefish 140, *140*
Fire worms 172
First aid 167–168
Fish-feeding **80,** *80,* 84, 173
Flags, warning
   water condition . . .**40,** 42, 46
   divers' 121
Flamingo tongue *94,* 163
Flounder
   peacock flounder **159**
Food hygiene 26–7

El Garrafón National Park .60, **64**
Goatfish **159**
   yellow goatfish 159
Gobies **156**
   cleaning gobies 106, 156
   neon goby 156, *156*
Great Maya Barrier Reef .12, **14,** 33, 105
Grouper **157**
   coney 73, *157*
   jewfish 157
Grunts 38, 112, **157**
   blue-striped 49
   porkfish *132*
   white grunt *157*
Guatemala 12, 29, 133
Gulf of Mexico .9, 12, 35, 36, 73
Gulf Stream 161

Haggling 28
Halocline 114, 150
Hamlets **159**
   barred hamlet 159
   golden hamlet 159
Hawkfish **159**
   redspotted *119,* 159
Health *26–27,* 28, **167–73**
Hogfish **159**
   common hogfish 159
   Spanish hogfish . .*83,* 84, 159
Holbox Island 71
Honduras 16, 29, 33
Hurricanes . . 20, 33, 48, 63, 76, 88, 125
Hydroids **162,** 172, 173
Hygiene 26–7, 167–73
Hyperbaric chamber 43

Invertebrates . . .84, 85, 98, 12 155, **161–62**
Ironstone shore 73, 135
Isla Blanca 46
Isla Contoy . .12, *24,* 33, 34, 46, **61,** *61,* **68,** 71, 162
Isla Mujeres . .12, 25, 33, 34, 46 58, **59–65,** *67,* **70–71,** *70, 71,* 91, 162
Ixlache Reef 61, **68**

Jacks **157**
   bar jack *157*
Jawfish **159**
Jewfish 157
Jellyfish 130, **162,** 172

Lettuce sea slug 161, *161*
Lights, divers down 126
Live-aboards 15, **38,** 46, 75, 103,
Lobsters 128
   spiny *128*
Lizardfish **159**

Manatees .14, **122–23,** *122, 123*
Marine-related ailments .172–73
El Matancero wreck . . .132, 133
Maya, the . . . .9, 12, 16, 18, 19, 29, 30, 46, 73, 75, *107,* . . . .

Index

112–13
  ruins **30–1**, *31*,103, 105, 112
Mayan Riviera 34, **105–137**
  water visibility 34
  See also Cenotes
Mariachi singers *8*
Mérida 9, 18, 30
Mesoamerican civilizations 16–17, 143
Mexico
  history 16–19
  language 17
  law 25
Mexico City 16, 17, 19, 23
Microatolls 98
Molluscs .89, 95, 111, 125, **161**, 162
Money 25, 27–28,

NAUI (National Asociation of Underwater Instructors) ...38
Nautibus submarine 48, 55
Night-diving 34, 37, 82, 108, 111,126, 155
Nitrogen narcosis 170
Nitrox diving 43
Nudibranchs (sea slugs) **161**, 173
  lettuce sea slug 161, *161*
  painted elysia 161

Octopus 162
Olives 162

PADI (Professional Association of Diving Instructors) 38
Painted elysia 161
Palapas *12, 28*
Parrotfish **157**
  princess parrotfish 157
  queen parrotfish 115
  redband parrotfish ..157, *157*
  stoplight parrotfish ..*91, 105,* 157
Petrol stations 25, **139**
Photography ...40, **164–65**, 94
  film-processing ..55, 71, 103, 139, 151
  macro 165
  wide-angle 164
Plankton 34–35, 61, 141
  stinging 42, **173**
Playa del Carmen 20, 25, *29*
Porcupinefish 160
Porkfish *131*
Prehistoric ocean life ...140–41
Puerto Aventuras 31
Pudding wife *158, 158*
Pufferfish **159–60**, 163
  Bandtail puffer 160
  sharpnose puffer *50,* 159
Purchase tax *(IVA)* 27

Qintana Roo state .9, 12, 19, 21, 23, 30, 107, 157

Reef structures 15, **34, 155**
  See also Coral reefs
Rays **158, 159**
  electric **158,** 173
  manta 140, 159
  Narcine brasiliensis 158
  spotted eagle ray 159
  stingray 124, **158,** 173
  southern stingray .*132,* 157
  yellow stingray ...158, *158*

Safety 36, 40, 42, 43, **167–173** .
San Miguel 26, *72, 75,* **75**
Sand chute ..34, 114, 115, 155
Sand tilefish 114, **160**
Saucereye porgy **160**
Scorpionfish **160,** 172
  plumed 160
  spotted *118*
Scuba-diving 14, 38, *45,* 59, 60, 112, 124, 133, 135, 147
Sea fans *See* corals, gorgonian
Sea horses 79, *79*
Sea pearls 110, *110*
Sea plumes *See* corals, gorgonian
Sea stars 162
Sea urchins ..80, 111, 124, 162 **163,** 172
Sea wasps 172
Security, personal **25**
Sergeant majors 140
Sharks ..62, 126, 129, 139, **160,** 171
  bull shark 160
  nurse shark *63,* 160
Shells **162**
Shrimps 69, **162**
  banded coral 69, *115,* 140, 162
  peppermint 162
  red night shrimp 162
Sian Ka'an Biosphere Reserve 13, ...**14,** *15,* 139
Siestas 28
Silver 28
Silversides *136,* 157, **160**
Sleeping Shark Caves ...**62,** 160
Smooth trunkfish 160
Snails **161**
Snapper 38, 112, **158**
  schoolmaster 158,
  yellowtail snapper ..158, *158*
Snorkelling ..**40–42,** *41, 42,* 52, 60, 64, 79, 92, 108, 112, 114, 121, 124, 132, 133, 135, 147
Soldierfish
  blackbar soldierfish 158
Sponges ..*65, 76, 93,* 125, **162,** 163
  giant barrel 162
  rope *120,* 162
  pink vase *50, 69,* 162
  tube *52, 162,* 162

Spur and groove reef 15, 34
Squid 162
Squirrelfish **158**
  blackbar soldierfish 158
  common squirrelfish 158, *158*
Street directions 29
Suckerfish (remora) **160**
Sunburn 42
Surge 36, 105, 155
Surgeonfish **158,** 173
  ocean surgeonfish 158
Swimming safety 40
Swimthroughs 34, *96,* 108

Taxis 25, 37, 71
Telephones 26
Tidal streams 35, 140
Time, Central Standard 20
Tipping 25
Toadfish 38, **100,** *100*
Toltecs 17, 30, 46
Tourist Corridor .12, 13, 35, 46, 143, 147
Tourist offices 20, 53, 137
Triggerfish 172
Trumpetfish 75, **160**
Tube worms 160, **162**
  Christmas tree worm 162
  magnificent featherduster 162
  social featherduster .*162, 162*
TUBS 135–5, *134,* 137
Tulum ..13, 20, 26, 30, *30 104,* 135, *135,* 163
Tunicates (sea squirts) **162**
Turtle grass 155
Turtles .14, 71, 92, *97, 98,* 125, *120,* 163
  green *97*
Vehicle-hire **25,** 37
Video, underwater 166

Wall (drop-off) 34, *117,* 155
War of the Castes 19, 75
Water visibility 34–5, 105
Wet suits 42
White margate 157
Wrasse **158**
  bluehead wrasse 158
  pudding wife 158, *158*
  yellowhead wrasse 158
Wreck-diving 14, 40, 46, 62, 68, ...*68,* 78, 81, 107, 125–6

Xel-Há Tourist Lagoon 139
Xcalak 14, 105
Xcaret Ecoarchaeological Park ..
...........112–13, *112*

Yucatán Peninsula .9, 12, 16, 17, 18, 19–20, 29, 33, 139, 154, 156
  climate 20–21, 152
Yucatán state .9, 12, 21, 30, 139